THE PALGRAVE CONCISE
HISTORICAL ATLAS
OF
THE SECOND WORLD WAR

ALSO BY MARTIN FOLLY

Churchill, Whitehall & the Soviet Union, 1940–1945
The United States in World War II: The Awakening Giant

THE PALGRAVE CONCISE
HISTORICAL ATLAS
OF
THE SECOND WORLD WAR

MARTIN H. FOLLY
School of International Studies
Brunel University, UK

First published 2004 by
PALGRAVE MACMILLAN
Houndmills, Basingstoke, Hampshire RG21 6XS and
175 Fifth Avenue, New York, N.Y. 10010
Companies and representatives throughout the world

PALGRAVE MACMILLAN is the global academic imprint of the Palgrave Macmillan division of St. Martin's Press, LLC and of Palgrave Macmillan Ltd. Macmillan® is a registered trademark in the United States, United Kingdom and other countries. Palgrave is a registered trademark in the European Union and other countries.

ISBN 978-1-4039-0286-3   ISBN 978-0-230-50239-0 (eBook)
DOI 10.1057/9780230502390

This book is printed on paper suitable for recycling and made from fully managed and sustained forest sources.

A catalogue record for this book is available from the British Library.

Library of Congress Cataloging-in-Publication Data
The Palgrave concise historical atlas of the second world war
        p.   cm.
    Includes bibliographical references and index.
    1. Historical geography—Maps.   I. Title: Concise historical atlas of the second world war.
    II. Title: Historical atlas of the second world war.

    G1030.H3203 1997
    911—dc22   2004045000

    10   9   8   7   6   5   4   3   2   1
    13   12   11   10   09   08   07   06   05   04

For Nessa
– and for Tim

Contents

Preface

The Second World War affected most of the nations of the world in one way or another. It had long-lasting effects on the politics and economics of the world for the rest of the twentieth century. In those countries directly involved, the social and cultural impact was profound. Over 55 million people died, the majority of them civilian. Modern technology was matched by a callousness shown at times by all sides to produce a war of unprecedented destructiveness. For those living in the West, it has been seen as a 'good war', which resulted in the triumph of right over evil, though elsewhere the results have been regarded as more ambiguous. During the Cold War even in the West the expansion in power of the USSR seemed to be the major consequence of the war and this led many to see the Second World War as an incomplete, or fundamentally flawed, victory. There remains contention about many issues of the conflict, which is beyond the scope of this book to cover fully: the bibliography provides suggestions of texts for readers who wish to explore these more thoroughly. There is even dispute as to whether it should be regarded as one war or several. The thesis followed here is that it should be regarded as one, while recognising that the global nature of the conflict was only evident to some of its participants, and even for them for only some of its duration. But the fact that US participation, crucial to victory against Germany in the west, was precipitated by events in the Pacific, which were a culmination of the response by the US to the Japanese advance into Indo-China, which itself was made possible by the French defeat in Europe, demonstrates the layers of connection that link the different theatres of conflict around the world – while also demonstrating that it is essentially a Eurocentric viewpoint that sees the war beginning with the German invasion of Poland in September 1939 rather than the Japanese invasion of China in 1937.

The events of the war itself have been recounted and analysed in many forms, including in highly-detailed historical atlases. This atlas is designed to give a concise but rounded history of the war. It will regard the events of Asia and Europe as interrelated, and will treat the war as beginning in China in 1937. It is not intended to give detailed diagrams of military engagements nor supply the level of military details found in unit histories, but to provide an integrated geopolitical and strategic overview. The aim is to provide students and the general reader with a basic visual aid for understanding the course of events during the Second World War. The maps therefore have been kept as straightforward as possible. Too much detail can obscure as much as elucidate. For the details of key military engagements and fuller statistical data, readers are referred to the texts in the bibliography.

The purpose of the atlas is to clarify the major developments and movements of the war. Each map is accompanied by a page of text explaining the events depicted, and giving further information and interpretations. These essays are of necessity brief. There are also, inevitably, aspects of the war that evade rendition into maps. The present focus of much writing on the war is on covert activities, most particularly signals intelligence (when referring to the Allied side, often called Ultra). This aspect is not ignored here, but is not a major focus, as the emphasis of the atlas is on the outcome rather than the process. Even with such good intelligence, the battles still had to be won: it is worth noting that the French in 1940 had good intelligence of the German order of battle, but still suffered catastrophic defeat. Modern writing on the war, particularly popular writing, also focuses heavily on the personal rather than the strategic; the recent spate of Hollywood movies is a case in point. Putting ordinary people at centre stage is entirely right: it was *their* war. Again, such an approach is, however, hard to deliver in an atlas of this kind. What this book does is to give a tactical, strategic and political context to their experiences. Again, some reading suggestions are provided at the end for readers to follow some personal stories that flesh out and humanise the picture presented of the war as a whole given here. The Second World War was a total war, in which the major events were not always those on the battlefield, or involving young men in uniform. Sections here deal with the home front, with the economics of war, and with the politics of this most political of struggles. Inevitably, the individuals specifically named are statesmen or generals, and the ordinary people are referred to *en masse*. But the war was an amalgam of personal histories, usually tragic, often heroic, sometimes comic, as ordinary people found themselves caught up in extraordinary events. While they may not appear in its pages, this book was written with them in mind, in particular my personal heroes: Pearl Withrington, John Gillespie Magee, Wade McCluskey, Lilya Litvak, Donald Macintyre, Raoul Wallenberg. And, for giving us those two lasting iconic images of the victory of the Allies: Joe Rosenthal for the photograph of the US Marines' raising of the American flag over Mount Suribachi and Yevgeny Khaldei for the photograph of Alyosha Kovalyov raising the Soviet flag over the Reichstag. It is entirely fitting that both photographers were Jewish.

I would like to acknowledge with thanks the encouragement of my colleagues in American Studies and History at Brunel University, in particular Niall Palmer and Sean Holmes, who tolerated with quizzical stoicism my obsession with apparently arcane details like the operational range of the Messerschmitt Bf109E. Finally, this book is dedicated to Vanessa, without whose support it could not have been written, and to the memory of my colleague Tim Fernyhough, who took great interest in the project and whose untimely death has left a hole that cannot be filled.

A note on the maps

The prime aim of the maps is to demonstrate geopolitical and strategic developments, and the spatial relationship between important places. To achieve this a simplified form of Mercator's projection is used, while recognising the shortcomings of that method in geographical exactitude, in the belief that this is the best way to present the information that is the focus of this book. In most instances, the maps are aligned around a central vertical north–south axis (the major exception is Map 26).

As befits an historical atlas, in both the text and maps place names and country names are those used at the time (thus Beijing is cited as Peking, Sri Lanka as Ceylon, St Petersburg as Leningrad). The maps have been drawn with the versatile drawing tools of Microsoft Word.

Symbols used in individual maps are defined in keys to each one. Allied movements (American, British, French, Chinese, Soviet) are generally represented with green arrows. In both maps and text, in accordance with usual convention, the term 'British' is applied to armed forces units that also contained elements from the British Empire and Commonwealth: thus, the 'British' 8th Army contained significant numbers of troops from India, New Zealand, Australia and South Africa. Axis movements (German, Italian, Japanese) are generally represented with black. Minor allies of both sides are represented with grey, which is also used at times to depict specific elements of the major powers.

Map 1: The Uneasy Peace

The Second World War – in its European manifestation – has often been characterised as the final act of a thirty years war for domination of the continent. In this interpretation, the second war followed because the arrangements after the first war failed to settle the issues that caused it; principally the problem of a Germany that was the strongest nation in Europe, but was geographically constrained. The shared ambitions of the Kaiser's and Hitler's regimes for expansion in the east at the expense of the Slavs make this theory plausible.

An alternative theory was advanced by the Allies during the Second World War, and widely accepted afterwards: that the war was the product of Hitler's prejudices and ambitions (and generally that appeasement of such dictators is what causes wars). That theory, as A. J. P. Taylor pointed out in the early 1960s, tended to blame other nations only passively – in their failure to stand up to Hitler – rather than ascribing responsibility more generally to the ambitions and mistakes of statesmen from 1919 to 1939. Taylor's approach stimulated much debate, but generally Hitler is still regarded as the active element on the road to war in Europe, and also a man who welcomed war, when almost all of his victims and opponents were anxious, for various reasons, to avoid it at virtually any cost. That Hitler did not have the detailed timetable that traditionally he has been ascribed, does not remove that basic responsibility.

This is not to exonerate other leaders. Nor is it to downplay the importance of the instability of the international system in which Hitler operated. It is tempting – because Hitler and the other aggressive statesmen of the 1930s, Mussolini and Stalin, sought to revise them – to see the cause of this in the five treaties that ended the First World War (notably Versailles, which dealt with Germany). The defeat of Germany, Austria-Hungary and Turkey (and a year earlier, Russia) had allowed nationalities within their multi-ethnic empires to secure independence, encouraged by US President Woodrow Wilson who set self-determination of peoples as a war aim (and by implication, a right). The Paris Peace Conference had to deal with national units that were already spontaneously emerging. Given this situation, and the complex geography of European ethnicity, it is hardly surprising that the result was flawed.

Some peoples, who now regarded themselves as 'nations', found themselves still minorities, even in the new states. Old rivalries between peoples were maintained by the new states, and many states, old and new, had claims on the territory of their neighbours. Moreover, many of these states were small, and their natural economic ties had been damaged when the empires fell apart. Should the larger states, Germany and Russia (now the USSR), become stronger once again, these states would be very vulnerable. Wilson always intended that this eventuality could only be prevented by effective international management of the system, in the new League of Nations.

The peace settlement created strong resentments, particularly in Germany. The Versailles Treaty was seen as punitive and imposed on a country that had been defeated by a 'stab in the back' by elements at home, not on the battlefield. It had separated many Germans from the Fatherland. It is possible, however, to see the treaty as too soft, for though it punished Germany with territorial losses, disarmament and reparations, the country was left essentially intact, and potentially still the most powerful nation in Europe. During the 1920s, with American economic aid, the new German republic did indeed prosper, and was welcomed back into the community of nations. At Locarno in 1925, Germany accepted the Versailles frontiers – at least the western ones. In point of fact, although the 'thirty years war' theory is beguiling, in 1929 the system was working well, despite US isolation from the League. The Pact of Paris in 1928, which outlawed war except in self-defence, and was signed by all but five nations in the world, has often been derided as naïve idealism (and since it provided no sanctions against transgressors it was certainly weak), but at the time there was no apparent crisis on the horizon.

The event that changed this, and brought out the latent tensions in Europe (and beyond), was the Great Depression. It began with the crash of the US stock market, and as the American financial system collapsed, so too did European economies, tied heavily to that of the US by trade and by debts from the war. European businesses and banks closed, unemployment rose, and governments sought to balance their economies by nationalistic measures such as withdrawal from the gold standard and austerity measures that made the plight of the unemployed even worse. World trade slumped with the collapse of orderly currency exchange against gold. Old enemies or the new international order were blamed.

Extremist movements proposing simplistic solutions based on ideology or power emerged throughout Europe. This put strain on the practice of democracy, a new form of government for many. In an increasing number of states, it was replaced by authoritarian rule. Only the USSR did not experience the shattering economic, social, political and cultural dislocation of the Depression, but the situation there was even worse, as Stalin set about forced collectivisation of agriculture and a crash programme of industrialisation. Those who were opposed, or whom Stalin suspected of opposition, were liquidated – whole classes of Soviet society were wiped out.

ICELAND

Atlantic

Ocean

NORWAY

SWEDEN

FINLAND

Baltic

Sea

ESTONIA
[1934]

LATVIA
[1934]

LITHUANIA
[1926-29, 1936]

RUSSIA
[1917]

(USSR
estd.
1923)

North

Sea

DENMARK

IRISH FREE
STATE (Eire
after 1937)

Irish War for
Independence
and Civil War
1919-23

GREAT
BRITAIN

NETH.

BELG.

SAAR

SWITZ.

'Polish Corridor'

East Prussia
(Ger.)

DANZIG

GERMANY
[1933]

Silesia

P O L A N D
[1926]

Polish-Soviet
War, 1920-21

Teschen

CZECHOSLOVAKIA

AUSTRIA
[1933]

HUNGARY
[1919]

R O M A N I A

[1938]

Fiume
1919

FRANCE

PORTUGAL
[1926]

SPAIN
[1923-30,
1939]

CORSICA
(Fr.)

ITALY
[1922]

YUGOSLAVIA
[1929]

BULGARIA
[1923-30, 1934]

ALBANIA
[1925]

1919

SARDINIA
(Ital.)

GREECE
[1936]

Corfu
1923

1922

GIBRALTAR (Br.)

SPANISH
MOROCCO

Mediterranean Sea

Dodecanese
Islands (Ital.)

FRENCH   NORTH   AFRICA

MALTA (Br.)

CRETE (Gr.)

Key

▬▬▬ Frontiers of Russia before 1914

▬▬▬ Frontiers of Germany before 1914

▬▬▬ Frontiers of Austria-Hungary before 1914

▨ Rhineland de-militarised zone 1919-36

▨ Areas administered by League of Nations

▨ Memel: Allied 1919-23, then Lithuanian,
1923-24, then autonomous

••••• 'Curzon line' 1919: Polish eastern ethnic frontier

▤ Bulgarian territorial losses, 1919

▩ Vilnius: annexed by Poland 1920

O Areas partitioned by 1919 peace treaties

✵ Armed conflicts/disputes

▨ Authoritarian regimes gaining power 1919-29

▨ Authoritarian regimes gaining power 1930-39

☐ Parliamentary democracies throughout period

Map 2: The Road to War in Asia

Although it only emerged from 300 years of isolation in 1853, by 1900 Japan had become the leading Asian industrial power. War with China brought possession of Korea, Formosa and concessions on the Chinese mainland. Japan became the first Asian power to defeat a European one in the Russo-Japanese war of 1904–05. For fighting on the Allied side in the First World War, Japan was given German Pacific island colonies. Pressure tactics (the '21 Demands') used against China, however, worsened Japanese relations with the US, already strained by American restrictions on immigration from Japan. The Japanese had been allies with Britain – sharing a rival in Russia – and the British helped the development of the Imperial Navy. However, after the First World War, American pressure and British desire to reduce commitments, led the British to end the alliance. In the Washington Naval Treaties (1921) Japan was limited to just over half the number of capital ships of Britain and the US (who claimed they had two or more oceans to protect, where the Japanese had only the Pacific). The ratios were 5 (US): 5 (UK): 3 (Japan): 1.5 (Italy and France). The Japanese Navy regarded this as a humiliation. All parties also agreed not to fortify their Far Eastern possessions.

For an industrial country, Japan was extremely short of vital resources, notably iron ore, coal, oil and rubber. Many Japanese felt that they had the right to develop and exploit these resources in neighbouring territories. The Depression hit Japan hard, leading to an increase in power of the military, and the assassination of a number of political leaders as politics descended into factionalism. The War and Navy Ministers were serving officers, leaving the forces effectively free of civilian control. A consequence of this was the 'Manchurian Incident' (1931). Troops guarding Japanese concessions in this resource-rich Chinese province seized control from local warlords. China was in a state of semi-anarchy. There was a nationalist government, dominated by the Kuomintang party led by Jiang Jieshi (Chiang Kai-Shek), but many localities were controlled by warlords. Jiang devoted much of his attention to dealing with a growing Communist movement. The Japanese conquest of Manchuria prompted a League of Nations investigation which failed to condemn Japanese aggression in strong terms, yet did enough to prompt the Japanese to leave the League. The US kept aloof from League activities, but like the League refused to recognise the state of Manchukuo that the Japanese set up with a puppet regime under the former emperor of China.

In 1937, a clash with Chinese soldiers at the Marco Polo bridge near Peking (Beijing) led the Japanese Army to invade China, and again the government was dragged along in its wake. Peking soon fell, as did much of the coastal region. Shanghai was bombed, to international outrage, and the new Chinese capital of Nanking was captured in November 1937, to be followed by mass slaughter in the 'Rape of Nanking'. The US traditionally had sympathies for China, but it did nothing, such was the strength of domestic neutralism and isolationism. Even when a gunboat, USS *Panay*, was sunk on the Yangtse river and two Americans were killed, the US government was satisfied with an apology from the Japanese.

The war in China soon developed into a stalemate. Japan did not possess the means to conquer China, and Jiang would not give up the fight, though his strategy tended towards the passive – 'trading space for time' – even when forced by some of his officers into a pact with the Communists at Sian in 1936. The Japanese Army found the war a drain on resources. They were concerned about the danger of attack from the USSR – which supported Jiang in the 1930s – and two brief wars in 1938 and 1939 demonstrated Soviet military strength in the region. Japan had joined the anti-Comintern Pact with Germany in 1936 with this danger in mind. Invasion of Siberia was an option, but this would not solve the problem of resources. These lay southwards, in territory controlled by the European colonial powers. The defeat of these powers in 1940 offered the enticing prospect of a solution to Japan's long-term economic problems.

A new phase in the conflict began when the Japanese demanded the British close the Burma Road. Japanese conquest of coastal ports and closure of the railway to Haiphong were designed to starve Jiang of resources, and bring the victory that was proving impossible by force of arms alone. The Burma Road was the only remaining supply route to Jiang's capital, Chungking. The British agreed to do this temporarily in June 1940: since it was the rainy season, this had little material impact – but it did bring home to the Japanese how weak was even the strongest of the imperial powers. Pressure followed on the authorities in Indo-China after the French surrender to Germany. The French Vichy regime agreed to Japanese use of northern Vietnamese ports as bases. The American government saw this as a threat to resources vital to the British war effort, and as evidence of unlimited Japanese ambitions. US policy changed: the Japanese–American Trade Treaty was terminated, and, after the Japanese signed the Tripartite Pact with Italy and Germany in September, embargoes were placed on certain strategic materials. It seemed clear that they would oppose further expansion, and Japanese strategy now had to assume that the US ability to intervene needed to be neutralised.

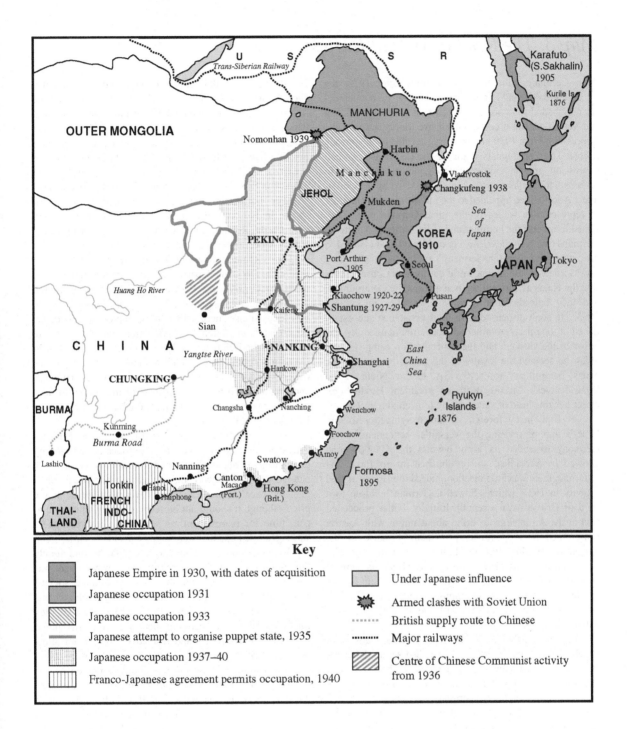

Key

	Japanese Empire in 1930, with dates of acquisition		Under Japanese influence
	Japanese occupation 1931	✹	Armed clashes with Soviet Union
	Japanese occupation 1933		British supply route to Chinese
	Japanese attempt to organise puppet state, 1935		Major railways
	Japanese occupation 1937–40		Centre of Chinese Communist activity from 1936
	Franco-Japanese agreement permits occupation, 1940		

Map 3: The Road to War in Europe

In Germany, with economic stability after 1923, the extreme right and left declined in popularity: but democracy had shallow roots, associated as it was with defeat and Versailles, and it could not survive the upheaval of the Depression. From 1930, the government ruled by emergency decree. The Communists, claiming the USSR had avoided depression, grew in popularity among industrial workers. In response, the National Socialists (Nazis), led by the charismatic Adolf Hitler, appealed to the middle classes, claiming to represent the values of the great German past. They aimed to reverse the humiliations of Versailles and unite all Germans (the '*volksdeutsche*') in one Reich, and claimed to have an explanation for Germany's problems in what they saw as a Jewish–Bolshevik world conspiracy. Conservatives saw the Nazis as a useful weapon against the Communists, and they helped Hitler become Chancellor in January 1933. He soon dispensed with their assistance and established a one-party totalitarian state, maintained by the terror of the Gestapo and the concentration camp. In July 1934, he secured the loyalty of the Army, by purging the Nazis' paramilitary force, the SA, in the 'Night of the Long Knives'. On the death of President Hindenburg, Hitler became head of state, calling himself simply *Führer*.

At first, many foreign statesmen sympathised with Hitler's aim of revising the Versailles settlement. When Germany expanded its army beyond the 100,000 men allowed by Versailles, and established an air force, the *Luftwaffe*, there was little reaction: indeed the British agreed a treaty in 1935, which allowed a German build-up to a third of British naval strength. Initially, Hitler proceeded cautiously. An attempt to bring about union with Austria (*Anschluss*) in 1934 failed, principally because of the opposition of Mussolini, the Italian Fascist dictator who saw Austria as part of his own sphere. Hitler set himself to woo Mussolini, aided by their ideological similarities and by Mussolini's own ambitions to build a new Roman empire, shown in his conquest of Ethiopia in 1935–36 and Albania in 1939.

The main potential obstacles to Hitler's plans were Britain, France and the USSR. France had set up defensive alliances with Germany's eastern neighbours, but the British in particular were reluctant to make any arrangements with the Soviets, whom they mistrusted more than the Nazis. France was wracked by internal discord, and increasingly came to rely on the defensive Maginot line and in foreign policy to follow Britain. The British, unready and unwilling to make war, believed Hitler could be dealt with by 'appeasement'. They looked to grant him economic concessions, to tempt him with colonies, and also sought the mediation of Mussolini. Crucially, when Hitler sent troops into the Rhineland, which had been de-militarised, the British and French did nothing. Emboldened, Hitler encouraged Austrian Nazis and in March 1938 he completed the *Anschluss*. He then made demands against Czechoslovakia, which contained a German minority, mostly living in the strategically important Sudetenland. The Czechs were prepared to fight, but fearful of a war for which they were not prepared, the British and French made a deal with Hitler at Munich in September 1938 that gave Hitler the Sudetenland.

The horrors of modern warfare had already been shown in the civil war in Spain that broke out in 1936 between the Republican government and right-wing forces led by General Franco. Other states had agreed to keep out, but Germany, Italy and the USSR all sent forces to Spain: the Germans in particular used it as a testing ground for the new *Luftwaffe*. Franco captured Madrid in March 1939 and thereby secured power. By that time attention was focused elsewhere. Hitler had occupied the rest of the Czech lands in March 1939. Bohemia and Moravia were taken into the Reich and Slovakia became a clerical-fascist German satellite state. As if to show the bankruptcy of collective security, Czechoslovakia's neighbours, Hungary and Poland, each took a small part of the spoils. In addition, Germany regained Memelland after an ultimatum to Lithuania on 23 March.

This was all too much for British Prime Minister Chamberlain, who in a dramatic about-face issued security guarantees to Poland, Greece and Romania, and reluctantly entered discussions with the Soviets. British rearmament gathered pace. Appeasement had never been 'peace at any price' (though it should not be seen as simply a measure to gain time for rearmament, as some have asserted: there was a genuine hope that war could be avoided). Hitler's aim for 'living-space' now seemed to extend far beyond merely the re-unification of the *volksdeutsche*. However, there was deep suspicion between the Anglo-French and the Soviets, and negotiations on political and military arrangements foundered on Soviet demands that they be able to deploy forces into the states between them and Germany should war threaten. The Poles and Romanians would not allow this. The British guarantees to those countries were therefore left without effective means of implementation.

Hitler then turned to pressure Poland over the so-called Polish corridor that separated East Prussia from the rest of Germany, and especially the internationalised city of Danzig. He too entered negotiations with the Soviets. With more to offer, he was successful, and on 24 August 1939, to the shock of the world, these two bitter ideological foes announced the signature of the Nazi–Soviet pact of non-aggression. What was kept secret was a protocol dividing eastern Europe between the two. Hitler could now go to war against Poland without fear of effective intervention.

SWEDEN

Baltic Sea

Memel   LITHUANIA

North Sea

Danzig   Königsberg   Vilnius

Kiel

East Prussia
(Ger.)

Hamburg

Elbe

Rhine

Poznan

•Berlin

Warsaw•

Brest-Litovsk

G E R M A N Y

P O L A N D

•Cologne

⊛ Bad Godesberg
23 Sept 1938

Sudetenland

•Lvov

Saar
(re-united to
Germany after
plebiscite, 1935)

Pilsen   •Prague

CZECHO-

Teschen

Ger protectorate
23 Mar 1939

SLOVAKIA

Ruthenia

⊛ Munich
29 Sept 1938

Vienna•

Bratislava•

SWITZERLAND

AUSTRIA

⊕ Obersalzburg
15 Sept 1938

•Budapest

H U N G A R Y

Milan •

Danube

R O M A N I A

Venice•

Zagreb•

ITALY

Y U G O S L A V I A

Belgrade•

Key

⊛   Chamberlain's conferences with Hitler

Rhineland re-militarised, March 1936

Annexed by Germany (*Anschluss*), March 1938

Annexed by Germany, October 1938 (ceded to Germany at Munich)

Annexed by Germany, March 1939

Bohemia and Moravia annexed by Germany, March 1939

Annexed by Hungary from Slovakia, November 1938

Autonomous from Sept 1938, annexed by Hungary, March 1939

Czech part of Teschen annexed by Poland, October 1938

Annexed by Lithuania from Poland, October 1939

Map 4: The Fall of Poland

Late on 31 August 1939, German SS men disguised as Polish soldiers staged an 'incident' at Gleiwitz, which gave Hitler his pretext for attacking Poland without a declaration of war. Hitler had been planning this war for months. Despite the British guarantee, he believed that they would not risk a general European war over Poland. By concluding the Nazi–Soviet Pact he had made it impossible for the British to directly affect the outcome in Poland, and he judged that they would accept the result of a quick, decisive war as unpleasant but unavoidable.

The Polish Army was not an insignificant force, but it was not ready for the new form of warfare the Germans employed. This was *blitzkrieg*, the 'lightning war'. The spearhead was the panzer division, a concentration of armour, with fully motorised infantry and close air support provided by the *Luftwaffe* in the form of the fearsome dive-bombers, the *Stukas*. Germany had only light tanks available, and the Army was not fully prepared for war, but the key to *blitzkrieg* was speed, which would overwhelm enemy defences before their strength could be mustered, or underlying weaknesses in the attacking forces exposed. Use of airpower against civilian targets would clog the roads with refugees and add to the disintegration of morale: a vital component of successful *blitzkrieg*. The Poles had numerical strength – 30 divisions and ten in reserve – but had outdated equipment and strategic doctrine. Their forces were deployed on their frontiers: it was Polish misfortune that their main industrial areas were in Silesia, right on their borders – and this made them highly vulnerable to *blitzkrieg*.

Britain and France issued an ultimatum for Germany to withdraw: when it expired on 3 September, Chamberlain regretfully announced that Britain was once more at war with Germany. The British Dominions followed suit. With no arrangement with the Soviets, it was not clear how Britain or France were going to help Poland. The French Army made a token movement over the German border in the Saar, but its military strategy was built around the defensive, based on the Maginot line.

German armies converged on Poland from three sides. Most significantly, General Guderian's five panzer divisions were concentrated in spearheads that made deep and rapid penetration, leaving their infantry far behind. The Poles, deployed too far forward, especially in the Polish corridor, lacked the mobility to respond. The Polish Air Force had half its strength destroyed on the ground by the end of 1 September and its aircraft were outperformed by those of the *Luftwaffe*. The Poles fought hard, but were overwhelmed. General von Bock's Army Group North from Pomerania and East Prussia overran the corridor by

3 September. The *Luftwaffe* disrupted communications and made organising a defence behind the Vistula–Narew line by the Polish commander, Marshal Smygly-Rydz, impossible. The panzers thrust towards Warsaw. Polish forces fell back on the city, but a double-pincer movement by Army Groups North and South met at Brest-Litovsk and encircled the Polish forces by 17 September. Only at Kutno was there an effective counter-attack, and that was overwhelmed by 19 September in the Battle of Bzura River.

The Germans bombed Warsaw from 17 to 27 September to demoralise by terror. On 17 September, the Soviets acted in accordance with the secret protocol, and invaded Poland from the east. As a consequence, many of the Polish forces fell into Soviet hands (220,000 out of 910,000 Poles taken prisoner). They were taken to camps in the USSR, where over 20,000 were murdered in the next 18 months. The Soviets incorporated eastern Poland into the USSR on the grounds that it was ethnically Ukrainian. Sovietisation and destruction of Polish culture followed.

The last organised resistance took place in Warsaw and the fortress of Modlin: after heavy bombardment Warsaw surrendered on 27 September and Modlin a day later. The defeat of Poland was complete by 5 October. The Polish armed forces suffered 70,000 killed, against 8,082 Germans. Some 90,000 escaped to Hungary, Romania, Lithuania and Latvia, and many made their way to the west to continue the fight. Members of the government who escaped by way of Romania set up a government-in-exile in France (and later London), headed by General Sikorski. They brought with them details of their attempts to crack the German Enigma encryption machine, which were to prove an invaluable asset to the Allied war effort.

Poles living in the Polish corridor were forced to leave, and replaced by Germans, and the area was incorporated into the Reich as Warthegau (Wartheland). The rest of Poland was put under the control of Hans Frank as the General Government. He embarked on a policy of national and cultural destruction in accordance with Nazi racial theories. Thousands of intellectuals, nationalists and professionals were murdered in an attempt to reduce Poland to a slave society. Frank, based at Krakow, put tens of thousands to forced labour, and ghettoised and then murdered Poland's 3 million Jews. Poland was to suffer a higher proportion of its population killed in the war than any other state.

Hitler expected that Britain and France would see the folly of maintaining hostilities after the disappearance of the country for which they went to war. When it became obvious that they intended to fight on, he ordered the General Staff (OKW) to prepare plans for the invasion of France (*Fall Gelb* – Operation Yellow).

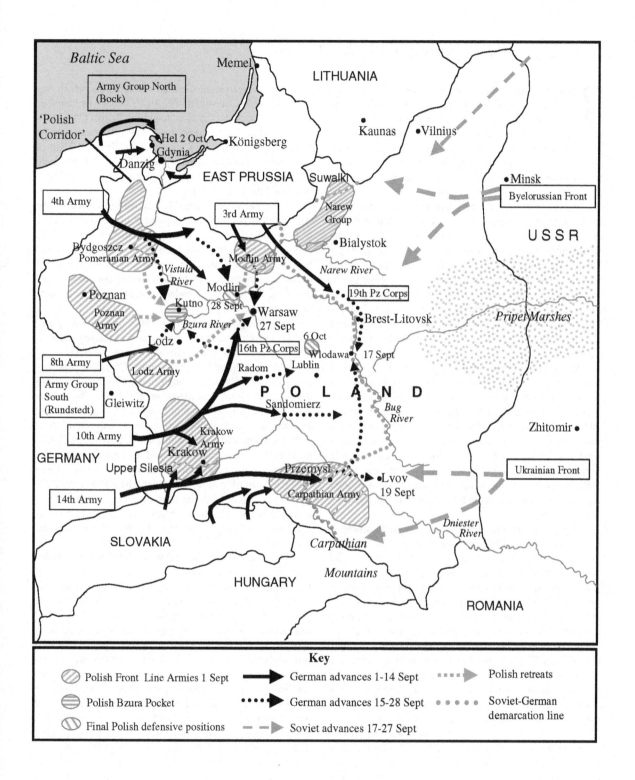

Baltic Sea

Memel

LITHUANIA

Army Group North
(Bock)

'Polish
Corridor'

Hel 2 Oct
Gdynia
Danzig

Königsberg

EAST PRUSSIA

Suwalki

Kaunas   Vilnius

Minsk

Byelorussian Front

4th Army

Modlin Army

Narew
Group

Bialystok

USSR

Bydgoszcz
Pomeranian Army

3rd Army

*Vistula
River*

Modlin

Narew River

19th Pz Corps

Poznan
Poznan
Army

Kutno
28 Sept

Bzura River

Warsaw
27 Sept

Brest-Litovsk

Pripet Marshes

Lodz

6 Oct
Wlodawa

16th Pz Corps

17 Sept

8th Army

Lodz Army

Radom

Lublin

P O L A N D

*Bug
River*

Zhitomir

Army Group
South
(Rundstedt)

Gleiwitz

Sandomierz

10th Army

Krakow
Army

Krakow

GERMANY

Upper Silesia

14th Army

Przemysl

Carpathian Army

Lvov
19 Sept

Ukrainian Front

*Dniester
River*

SLOVAKIA

Carpathian

Mountains

HUNGARY

ROMANIA

Key

Polish Front Line Armies 1 Sept

German advances 1-14 Sept

Polish retreats

Polish Bzura Pocket

German advances 15-28 Sept

Soviet-German
demarcation line

Final Polish defensive positions

Soviet advances 17-27 Sept

Map 5: Soviet Expansion 1939–41

The secret protocol of the Nazi–Soviet Pact divided Eastern Europe into German and Soviet spheres of interest. The Soviets began immediately to act upon this agreement, which, Stalin said, had 'been sealed with blood'. Stalin proceeded to force 'mutual assistance' pacts on Latvia and Estonia, under which he could station Soviet troops on their soil. Lithuania had been assigned to Germany, but under the German–Soviet Border and Friendship Treaty of 28 September, it was exchanged for German occupation of a larger part of Central Poland up to the Bug river and the Suwalki area, and it too was forced into such a pact. Stalin pressured his other neighbours Romania and Turkey, and also Bulgaria, for similar arrangements. Whether these moves were opportunistic expansionism or defensive responses to German expansionism is disputed. The likelihood is that they were both, as Stalin felt insecure about any areas not under his control. He preferred to deploy his troops right up to the frontier of a potential enemy.

Stalin also put pressure on Finland, but in this case it was not to gain a pact, but to gain actual territory, pushing the frontier further away from Leningrad and the important port of Murmansk. The Finns rejected his demands, and on 30 November, the Soviet Union attacked. Finnish resistance was fierce, and the Soviet performance, despite overwhelming numbers, was abysmal. Many of the Soviet units initially deployed were from Central Asia, the Soviet practice being to station troops well away from their home regions, and they were untrained and unequipped for winter warfare.

The success of the Finns attracted great sympathy in Britain and France. The Soviet attack confirmed for many that Stalin was as bad as Hitler, and it was widely assumed that they were colluding so closely as to be allies. The USSR was expelled from the League of Nations, and even for many of those left-wing sympathisers whose loyalty to the Soviet Union had survived the Nazi–Soviet Pact, it was the last straw. For strategists in France, the Winter War seemed to offer an opportunity to fight the war away from the Western Front. While the British military were less enthusiastic, it was felt in the governments of both countries that aiding Finland and attacking the USSR would be a way to strike at Germany. It was assumed, correctly, that the Soviets were supplying oil and other war materials to Germany, circumventing the Allied blockade. The purges of the military and political leadership, and collectivisation upheavals in the USSR in the 1930s, were believed to have made it economically and morally weak, so that a well-directed blow could bring the whole structure crashing down. This would neatly end the Bolshevik menace and

strike a blow against the German war economy, which was itself believed to be vulnerable. An air strike was therefore seriously mooted by the French and the British from bases in the Middle East against the Soviet oil installations at Baku and Batum in the Caucasus. The British Chiefs of Staff were cautious about the practicality of this, but were prepared to begin planning another operation, the despatch of ground forces to Finland.

The attraction of doing this was that in the process, the Allied forces could block the passage of Swedish iron ore to Germany. Winston Churchill, British First Lord of the Admiralty, was particularly keen on this plan, which would be a mortal blow against the German war effort. The Soviet military performance in Finland meant that few feared engaging the Red Army; indeed it seemed the weak point of the enemy front.

Two things prevented this operation going ahead, though French and British troops were gathered ready to go. Norway and Sweden refused to allow passage for the Allied troops through their territory. Churchill was prepared to force the way through, but while this was being debated, the Finns surrendered on 12 March. The Soviets had made drastic changes to their tactics and command structure and had launched successful assaults in the New Year, including the bombing of Finnish towns. They broke through the 'Mannerheim line' and the Finns bowed to the inevitable, and accepted terms that were worse than those they had been offered in November. The USSR gained the territory it wanted, at the cost of 200,000 casualties – though Finland did remain independent. It would increasingly look to Germany to help with its defences over the next year.

The Allied assumption that the USSR was in the enemy camp was only to be reinforced as Stalin took advantage of the war situation to extend his control over the states on his borders. In June 1940, Moscow demanded that 'friendly governments' be installed in the three Baltic States, and immediately invaded them. Rigged plebiscites were held, approving entry into the USSR. The secret police (NKVD) then embarked on wholesale arrests, murders and sovietisation. Further south, pressure was put on Romania which resulted in the annexation of Bessarabia, which had been part of Tsarist Russia, and Northern Bukovina, which had not. Romanian oil was vital to Germany, and Stalin was directly threatening German interests. With Britain's ability to keep Germany preoccupied with war in the west very uncertain at this time, these moves were very risky, and added very little to Soviet security: Romania and Finland had become enemies and the British and Americans convinced that Stalin was Hitler's closest collaborator.

Arctic Ocean

Petsamo

Nautsi

Murmansk

Gallivare

Kemijarvi • Salla

SWEDEN

Kemi

White Sea

Lulea

Gulf of
Bothnia

Suomussalmi

Soviet

Murmansk Railway

Kuhmo

Karelia

F I N L A N D

Ilomantsi

Lake
Saimaa

Tolvajarvi
Suojarvi
Kollaa

Karelian
Isthmus

Lake
Ladoga

USSR

Helsinki Porvoo Viipuri

Turku

Baltic
Sea

Hangö Gulf of Finland

Tallinn

Leningrad

Novgorod

Key

Above: The Soviet-Finnish War, 1939-40

Soviet attacks Nov 1939-Jan 1940
Finnish counter-attacks Jan 1940
'Mannerheim line'
Finnish defensive holding positions
Abortive Soviet naval assaults
Soviet attacks Feb 1940
New Soviet frontier March 1940
(Hangö leased to USSR)

Right: Soviet territorial expansion

Annexed from Poland Oct 1939
Annexed by Lithuania Oct 1939
Gained from Finland, Treaty of
Moscow, March 1940
Annexed June 1940 after fake
plebiscites
Annexed from Romania June 1940

NORWAY

SWEDEN

FINLAND

ESTONIA

LATVIA

LITHUANIA

USSR

Berlin

P O L A N D

GERMANY

SLOVAKIA

Vienna

BUKOVINA

HUNGARY

BESSARABIA

Budapest

ROMANIA

ITALY

Belgrade

Bucharest

YUGOSLAVIA

BULGARIA

Map 6: The 'Phoney War' and the Invasion of Norway

Allied strategy was based on the belief that the German economy was fundamentally weak, and that holding defensive positions and implementing a naval blockade would win victory by attrition. Unable to deliver a decisive victory against the Allied defensive position in the west, Hitler would be overthrown, bringing peace and the restoration of Polish independence. There were serious flaws to this approach, both in its fundamentals and in its implementation. The Nazi–Soviet Pact reduced the likelihood that Germany would need to station many troops on its eastern frontier, and also constituted a serious breach in the blockade.

Hitler offered peace to the Allies after completing the conquest of Poland, but Chamberlain no longer trusted him, and the war was now less about Poland than about the whole European balance of power. The period from October to April 1940 is often called the 'phoney war', a derisive term applied by an isolationist American senator. There was action elsewhere, but certainly it was a time of inaction on the Western Front – disastrously so for the Allies. The attrition strategy created a state of mind that avoided bold risks; passivity was all that was necessary. They failed even to develop an effective defensive strategy. The French and British continued to rearm, and a sizeable British Expeditionary Force (BEF) was deployed to France. The problem was the northern part of the line. Belgium and the Netherlands were determined to remain neutral, so refused to engage in any military planning and would not allow Allied forces into their countries. Allied planning had either to be based on leaving the Low Countries to the Germans or on guesses as to their defensive deployments and capabilities. The first option was rejected because it would compromise the whole defensive position. It was planned therefore to advance to the natural defensive lines in Belgium formed by the canals, in the hopes of forming a line with the Belgian Army. Unfortunately, German planning accurately predicted this move, and indeed welcomed it as it would draw the Allied forces forward into the trap to be sprung through the Ardennes.

There was more action at sea. The German Navy (Kriegsmarine), like the Army, was unprepared for war in 1939. The submarine force was small, and the two new battleships, *Tirpitz* and *Bismarck*, and the aircraft carrier *Graf Zeppelin*, were nowhere near completion (the latter never was). As it was, the submariners scored some spectacular early successes, aided by British tardiness in introducing up-to-date anti-submarine measures. Günther Prien in *U-47* became the first German Second World War hero when he penetrated the fleet anchorage at Scapa Flow and sank the battleship HMS *Royal Oak* on 14 October 1939. The aircraft carrier *Courageous* was another early victim of the U-boats,

as, more controversially, was the liner *Athenia* on 3 September. At the outbreak of war, some surface commerce raiders were at sea, and caused great disruption to merchant shipping. One, *Graf Spee*, was tracked down in the South Atlantic and engaged in the Battle of the River Plate by two British cruisers, *Ajax* and *Exeter* and the New Zealand-manned *Achilles*. After battering *Exeter*, *Graf Spee* took refuge in Montevideo. Deceived into thinking that a larger British force was waiting outside, its captain, Langsdorff, scuttled the ship and committed suicide.

One of *Graf Spee*'s supply ships, *Altmark*, was intercepted in February in Norwegian coastal waters by HMS *Cossack* and British prisoners-of-war on board were liberated. The British and French were still considering intervention in Scandinavia to interdict the ore traffic to Germany, at the least by mining Norwegian waters. After the *Altmark* incident, Admiral Raeder, commander-in-chief of the *Kriegsmarine*, convinced Hitler that he should pre-empt this in order to protect German interests and prevent the Allies gaining control of key Norwegian ports.

Not for the last time, the Germans moved faster than the Allies. On 9 April, without warning, German forces entered Denmark, which, being virtually unarmed, capitulated without a struggle. Naval forces, mountain troops and airborne units were sent to Norway to land at six points simultaneously. Despite the betrayal of the collaborator Vidkun Quisling, the Norwegians were able to hold up the Germans in time for Anglo-French forces to land. The Royal Navy had significant forces close by: they were unable to stop the Germans landing, but the *Kriegsmarine* suffered serious losses in the campaign, which it could ill afford. The new cruiser *Blücher* was sunk by a shore battery in the approaches to Oslo, two other cruisers were sunk and the cream of German destroyer forces was sunk in the two battles of Narvik. The two largest German ships, the battle-cruisers *Scharnhorst* and *Gneisenau*, plus the pocket battleship *Lützow*, were damaged – though the aircraft carrier HMS *Glorious* had been sunk in return.

The Germans, however, seized important airfields, enabling them to fly in further troops. The invasion of Norway was the world's first offensive airborne operation. The Allied response was poorly planned and executed, and German land forces fought effectively. The Allies landed at Andalsnes and Tromso and engaged the Germans at Trondheim, then were forced to withdraw within two weeks. Their forces further north in Narvik held on until June, when events on the Western Front heralded the end of the 'phoney war' and forced a withdrawal. The campaign demonstrated the close and effective inter-service cooperation that was to be the hallmark of German military operations throughout the war, and gave Germany important air and naval bases.

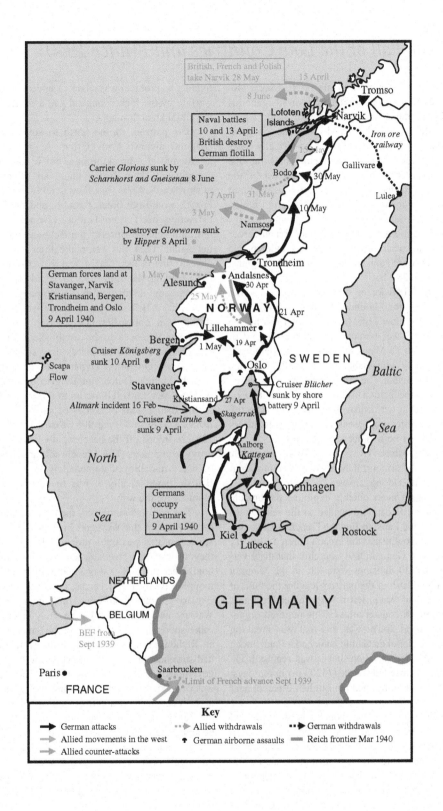

British, French and Polish take Narvik 28 May

15 April

Tromso

8 June

Lofoten
Islands

Narvik

Naval battles
10 and 13 April:
British destroy
German flotilla

Iron ore
railway

Gallivare

Carrier *Glorious* sunk by
Scharnhorst and *Gneisenau* 8 June

Bodo

30 May

Lulea

17 April

31 May

3 May

10 May

Namsos

Destroyer *Glowworm* sunk
by *Hipper* 8 April

18 April

Trondheim

German forces land at
Stavanger, Narvik
Kristiansand, Bergen,
Trondheim and Oslo
9 April 1940

1 May

Andalsnes

Alesund

30 Apr

25 May

N O R W A Y

21 Apr

Lillehammer

Bergen

Cruiser *Königsberg*
sunk 10 April

1 May

19 Apr

S W E D E N

Oslo

Baltic

Scapa
Flow

Stavanger

Cruiser *Blücher*
sunk by shore
battery 9 April

Altmark incident 16 Feb

Kristiansand

27 Apr

Sea

Cruiser *Karlsruhe*
sunk 9 April

Skagerrak

North

Aalborg

Kattegat

Sea

Copenhagen

Germans
occupy
Denmark
9 April 1940

Kiel

Lübeck

Rostock

NETHERLANDS

G E R M A N Y

BELGIUM

BEF from
Sept 1939

Paris

Saarbrucken

Limit of French advance Sept 1939

FRANCE

Key

→ German attacks
▸ Allied withdrawals
▸ German withdrawals
→ Allied movements in the west
♦ German airborne assaults
▬ Reich frontier Mar 1940
→ Allied counter-attacks

Map 7: The Fall of the Low Countries and France 1940

The Western Front burst into life on 10 May 1940. Hitler had imposed his preferences on his generals and forced them into an offensive plan, which General von Manstein had refined into one of great boldness, 'Sickle Stroke'. The plan worked virtually flawlessly. German forces overran the Netherlands rapidly, reaffirming a reputation for terror-bombing when the *Luftwaffe* attacked Rotterdam. Parachute troops captured the Belgian frontier fortress of Eben Emael. The Belgian Army lost its best defensive positions, but fought bravely. As Sickle Stroke anticipated, the BEF and French forces moved forward to what proved to be an indefensible position, and they were soon separated from the Belgians, who surrendered on 28 May.

By then, the Allied forces were being squeezed into an ever-diminishing area, hounded by the *Luftwaffe*. The *Schwerpunkt* ('main blow') of Manstein's plan had hit the French line where it was weakest, just above the end of the Maginot line. On 13 May Guderian's panzers emerged from the supposedly impassable narrow valleys of the Ardennes forest, at Sedan. The 1st Panzer Division secured a bridgehead, and the French forces, already numbed by *Stuka* attack, failed to act decisively in response. The 9th and 2nd French Armies were weak and poorly organised: this was expected to be a quiet sector, protected by the Ardennes and the Meuse river. In addition, while the French had plenty of armour, they divided it among their infantry units, and had no answer to the concentrated panzers. The German tanks quickly exploited the breach. They burst out from Sedan and headed to the sea. On 16 May, Churchill visited Paris, to find the French commander, General Gamelin, gloomy and the French Foreign Ministry burning its archives. Gamelin told Churchill that there was no reserve (though 30 divisions were idle in the Maginot line). The headlong rush of the panzers leaving the bulk of their infantry in their wake, left a long vulnerable flank, open to a determined counter-attack. This required organisation and command and it was this that was breaking down. As it was, Colonel de Gaulle launched a flank attack with the 4th Armoured Division, but it was repulsed. On 19 May, having advanced 200 miles (320 km) in ten days, the 2nd Panzer Division reached the English Channel near Abbeville.

The French command was hopelessly divided, and though Gamelin was replaced by Weygand, and the hero of Verdun, Marshal Pétain, called into the government, it could come up with no effective strategy to rally the French Army. It is often suggested that France was defeated in 1940 because it was a divided society, demoralised and decadent. However, individual French units fought like tigers. The problem was a lack of understanding of modern warfare by the high command and a certain fatalism after the initial breakthroughs.

The panzers turned north to squeeze the Allies in Belgium against Army Group A. Weygand organised an attempt at a breakthrough, but it was never properly coordinated. The British made an effective armoured push towards Arras, but they quickly concluded that the French would not break through, and the BEF turned to extracting itself from France. Dwindling supplies and the imminent collapse of the Belgians left their position untenable. They did not make their intentions entirely clear to their allies. On 24 May Hitler ordered a two-day halt, leaving the *Luftwaffe* to attack (possibly to give Göring some distinction in the campaign, possibly in the hopes that a British separate peace would be more likely if they did not suffer heavy casualties). This allowed perimeter defences to be established. Bravely held by French and British rearguards they enabled a successful evacuation, Operation Dynamo, to be organised. Forty British, French, Dutch and Belgian destroyers were sent in, but larger ships fell victim to mines and the *Luftwaffe*, so the British sent in hordes of small civilian craft, and from 26 May to 4 June 900 vessels succeeded in lifting 338,226 troops off the beaches, albeit without any of their heavy equipment. The French soldiers who were taken off were re-deployed immediately to Normandy. For the British, paradoxically, it was to be one of the defining moments of the war.

The end in France was then swift. The French were established on the Weygand line on the Somme and the Aisne, but this was not a proper defensive line, and while they resisted the first attack on 5 June, they could not hold. Once through, it was a matter of speedy advance and mopping up for the Germans. Paris was declared an open city to prevent it suffering the fate of Rotterdam and Warsaw, and it fell on 14 June. Italy entered the war for some spoils and on 22 June, in the same railway carriage at Rethondes near Compiègne in which the Germans had surrendered in 1918, the representatives of the French government, now headed by Pétain, surrendered. France was divided. Northern France and the Atlantic coast were to be occupied. Alsace-Lorraine would become part of the Reich, and the industrial north-east around Lille was to be administered by the German command in Brussels. Italy gained small parts of Savoy and an occupation zone that included Corsica. Unoccupied France would be governed by Pétain from Vichy. French soldiers who were prisoners-of-war would remain so, and France was required to make economic reparations.

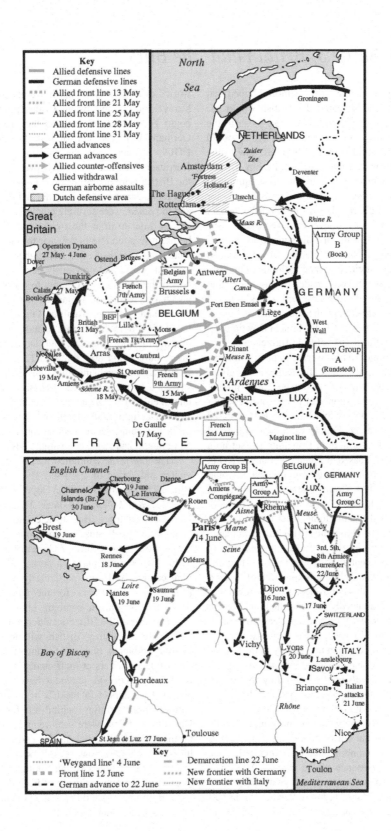

Map 8: The Battle of Britain and 'the Blitz'

Hitler, an admirer of the British Empire, hoped that once France was defeated the British would see sense and sue for peace. There were those in the British ruling elite who wished to, fearing that Britain would be bankrupted by the war. However, Churchill, now Prime Minister, made it clear that under his leadership, Britain would fight on. The Germans had no specialist equipment for an opposed sea crossing. As a precondition for Operation Sealion, which would cross the English Channel at its narrowest point with converted river barges, the *Luftwaffe* had the task of achieving air superiority, so that it could prevent the Royal Navy interfering. Britain's ground forces had left most of their equipment behind at Dunkirk, so if a successful crossing was made, it was likely that another German victory would follow very quickly. In the way stood the RAF – effectively, the squadrons of Fighter Command, commanded by Air Chief Marshal Dowding.

Dowding had held back his valuable fighter squadrons from the battle in France. They were equipped with two excellent aircraft, the Spitfire and Hurricane. Numbers of aircraft were adequate, with production at 500 a month. The main problem was the supply of pilots: only 200 per month to go with the 1,450 with which the RAF entered the battle. The greatest assets Fighter Command possessed were organisation and information. Dowding had set up a system of central control based at Fighter Command HQ at Stanmore. Ground commanders in the control centres would vector in fighters against German attacks, by utilising information from the Observer Corps and from a network of radar stations, called Chain Home. This meant that 11 Group, the south-eastern command of Fighter Command, could keep its aircraft on the ground, 'scrambling' in response to German concentrations gathering over their air-fields in the Pas-de-Calais. While this approach of feeding aircraft into the battle in this controlled, piecemeal manner had its critics, it was undoubtedly suited to the limitations of forces that Dowding and Air Vice-Marshal Park, command-ing the 23 squadrons of 11 Group, had at their disposal.

They were helped by German uncertainty as to strategy. The two Air Fleets in France attacked shipping and ports in the Channel (the '*Kanalkampf*'), from July to August. Göring then launched Operation Eagle to attack the RAF's infrastructure, including aircraft factories. Only scattered attacks were launched on the Chain Home stations; while some were temporarily put out of action, the radar towers were hard to destroy by bombing, and German intelligence underestimated the importance of the system. The crisis for the RAF began when the attack was switched to their airfields on 24 August. Manston, North Weald, Biggin Hill and others were seriously damaged. The RAF was being worn down. The Germans however, were also suffering heavy losses – and where British pilots who bailed out could fight again as soon as they had another aircraft, Germans were captured or lost. The fine Messerschmitt Bf109, a match for the Spitfire and superior to the Hurricane, only had fuel to stay over England briefly, while the British were operating close to their bases. Some of the German aircraft – especially the Bf110, the Dornier Do17 and the *Stuka*, were severely outclassed.

In order to draw the fighters out for a decisive battle before it was too late in the year for Operation Sealion, the tactic was switched on 7 September to daylight raids on London. These had previously been avoided as Hitler still hoped the British would agree to a negotiated peace, and also feared retaliation against German cities. While causing damage and civilian casualties, this was a crucial relief for the RAF. On 15 September a mass raid was launched to overwhelm the defences, but Dowding had husbanded his resources and now threw in 12 Group as well. To the Germans, not realising that the British resources were stretched to the limit, the strength of the RAF appeared unbroken. On 17 September, Sealion was postponed for 1940. Daylight raids continued, as Göring believed his *Luftwaffe* could secure victory on its own, but by mid-November it had switched to night raids, such were its losses.

The *Luftwaffe* continued these attacks throughout the winter and spring of 1940–41. The British dubbed it 'the Blitz'. The Germans had developed radio beam guidance systems, *Knickebein* and later *X-Gerät* that gave them increased accuracy. British scientists eventually devised ways to jam the beams, but not soon enough to prevent the destruction of the centre of Coventry on 14/15 November 1940. Attacks took place on ports, industrial centres, cul-tural centres, and most particularly on London. Germany had no heavy bombers, for the *Luftwaffe* had not been developed for strategic bombing, but the damage was great.

The aim of the Blitz, once Sealion was cancelled, was essentially to destroy British will to continue the war. Despite outbreaks of local discontent (usually over provi-sion of deep shelters or inefficiency in re-housing, feeding or clothing victims) it tended to have the opposite effect. It also had an impact in the US in moving hesitant public opinion more strongly behind aid for Britain. Although Dowding and Park were soon relieved of their commands, on the grounds that their tactics had been mistaken, most historical opinion now sees Park and Dowding as the victors of the Battle of Britain, along with their small cadre of pilots – not only British, but from the Dominions (with some from the US) and Poles and Czechs who had escaped when their own countries fell.

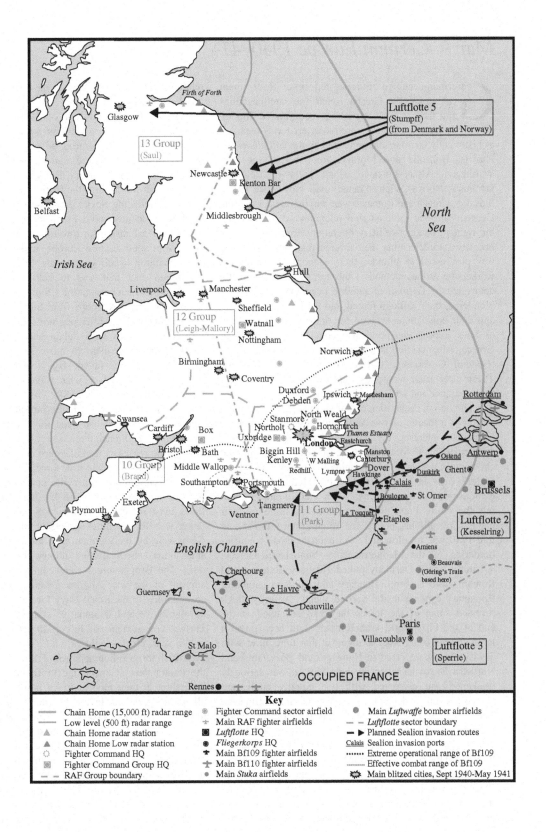

Key

——— Chain Home (15,000 ft) radar range	⊙ Fighter Command sector airfield
——— Low level (500 ft) radar range	✚ Main RAF fighter airfields
▲ Chain Home radar station	▣ *Luftflotte* HQ
▲ Chain Home Low radar station	● *Fliegerkorps* HQ
○ Fighter Command HQ	✚ Main Bf109 fighter airfields
▣ Fighter Command Group HQ	✚ Main Bf110 fighter airfields
– – RAF Group boundary	● Main *Stuka* airfields
	● Main *Luftwaffe* bomber airfields
	– – *Luftflotte* sector boundary
	▬▶ Planned Sealion invasion routes
	Calais Sealion invasion ports
	······· Extreme operational range of Bf109
	······· Effective combat range of Bf109
	✺ Main blitzed cities, Sept 1940–May 1941

Map 9: German Europe 1940–41

German-occupied Europe fell into three main categories: the Greater Reich, the satellites/allies and the occupied territories. Incorporated directly into the Reich immediately were those territories regarded as historically German and populated by the *volksdeutsche*: Austria, Bohemia and Moravia from before the war, Warthegau, Alsace-Lorraine, small parts of Belgium. Denmark, Norway, Vichy France (until November 1942), Slovakia, Croatia and Romania were run by regimes that the Germans allowed some internal autonomy, while reserving the right to conduct military operations from there when necessary, to determine their foreign relations and as the war progressed to plunder their economies and obtain workers by various methods. Other territories were directly controlled by German or satellite occupying forces, and plundered, their workers forced into labour for the Reich, and their populations scoured for 'impure' elements such as Jews, gypsies and political opponents. These included Greece, Albania, Serbia, central and eastern Poland (the 'General Government'), Byelorussia and the Ukraine. These three latter territories were earmarked for population clearance and settlement by Germans.

The Italian declaration of war established the Mediterranean as a theatre of war. While this was clearly a threat to British interests, the region offered an opportunity for British naval forces to strike at places of their own choosing in a strategy of stretching the enemy's resources. Hitler's early lack of interest in the Mediterranean was demonstrated in the settlement with Vichy France, which left the entire French Mediterranean coastline in their hands. Overall, his policy for south-eastern Europe in mid-1940 was to allow Italy to dominate those countries bordering on the Mediterranean – Yugoslavia, Greece, Albania – while Germany pulled Hungary, Bulgaria and Romania into its orbit. Hungary and Bulgaria gained at Romania's expense in the Second Vienna Awards, which reversed some of the losses they had sustained at the end of the First World War. Romania had been given a large amount of territory to digest at that time; now, with Transylvania transferred to Hungary, and Bessarabia and Northern Bukovina taken by the USSR, it was seriously weakened and presented with two equally unpleasant choices: to fall under either Soviet or German influence. There was never any doubt that Romania's right-wing regime under Antonescu, despite the humiliation at Vienna, would side with the Germans. Hitler began to deploy troops into the country in October, with the primary objective of securing the flow of oil from the vital wells at Ploesti. It was Bulgaria that was most resistant to joining the Tripartite Pact, mainly out of caution and a desire not to offend the USSR (Bulgaria had a tradition of close relations with Russia). Yugoslavia kept its distance, but avoided a breach.

During the second half of 1940, there was some uncertainty as to where German policy would lead next. Foreign Minister Ribbentrop advocated a grand design linking all the 'dissatisfied' nations (the USSR, Germany, Italy, Japan, Spain, Hungary, Bulgaria), producing a great coalition that would force the British to negotiate peace: he worked at reducing Soviet–Japanese tensions and encouraged Hitler to meet with Franco. The Soviets refused to direct their expansionism towards the British Empire and away from south-eastern Europe, and the main outcome of Ribbentrop's policy was the Soviet–Japanese non-aggression pact that was to help divert the Japanese southwards, which brought the US into the war and allowed Stalin to bring back troops from Siberia to save Moscow in December 1941. Hitler was not fully committed to the idea: his meetings with Pétain and Franco in October 1940, to persuade them to move against the British in the Mediterranean, failed. By November 1940, Hitler had already resolved on what was anyway his preferred strategy – invasion of the USSR.

For the British, the Mediterranean had always been significant. The plan had been for Britain to control the eastern half, the French the western. Now, if Britain wanted to keep the sea-lanes to its Eastern empire open, it had to do the job itself. A naval task force, Force H, was formed under Vice-Admiral Somerville at Gibraltar. The Italian Navy had fine ships, but was handicapped as were other fleets by a reluctance of the high command to risk its larger vessels. The most successful attacks on the British Navy were by the German and Italian air forces and by small units – especially the 'human chariot' guided torpedoes. The British forces were commanded by their best admiral of the war, Andrew Cunningham. Operating in seas familiar to the Royal Navy for 150 years, he adopted an aggressive and imaginative strategy from the outset. Surface engagements in July 1940 set the pattern. Later in the year, on the night of 11/12 November, antiquated Swordfish torpedo-bombers from HMS *Illustrious* attacked the Italian fleet at anchorage in Taranto and sank three battleships at their moorings. Air power was to dominate all naval operations in the Mediterranean, but the navy to learn the fullest lesson from Taranto was the Japanese.

The British bombarded Genoa on 9 February 1941, and then on 28 March off Cape Matapan, Cunningham's forces engaged and sank three modern Italian cruisers. Though the battleships escaped, they were to play an insignificant part in the rest of the war. The arrival of German airpower, however, on the Mediterranean shores, would alter the whole naval balance, and put Britain's hold there in jeopardy.

ICELAND

FINLAND

NORWAY

SWEDEN

ESTONIA

LATVIA

LITHUANIA

U S S R

SUWALKI

EIRE

GREAT
BRITAIN

London

DENMARK

NETH.

BELG.

DANZIG

ZICHENAU

Berlin

WARTHEGAU

Warsaw

GENERAL
GOVERNMENT

Paris

LORRAINE

ALSACE

F R A N C E

Vichy

SWITZ.

Under
Italian
supervision

Genoa

GERMANY

SLOVAKIA

Vienna

HUNGARY

Budapest

TRANSYLVANIA

N. BUKOVINA

BESSARABIA

ROMANIA

Ploesti

Bucharest

S. DOBRUJA

PORTUGAL

SPAIN

Toulon

CORSICA

ITALY

YUGOSLAVIA

Belgrade

BULGARIA

Sofia

Rome

ALBANIA

Gibraltar (Br.)

Mediterranean Sea

SARDINIA

Naples

Brindisi

Taranto

Salonika

GREECE

TURKEY

Force H
3 July 1940

Cape Spartivento x
27 Nov 1940

from
Jan
1941

SICILY

x Cape
Spartivento
9 July 1940

Athens

CRETE (Gr.)

SPANISH MOROCCO

Mers-el-Kebir

Algiers

ALGERIA

TUNISIA

MALTA (Br.)

Cape Matapan
28 Mar 1941

x

MOROCCO

FRENCH   NORTH   AFRICA
(under Vichy control)

Tripoli

Benghazi

Tobruk

EGYPT

L I B Y A

El Agheila

Key

German reich	German satellite	Italy
Incorporated into Reich	Under German influence	Annexed by Italy June 1940
Occupied by Germany	Ceded to Bulgaria by Romania Aug 1940	Annexed by USSR 1939-40
Allied to Germany	Ceded to Hungary by Romania Sept 1940	Allied Mediterranean convoys
	Luftwaffe attacks on Malta convoys	Axis Mediterranean convoys

Map 10: The War in Africa and the Middle East

Like the British, the Axis powers, though less whole-heartedly, sought to stretch their enemy's resources, in particular in East Africa and the Middle East. In East Africa, Italian forces took advantage of Britain's distraction to invade British Somaliland from Ethiopia on 5 August 1940, and conquer it easily. The previous month they had penetrated into Kenya and had occupied frontier towns in Anglo-Egyptian Sudan. Italian forces were larger than the British Empire forces in the area, but they were isolated from reinforcements. In September, despite the threat posed to Egypt by Italians in Libya, the British C-in-C Middle East, General Wavell, sent the 5th Indian Division to the Sudan. The 1st South African Division was formed in Kenya. After Wavell's successes in the Western Desert in December (see Map 11), the 4th Indian Division was sent up the Nile as well.

There was a number of reasons why the British wished to fight a campaign in Ethiopia, despite it being so far from the major theatres of war. South African premier Jan Smuts needed a victory to get public support for the war. The British were concerned to counter growing German influence with some Muslims in the Middle East by gaining a victory at the nexus of the African and Asian parts of the Islamic world. Strategically, it commanded the approaches to the Suez Canal, though the Italians never had the naval force there to make this a serious threat. Campaigning began when irregular forces called 'Gideon Force' under Colonel Orde Wingate, including Ethiopian patriot forces and Emperor Haile Selassie himself, crossed from Sudan into Ethiopia. The Indian Divisions did so too, on 19 January. On 11 February the South Africans, with West and East African forces, under General Alan Cunningham, attacked from Kenya.

There followed an old-fashioned campaign of mountain strongholds and desert forts. The Indians took Eritrea by 2 April, after fierce fighting around Keren. Having taken Italian Somaliland easily, Cunningham fought a tough battle at Harar, won by his Nigerian troops of the Royal West African Frontier Force. On 5 April, the Italians' colonial troops having melted away, Addis Ababa fell, and Haile Selassie made a triumphant return with Wingate on 5 May.

Among the units fighting at Keren were parts of the French Foreign Legion, fighting under de Gaulle's Free French banner. Many parts of French Africa remained loyal to Vichy. More worrying to the British in 1940–41 were French naval forces, still formidable, and French colonies in the strategically sensitive Levant. After the French surrender, Churchill had moved quickly and ruth-lessly to deal with the naval issue. Fearing that French ships would be a dangerous addition to German naval strength, he sought to neutralise them. In some places this was achieved, notably Alexandria, where French ships remained for the duration of the war, having given up their ammunition and fuel. In others the French Navy proudly refused to sacrifice its honour. At Mers-el-Kebir in Morocco on 3 July 1940, in a sad finale for the Anglo-French alliance against Hitler, Somerville's Force H demanded the French scuttle or surrender. Vice-Admiral Gensoul refused and the British then sank one battleship and damaged two others. Aircraft from HMS *Ark Royal* then torpedoed the battleship *Dunkerque*. About 1,200 French sailors were killed in this sad incident – though it may have had a significant outcome in that it signalled to those in the US who doubted Britain's resolve that they were ruthlessly determined to fight on.

In the Middle East, German agents received a ready response from Iraqi nationalists led by Rashid Ali and from Arabs disgruntled at Britain's failure to halt Jewish immigration into Palestine (Zionist groups were equally aggrieved with the British for the limitations they placed on this immigration, and waged a campaign against them throughout the war). Rashid Ali seized power on 3 April 1941. British signals decrypts revealed the Axis to be supplying aircraft to him through Syria. British forces were too strong, however: those besieged in the air-base at Habbaniya chased their besiegers away, and the 10th Indian Division landed at Basra and restored the pro-British regent in Baghdad on 31 May. These events underlined how the Vichy regimes in Lebanon and Syria threatened the security of British forces in Egypt. On 23 June, British, Australian, Indian and Free French forces moved in. A short and bitter war, pitting Frenchman against Frenchman, followed. Finally, a breakthrough by the 7th Australian Division south of Beirut induced the French commander General Dentz to seek terms. Less than 6,000 of his 38,000 troops opted to join the Free French.

Further south, concerned that the Japanese might spread their operations across the Indian Ocean, British, Free French and Empire forces landed on Madagascar in Operation Ironclad in May 1942. The French fought hard, and though Diego Suarez fell on 7 May, Tananarive (Antananarivo), the capital, held out till September. This operation was not well-handled and its principal legacy was to reinforce the impact of the Levant operations the previous year in further damaging de Gaulle's patriotic standing with many Frenchmen.

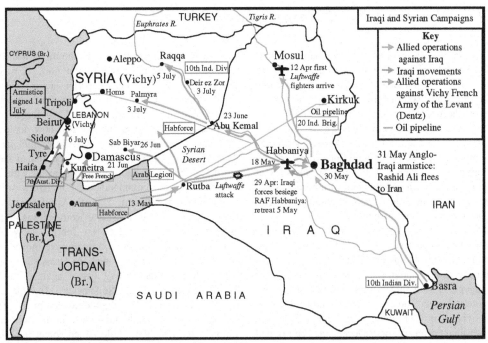

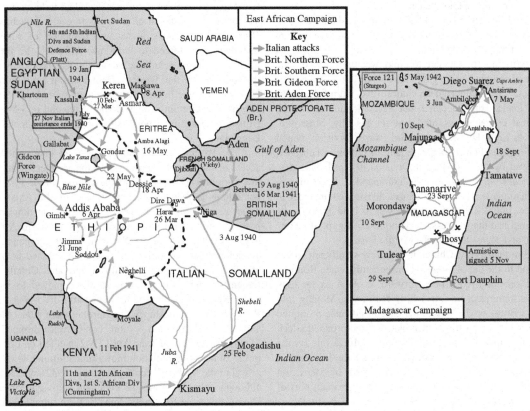

Map 11: Western Desert Campaigns 1940–41

The war in the Western Desert had a character of its own. Fought on open country for the most part, with a scattered population, and between armoured and mobile forces that were relatively small by the standards of other theatres, there was much less bombing of civilians, no atrocities, and both sides treated the other generally with a respect not shown elsewhere. Indeed, they shared a common foe: the harsh conditions of the desert. It was a campaign determined ultimately by logistics of supply and material, but it had the aura of a pure clash of arms – not least because the Axis commander, General Rommel, preferred to ignore such matters.

The theatre opened in June 1940 when Italian forces under Marshal Graziani moved slowly into Egypt from Libya, halting at Sidi Barrani. Despite Britain being under threat of German invasion, Churchill sent armoured reinforcements to Egypt, to join three Commonwealth Divisions as the Western Desert Force (13 Corps) under General O'Connor. The C-in-C Middle East, General Wavell, launched a brilliant offensive on 9 December. They routed the numerically superior Italian forces, conquered Cyrenaica and by February 1941 130,000 Italian soldiers had surrendered after O'Connor had sped across the desert to get ahead of them at Beda Fomm.

With the British and Commonwealth forces on the verge of complete victory, and thus control of a vital part of the southern Mediterranean littoral, two fateful decisions were made. Hitler decided that he could not accept the political consequences of defeat for his ally, Mussolini. The 5th Light Division of the 3rd Panzer Division, which had fought in France, began to land in Tripoli in February, followed by the 15th Panzer Division in April. This new *Deutsches Afrika Korps* was commanded by Rommel, who had made a name as a panzer division commander in France. Initially, its sole purpose was to hold Tripolitania. Rommel had bigger ideas: the conquest of Egypt, the Suez Canal and access to oil in the Middle East.

Simultaneously, Churchill withdrew significant forces to send to the aid of Greece. Consequently, when Rommel made unauthorised probes forward as soon as he took up his command, he found little resistance. Moving into Mersa Brega on 31 March, the ease of advance prompted Rommel to a typically bold stroke. A three-pronged attack took the *Afrika Korps* to the Sollum–Halfaya line on the Egyptian border in two weeks, capturing the key port of Benghazi and the *Beau Geste*-style forts of Msus and Mechili along the way and placing the other main port of Cyrenaica, Tobruk, under siege.

Rommel was unable to breach the defences of Tobruk – a vital target for him as otherwise his supply-lines stretched back as far as Benghazi. On 15 June the British launched Operation Battleaxe to relieve the port. It was poorly coordinated and Rommel's superior tactics thwarted the British. The next British and Commonwealth offensive was Operation Crusader in November. Their forces had been renamed 8th Army in September and now deployed over 750 tanks. Against this, the Axis forces, *Panzergruppe Afrika*, had 320 tanks, of which 146 were Italian and mostly obsolete. Churchill had replaced Wavell with General Auchinleck, and command of 8th Army was given to General Cunningham. The 8th Army attacked on 18 November, achieving surprise as Rommel was in the midst of preparing another attack on Tobruk. However, once again, by quick thinking and aggressive moves, Rommel was able to retrieve the situation. Unsatisfactory British tank tactics brought heavy losses against the German 88 mm anti-tank guns. Nonetheless, five days' heavy fighting around Sidi Rezegh reduced Rommel to 100 tanks. He then made a typically bold dash for the frontier, threatening to outflank the whole Allied force, but ultimately failed to destroy them. Crusader itself had failed to relieve Tobruk or inflict defeat on the Axis forces, but such were *Panzergruppe Afrika*'s losses and depletion of supplies that they were forced to withdraw. Although the Italian generals insisted on holding at Gazala, Rommel knew that the logistics of the Western Desert meant pulling right back to El Agheila, whence they had started in March. Tobruk was therefore relieved and at the end of 1941 the British were again in possession of Cyrenaica, including Benghazi.

The Western Desert campaigns were determined by access to supplies. The naval war in the Mediterranean was therefore crucial to their outcome. At the end of 1941 the pendulum had swung back in favour of the Axis. The issues centred on a tiny British colony. As an important base for interfering with Axis convoys to North Africa, Malta was the key to the Western Desert campaign. Its air defences at one point early on were reduced to three obsolete biplanes named Faith, Hope and Charity. In December 1941, Fliegerkorps X was deployed to Sicily under Kesselring, along with a squadron of U-boats. *Ark Royal* and the battleship HMS *Barham* were sunk. Malta was close to starvation – more bombs were dropped on Malta between January and April 1942 than fell on London in the Blitz. The population moved underground. Only the arrival of the 'Pedestal' convoy in August 1942 saved Malta, although only five of its 12 merchant ships got through. During this time Rommel's convoys were unmolested, so he was able to grow strong and harbour grand ambitions once again.

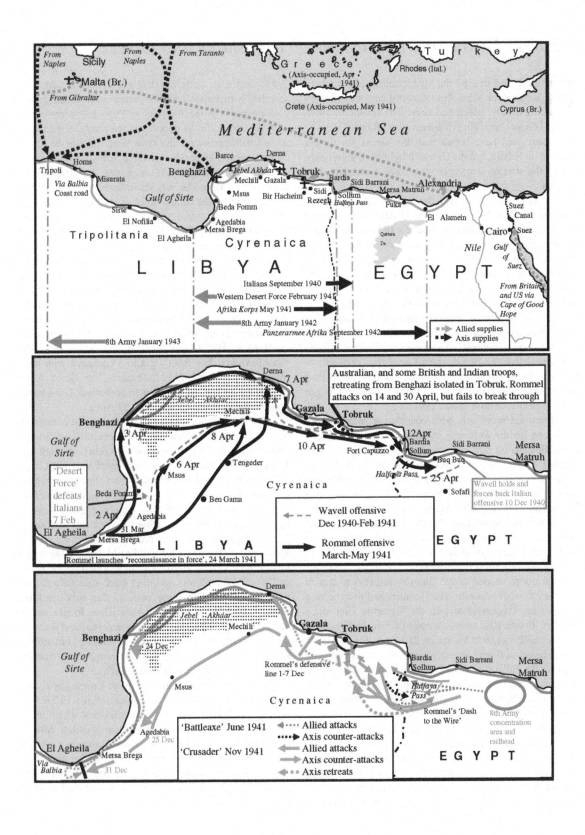

Map 12: The German Invasions of Yugoslavia and Greece

Hitler's plan to leave the Mediterranean and southern Balkans for Mussolini to control began to go awry when Italy, which had occupied Albania in 1939, attacked Greece with Hitler's approval on 28 October 1940. Hitler may well have hoped that this would put further pressure on Britain, but the Greeks fought back vigorously, and by the start of December were counter-attacking into Albania.

By that time Hitler had decided to save Mussolini from humiliation. He also wished to deprive the British both of a propaganda coup and access to bases in Greece that they could use to attack vital resources in the Balkans. The Greeks, in point of fact, were taking pains not to allow the British to get heavily involved, so as not to provoke the Germans, and this was to have an impact on finding an effective coordinated strategy when they did attack.

The Greek dictator, Metaxas, died on 19 January. The Greek army commander-in-chief, General Papagos, was less concerned than Metaxas about aggravating the Germans and agreed that the British should send four divisions to reinforce the 18 Greek ones facing the Italians. The British forces were withdrawn from Wavell's forces and began arriving in Greece on 4 March 1941.

Hitler had previously been considering seizing bases in Greece for the *Luftwaffe* to keep Britain from threatening Balkans oil and other resources. The British move decided him to go for a full occupation. On 1 March, Bulgaria, fearful of German strength, had come into line and joined the Tripartite Pact. German forces from Romania began deploying through Bulgaria towards the Greek frontier. Hitler was determined that the British would not be able to use their seapower to strike against the flanks of his forthcoming campaign against the USSR.

For the operation (code-named 'Marita') to succeed, German troops needed to use Yugoslav railways to launch an attack through Monastir. The Germans had been putting pressure on Yugoslavia to join the Tripartite Pact since October. Prince Paul, who was pro-British, had resisted, but eventually did so in Vienna on 25 March. On 26 March a coup began in Belgrade, led by Serb officers and encouraged by the British, forcing Paul to resign as regent. The new government under General Simovic had little chance of survival. Yugoslavia was surrounded by countries with claims to its territory, and itself contained internal divisions, especially between Serbs and Croats. The coup gave Hitler the pretext to act fast and ruthlessly. The Yugoslav Army was ill-prepared and poorly deployed in an attempt to defend the whole length of its long frontier. The air force, which had led the coup, was overwhelmed within hours of the German assault on 6 April. The same air offensive caused 3,000 deaths in raids on Belgrade. The German Army, together with Italian and Hungarian units struck quickly, causing panic in the ill-prepared Yugoslav forces. Croats and Slovenes took the opportunity to proclaim themselves as independent states: the right-wing Ustashi in Croatia in particular collaborated actively with the invader. The attackers suffered only 151 casualties. An armistice was signed on 17 April. The only senior Serbian officer prepared to fight on was the deputy chief of staff of the 2nd Army, Draza Mihailovic, who led a small band into the mountains, which later became the Četnik resistance movement.

The plans for the defence of Greece were fatally compromised by the collapse of Yugoslavia, for forces had been deployed by Papagos on the Bulgarian frontier, the Aliakhmon line and the Albanian frontier, all with flanks resting on the Yugoslav defences in Macedonia. As they were now breached, the Allied forces in Greece were forced into helter-skelter retreat. The Metaxas line surrendered on 9 April. British and Anzac forces began evacuating the Aliakhmon line from 16 April. Equipped with motor transport, they were able to escape. The Greek forces, dependent on horses, were not so fortunate. The swastika was hoisted over the Acropolis on 27 April.

The final act was played out in Crete. The commander of the *Luftwaffe* airborne troops, General Kurt Student, volunteered for the job (Operation Merkur) – though most in the OKW thought Malta a much more important target. Although the British had warning from signals intelligence of what was coming, they were poorly equipped and disorganised after the retreat from Greece. Despite inflicting heavy casualties on the parachutists when they attacked on 20 May, they were unable to prevent the Germans securing a foothold on the crucial airfield at Maleme. Able then to land more troops by air, the Germans rolled up the British and New Zealand forces, to inflict another decisive defeat – though one that had some cost, as the airborne forces suffered such destruction that they never fought another such campaign. The Royal Navy intercepted and destroyed German reinforcements, escorted by Italians, but suffered heavy losses off Crete on 22 May (four cruisers and four destroyers lost and many more damaged).

The greatest significance of these campaigns is often said to be the effect on the invasion of the USSR. It is argued that Marita forced a six-week delay which was to be crucial in preventing the Germans taking Moscow before the Russian winter intervened. However, the timing of the invasion was probably not affected by these operations, and they were in any case regarded by Hitler, probably rightly, as vital for the success of Barbarossa by protecting its flank.

AUSTRIA

HUNGARY

German 2nd Army (Weichs)

Slovenia

Ljubljana

Itd 2nd Army
Fiume

Zagreb
10 Apr

Croatia

Hungarian 3rd Army

Banat

Novi Sad

41st Pz Corps

ROMANIA

Belgrade
12 Apr

Serbia

Zara (Ital)

Split

Bosnia

Sarajevo
16 Apr

Uzice

YUGOSLAVIA

Nis
8 Apr

Pz Group 1
(Kleist)

*Adriatic
Sea*

Dubrovnik
17 Apr

Montenegro

Italian
9th Army

ALBANIA

Skopje
7 Apr

6 Apr
Veles

BULGARIA

Sofia

German 12th Army
(List)

Durazzo

ITALY

Italian
11th Army

Macedonia

9 Apr Monastir

Metaxas Line

Salonika
9 Apr

Thassos
16 Apr

Aliakhmon
Line

Greek 1st
Army
(Surr 23 Apr)

Ioannina
20 Apr

Corfu

Larissa
19Apr

Br 'W'
Force
(Wilson)

*Aegean
Sea*

Lemnos
25 Apr

GREECE

26 Apr
Thermopylae

Lamia
Missolonghi

Euboea

Khios
4 May

Ionian Sea

Patras

Corinth

Athens
27 Apr

Piraeus

Peloponnese

Kalamata
28 Apr

Peloponnese

British Evacuation to Crete:
completed 30 Apr

Key

--- Limits of Greek advance 1 Mar 1941
— Italian-Greek front line 6 Apr
— Anglo-Greek defensive lines
······ British 'W' Force front line 16 Apr
······ 'W' Force front line 20 Apr
—·— Greek front line 23 Apr
→ Hungarian attacks
→ Italian attacks
→ German attacks
↟ German airborne assaults

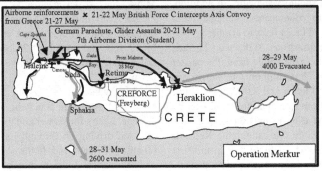

Airborne reinforcements
from Greece 21-27 May

✗ 21-22 May British Force C intercepts Axis Convoy

German Parachute, Glider Assaults 20-21 May
7th Airborne Division (Student)

Cape Spatha

Suda
Bay

From Maleme
28 May

28-29 May
4000 Evacuated

Maleme

Canea

Suda

Retimo

Sun 30 May

CREFORCE
(Freyberg)

Heraklion

Sphakia

C R E T E

28-31 May
2600 evacuated

Operation Merkur

Map 13: The Invasion of the USSR 1941

For Hitler, the real struggle was with the USSR. By the end of July, he ordered planning to begin for Operation Barbarossa. The Soviet–German alliance was one of convenience, but the tensions were never far below the surface. Stalin supplied Germany with significant war materials, particularly oil, but during 1940 slowed down on the delivery of them. The Soviets would not accept the geo-strategic position they were offered, refusing to concede eastern and south-eastern Europe in return for promises of British territory in India and the Middle East. Stalin was apparently confident that Germany, embroiled with Britain, would not risk a war in the east. Recognition of the Simovic government in Belgrade in April 1941 demonstrated that he still believed this, even though the Germans had begun to build up their forces in Poland. After the German invasion of the Balkans, Stalin reversed course and the flow of supplies was restored, to continue right up to the day the Germans invaded.

Stalin still hoped a German attack could be avoided or delayed. His forces remained under orders to avoid provocation. Stalin received plenty of warnings during the spring of 1941 that Hitler's military build-up in Poland and Romania was not just the prelude to economic or territorial demands. The evidence suggests he was under the delusion that he could still come to terms with Hitler. To make matters worse, Soviet forces were stationed too far forward, in territory only recently acquired, poorly prepared for defence and unconnected to the Soviet railway system – Stalin's annexations in 1939–40 had put his forces among a resentful population and ahead of the prepared defensive position, the Stalin line. There were preparatory deployments before 22 June, but they were incomplete, and headquarters units in particular were not in place. Moreover, the Red Army had neglected defensive strategic theory and training, and Stalin believed that the way to counter *blitzkrieg* was by taking the offensive, so that far from preparing for defence in depth, his army was deployed for advances into East Prussia should war begin. In addition, Stalin was not prepared to countenance strategic withdrawal from territories he had taken risks to acquire.

The consequences were disastrous. At dawn on 22 June, the *Wehrmacht* advanced along the whole front, the panzer divisions in the spearhead. Three million German troops went into action, with 3,300 tanks and 7,000 heavy guns, accompanied by divisions from Romania, followed later by Finns, Slovaks, Italians and even a division from Spain. The 2,000 aircraft of the *Luftwaffe* caught the Red Air Force on the ground, destroying 1,200 aircraft in the first day (one quarter of its front-line strength). The panzers made rapid progress and their penetrative thrusts left the defenders surrounded in large but isolated pockets, to be mopped up by the infantry following behind. It looked as if Hitler's expectation – that 'once the door had been kicked down, the entire structure will collapse like a house of cards' – would be proved correct.

German forces were divided into three, under Leeb, Bock and von Rundstedt. Leeb's forces would push up through the Baltic States – the fighting-ground of the Teutonic Knights – with Leningrad the ultimate objective. They would be aided by Finnish attacks in Karelia in revenge for the defeat of 1940. Bock would advance along Napoleon's route, through Minsk and Smolensk to Moscow. South of the 40,000 square mile Pripet Marshes (impenetrable to modern armed forces), Rundstedt was to advance into the rich agricultural land of the Ukraine and on to the great industrial areas of the Don and Donets river basins, and the oil-rich Caucasus. There had been considerable disagreement between Hitler and his army chiefs over strategy. OKH (Army high command) preferred a thrust at Moscow, which they believed the Soviets would defend with their main armies. Such an advance would therefore bring what they believed to be the optimum aim, the destruction of an enemy's armies, and then the capture of their capital. They had broadened their ideas to include thrusts towards Leningrad and Kiev. This was the strategy that was approved in Hitler's Barbarossa directive in December 1940. Unlike his generals, Hitler saw the principal strategic objective to be the capture of resources, which would destroy the enemy's ability to continue fighting, while strengthening Germany's own forces and easing the economic burdens that Hitler was always cautious about imposing on the people of the Reich. These issues were not to come to a head until July. Initially, the Soviet dispositions allowed all three Army Groups to make stunningly rapid advances in the dry high summer, across the steppes that were ideal territory for mobile warfare. Bock's spearheads, Panzer Groups Two (Guderian) and Three (Hoth) advanced at 50 miles (80 km) a day. After closing the pincers around Minsk, they struck eastwards again, now designated 4th Panzer Army under von Kluge. The Minsk pocket surrendered on 9 July. The Smolensk encirclement was completed by 17 July and contained 25 Soviet divisions. Resistance lasted until 5 August. Some 310,000 Soviet prisoners were taken.

Meanwhile, Army Group North was racing towards Leningrad. Although achieving no mass encirclements, by 30 June, Leeb's forces were on the Dvina, piercing the Stalin line and driving on through Latvia during July to within 60 miles of Leningrad. In the south, Rundstedt's Romanian and Hungarian divisions headed across the Dniester and Yuzhni Bug rivers towards Odessa while his German forces crossed the Ukrainian steppe heading for Kiev.

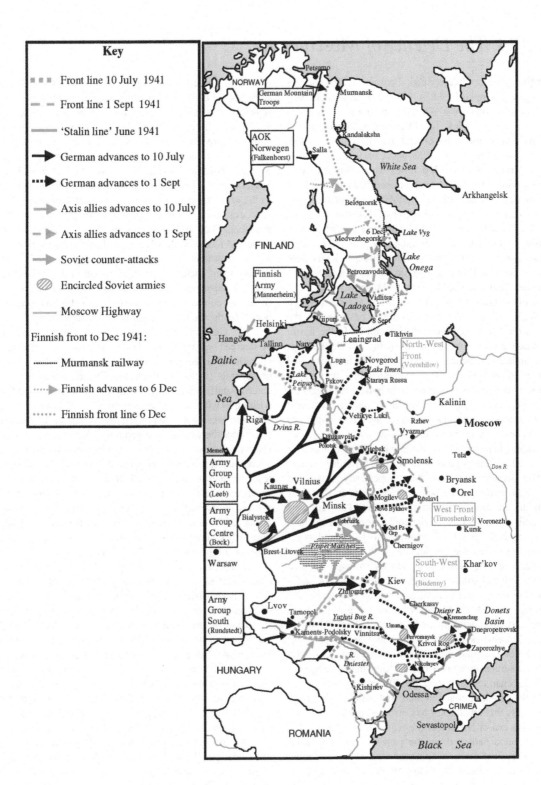

Key

.... Front line 10 July 1941

--- Front line 1 Sept 1941

—— 'Stalin line' June 1941

→ German advances to 10 July

....▶ German advances to 1 Sept

▶ Axis allies advances to 10 July

--▶ Axis allies advances to 1 Sept

➔ Soviet counter-attacks

▨ Encircled Soviet armies

—— Moscow Highway

Finnish front to Dec 1941:

.... Murmansk railway

....▶ Finnish advances to 6 Dec

...... Finnish front line 6 Dec

NORWAY

Petsamo

German Mountain
Troops

Murmansk

Kandalaksha

White Sea

AOK
Norwegen
(Falkenhorst)

Salla

Belomorsk

Arkhangelsk

FINLAND

6 Dec
Medvezhegorsk

Lake Vyg

*Lake
Onega*

Petrozavodsk

Finnish
Army
(Mannerheim)

Vidlitsa

*Lake
Ladoga*

Helsinki

Viipuri

8 Sept

Tikhvin

Hangö

Tallinn

Narva

Leningrad

North-West
Front
(Voroshilov)

Baltic

*Lake
Peipus*

Pskov

Luga

Novgorod

Lake Ilmen

Staraya Russa

Kalinin

Sea

Riga

Dvina R.

Velikye Luki

Rzhev

Vyazma

Moscow

Daugavpils

Polotsk

Vitebsk

Smolensk

Tula

Don R.

Memel

Army
Group
North
(Leeb)

Kaunas

Vilnius

Minsk

Mogilev

Novo Bykhov

Roslavl

Bryansk

Orel

Army
Group
Centre
(Bock)

Bialystok

Bobruisk

2nd Pz
Grp

West Front
(Timoshenko)

Voronezh

Kursk

Brest-Litovsk

Pripet Marshes

Chernigov

Warsaw

South-West
Front
(Budenny)

Khar'kov

Army
Group
South
(Rundstedt)

Lvov

Tarnopol

Kiev

Zhitomir

Cherkassy

Dniepr R.

*Donets
Basin*

Yuzhni Bug R.

Uman

Kremenchug

Kaments-Podolsky

Vinnitsa

Pervomaysk

Krivoi Rog

Dnepropetrovsk

HUNGARY

*R.
Dniester*

Nikolayev

Zaporozhye

Kishinev

Odessa

CRIMEA

ROMANIA

Sevastopol

Black   Sea

Map 14: The Defence of Moscow

The strategic disagreement between Hitler and his generals re-surfaced in July 1941. Rundstedt was heading down the 'Zhitomir corridor' towards the Ukrainian capital, Kiev. To Hitler, the resources of the Ukraine and beyond were crucial and his will prevailed, after a 19-day pause during the best campaigning month, and Guderian's panzers, 200 miles from Moscow, were diverted south. Despite the long exposed flank they offered by doing so, they held off the Red Army and met up with Kleist's Panzer Group 1 at Lokhvitsa, 100 miles east of Kiev. By 26 September they had encircled 665,000 Soviet soldiers, including the force Stalin had sent in as a counter-offensive on 16 August. Three million Soviet soldiers were now prisoners; half a million would not survive through to the winter. Guderian sped back to the Moscow road.

Further south the Romanians found Odessa a tough proposition, though Manstein had driven past them to the neck of the Crimea by the start of October. In the north, Leeb had cut off Leningrad by advancing to Lake Ladoga, but Stalin had sent General Zhukov, whom he had dismissed as chief of staff in July (for recommending withdrawal from Kiev before it was encircled), to bolster the defences, and under his urging the 3 million Leningraders had erected extensive anti-tank barriers. The Finns would not advance beyond their pre-1940 frontier, and Leeb's forces were unable to penetrate into the city itself. As their assault came to a halt, Leeb's tanks were diverted towards Moscow.

The Germans had a two-to-one superiority in men and tanks, and controlled the air. Fourteen Panzer Divisions began the advance in Operation Typhoon. The race was now against the weather. Soviet forces continued to show remarkable resilience, but their strategists had found as yet no answer to *blitzkrieg*, particularly with Stalin as averse as Hitler to giving up territory, even for strategic reasons. Another 650,000 soldiers – many of them now partially-trained militias – were encircled between Smolensk and Vyazma, and others around Bryansk. Amid panic in Moscow, Stalin called Zhukov back on 10 October, and he set the Muscovites (a population that was 75 per cent female) building line after line of static defences. The weather, traditionally a saviour of the Russian people against invaders, began to play a part. By 30 October, heavy rains turned the primitive roads to mud, and seriously impeded the mobility that was the key to German success.

At the end of November the winter freeze began, and as the ground hardened, so the panzers moved forward again. The final stage of Typhoon was to be a double pincer around Moscow, north to Kalinin and south to Tula. By 28 November Panzer Group 3 was 18 miles (27 km) from Moscow at Krasnaya Polyana. However, the Soviet Mozhaisk line offered stiffer resistance, and the Germans were poorly equipped for the freezing temperatures. The lightning campaign was supposed to be over before the winter, but the diversion of Army Group Centre to Kiev and the brave resistance of Smolensk had made the difference. By 5 December, German forces were stuck short of Moscow, north and south. They had failed to encircle the Soviet capital, allowing its continued supply from the east. In the great panic in October, government departments had been evacuated to Kuibyshev on the Volga, but Stalin had remained. He had one ace up his sleeve. A strong Soviet army had remained in Siberia, to guard against a Japanese attack. Comintern agent Richard Sorge reported in the autumn from documents in the German Embassy in Tokyo that the Japanese had no intention of doing so, giving Stalin the courage to move elements of this force, unsuspected by the Germans, towards the Moscow front.

As German forces suffered in temperatures of 40 degrees below freezing, Hitler declared a suspension of operations for the winter, while dismissing a large number of generals (including Bock and Guderian and the army chief-of-staff, Brauchitsch, replaced by Hitler himself) for wishing to withdraw to better positions. The Soviet armies, however, were better equipped for the cold. The respite offered by the weather had given the chance for the Soviet High Command (*Stavka*) to get a better grip of the situation. Inspired by the similar situation in 1812, strategic reserves painstakingly marshalled in the previous few weeks and the fresh forces from Siberia were launched in a great counter-offensive against the static German line. Using ski troops, Cossack units and guerrilla forces they struck through the snow-fields to hit the Germans, dependent on the roads, in flank and rear.

Kalinin and Tula were recaptured, relieving the immediate threat to Moscow. Similarly, in the north, Leeb was driven from Tikhvin and supplies began to get through to Leningrad (over the frozen lake) just in time to avert starvation of the whole population. In the south, Kerch was re-taken and Soviet forces re-entered the Crimea. Timoshenko had earlier re-captured Rostov, the gateway to the Caucasus, on 28 November. By the time their offensives had lost momentum in late February 1942, they had advanced in the centre as far as Kirov and Demidov, though Hitler had ordered 'no retreat' and German forces remained in some heavily defended enclaves, supplied through the winter from the air. When he addressed the Soviet people on Red Army Day, 23 February 1942, Stalin was brimming with confidence – indeed with over-confidence, for he promised them they could anticipate the complete defeat of the 'Hitlerite' invaders in 1942.

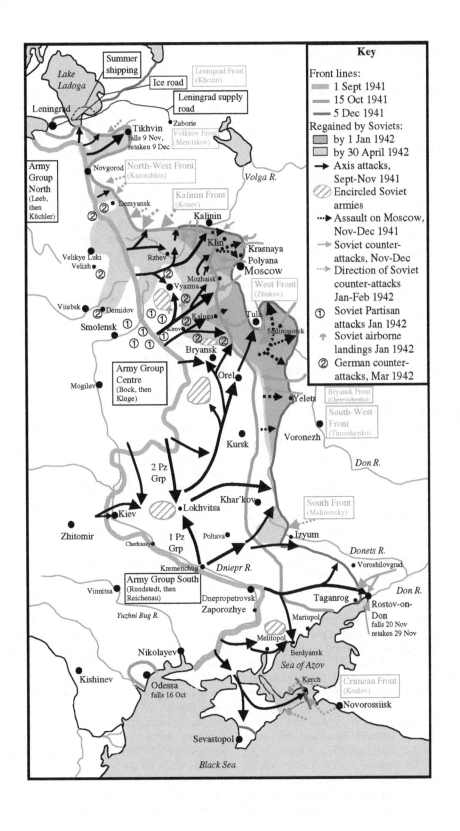

Key

Front lines:
- 1 Sept 1941
- 15 Oct 1941
- 5 Dec 1941

Regained by Soviets:
- by 1 Jan 1942
- by 30 April 1942
- → Axis attacks, Sept–Nov 1941
- Encircled Soviet armies
- ┅▶ Assault on Moscow, Nov–Dec 1941
- → Soviet counter-attacks, Nov–Dec
- ┅▶ Direction of Soviet counter-attacks Jan–Feb 1942
- ① Soviet Partisan attacks Jan 1942
- ♇ Soviet airborne landings Jan 1942
- ② German counter-attacks, Mar 1942

Lake Ladoga

Summer shipping

Ice road

Leningrad supply road

Leningrad Front
(Khozin)

Leningrad

Tikhvin
falls 9 Nov,
retaken 9 Dec

Zaborie

Volkhov Front
(Meretskov)

Army Group North
(Leeb, then Küchler)

Novgorod

North-West Front
(Kurotchkin)

Volga R.

Demyansk

Kalinin Front
(Konev)

Kalinin

Velikye Luki
Velizh

Rzhev

Klin

Krasnaya Polyana

Moscow

Vitebsk

Demidov

Mozhaisk

Vyazma

West Front
(Zhukov)

Smolensk

Kaluga

Kirov

Tula

Stalinogorsk

Bryansk

Mogilev

Army Group Centre
(Bock, then Kluge)

Orel

Yelets

Bryansk Front
(Cherevichenko)

South-West Front
(Timoshenko)

Voronezh

Kursk

Don R.

2 Pz Grp

Khar'kov

Kiev

Lokhvitsa

South Front
(Malinovsky)

Izyum

Zhitomir

1 Pz Grp

Poltava

Cherkassy

Donets R.

Voroshilovgrad

Kremenchug

Dniepr R.

Army Group South
(Rundstedt, then Reichenau)

Vinnitsa

Dnepropetrovsk

Zaporozhye

Don R.

Taganrog

Rostov-on-Don
falls 20 Nov
retaken 29 Nov

Yuzhni Bug R.

Mariupol

Nikolayev

Melitopol

Berdyansk

Sea of Azov

Kishinev

Kerch

Crimean Front
(Kozlov)

Odessa
falls 16 Oct

Novorossiisk

Sevastopol

Black Sea

Map 15: The Outbreak of War in the Pacific

The war in China continued to be stalemated for the Japanese Army in 1941, and resources began to decline as American embargoes on scrap metal, aviation engines and other materials began to take effect. In July 1941, Japanese forces moved into southern Indo-China, giving them a jumping-off place for attacking southwards. Roosevelt announced the freezing of Japanese assets in the US, and this quickly became a full-scale embargo (initially on the initiative of lesser officials), including, most significantly, oil. The United States now set out its line unequivocally: nothing less than withdrawal from China would bring an end to the embargo. When Roosevelt and Churchill met in August 1941, they agreed that Germany was a greater menace than Japan, but also that Japan might be deterred by a firm stance – and doing so was a concrete contribution the US could make to British prospects, if it restrained the Japanese from attempting to seize the vital resources of Malaya and the East Indies.

The policy, unfortunately, had the opposite effect. The Japanese Army was not inclined to withdraw from China undefeated, but could not secure victory without putting more pressure on Jiang, which it could not do without more resources. The Navy, which saw the US as its major enemy, believed the US would intervene from the Philippines, should Japan attack southwards. Having made a non-aggression pact with the Soviets in April 1941, the Japanese ignored the temptation of war with the Soviets when Germany attacked. The government under Prince Konoye continued to try to find a diplomatic solution, offering to withdraw from Indo-China once the 'China Incident' was settled, but the Americans would not budge. Konoye was replaced by the Minister for War, General Tojo, in October, and while negotiations continued, a deadline was set for the end of November. After that point, it would be war.

The Commander of the Combined Fleet, Admiral Yamamoto, came up with a bold plan to prevent American intervention. As the months passed and no breakthrough was made in Washington, the First Air Fleet under Vice-Admiral Nagumo secretly left its berth in the Inland Sea and sailed under strict radio silence across the empty Northern Pacific.

American cryptanalysts had succeeded, in Operation Magic, in breaking the Japanese diplomatic encryption machine (code-named Purple), and from it began to get clear warnings that the Japanese were preparing military action. It was not clear where this would be, but on 25 November, the US Army Chief of Staff, General Marshall, issued a war warning to all US bases in the Pacific.

However, because of the lack of specifics, and poor coordination of communications, when the blow fell it did so with complete surprise. At dawn on Sunday 7 December, aircraft from Nagumo's six carriers attacked the US Pacific Fleet at its moorings at Pearl Harbor in Hawaii, whence it had been sent in April 1940 as a deterrent. It was assumed that the fleet was safe from torpedo attack in this shallow harbour, but the skill of the Japanese pilots disproved this. In two waves, they sank 18 ships, seriously damaging all the American battleships (destroying two), but missing the carriers, which were absent on exercises. They also destroyed 187 aircraft, most of which had been conveniently gathered in the centre of the airfields as protection against sabotage. 2,403 were killed. A third wave was being prepared to attack repair facilities and oil installations, when Nagumo, fearing the fleet would soon be detected (they were actually in little danger), decided to turn for home. This failure to complete the job was to be a grievous mistake, though at the time it appeared that Japan had struck a great blow. Certainly the US Navy was unable to intervene against the main Japanese thrusts into South-East Asia. By attacking before making any declaration of war, while negotiations were proceeding, however, the Japanese made for themselves an implacable foe, which, far from being prepared to accept Japanese conquests as an unpleasant accomplished fact, was now committed to complete victory.

Churchill was elated that the US was finally in the war, and believed that victory was now assured. However, although conspiracy theorists have argued that Roosevelt knew of Japanese intentions and allowed the Pacific Fleet to be attacked so as to overcome isolationist sentiment in the US, it was by no means certain that the Japanese attack would bring the US into the war against Germany, though Britain and the US immediately became allies against Japan. To most Americans, the US's enemy was now Japan, and the Navy wished to transfer ships to the Pacific from their convoy protection activities in the Atlantic. For four days, US involvement against Germany was less likely than it had been for a year. Then Hitler effectively sealed his fate by declaring war on the United States on 11 December. The war was now truly a global conflict. It is likely that he did so to stretch American resources, and give the Japanese better chances of success (thus reducing American ability to supply Britain and the USSR) while also giving his U-boats free rein in the Atlantic, confident that this would tip the balance and secure victory in 1942. If it failed to do so, with US industrial resources fully committed to the war, then in the long term, Hitler, like the Japanese, had sealed his fate.

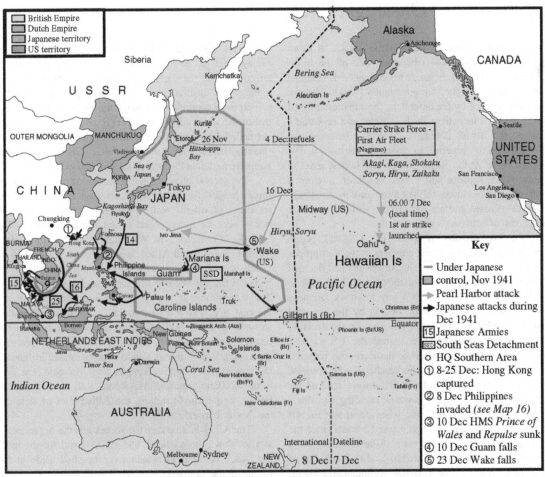

British Empire
Dutch Empire
Japanese territory
US territory

Siberia

Alaska

Anchorage

CANADA

USSR

Kamchatka

Bering Sea

Aleutian Is

OUTER MONGOLIA

MANCHUKUO

Kurile
Is
Etorofu · 26 Nov
Hittokappu
Bay

4 Dec: refuels

Carrier Strike Force -
First Air Fleet
(Nagumo)

Seattle

UNITED
STATES

Vladivostok

Sea of
Japan

Akagi, Kaga, Shokaku
Soryu, Hiryu, Zuikaku

San Francisco

CHINA

KOREA

Tokyo
JAPAN

16 Dec

Midway (US)

06.00 7 Dec
(local time)
1st air strike
launched

Los Angeles
San Diego

Chungking

Kagoshima Bay
Ryukyu
Is

Iwo Jima

Hiryu Soryu

Oahu

BURMA
FRENCH
THAILAND INDO-
CHINA
Rangoon
South
China
Sea

①

Fomosa

②

Philippine
Islands

14

Mariana Is

④

Guam

⑤

Wake
(US)

Hawaiian Is

Pacific Ocean

Manila

SSD

Marshall Is

Saigon

Davao

Palau Is

Truk

15

16

25

Caroline Islands

③

Gilbert Is (Br)

Christmas (Br)

Equator

MALAYA
Singapore

Borneo

SARAWAK

NETHERLANDS EAST INDIES

Sumatra

Java

New Guinea
Papua New Britain

Bismarck Arch. (Aus)

Solomon
Islands

Ellice Is
(Br)

Phoenix Is (Br/US)

Key

Under Japanese
control, Nov 1941

Pearl Harbor attack

Japanese attacks during
Dec 1941

15 Japanese Armies

SSD South Seas Detachment

⟡ HQ Southern Area

① 8-25 Dec: Hong Kong
captured

② 8 Dec Philippines
invaded (see Map 16)

③ 10 Dec HMS Prince of
Wales and Repulse sunk

④ 10 Dec Guam falls

⑤ 23 Dec Wake falls

Timor

Timor Sea

Darwin

Coral Sea

New Hebrides
(Br/Fr)

Santa Cruz Is
(Br)

Samoa (US)

Tahiti (Fr)

Indian Ocean

AUSTRALIA

New Caledonia (Fr)

Fiji Is

Melbourne Sydney

NEW
ZEALAND

International Dateline

8 Dec 7 Dec

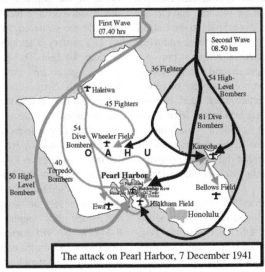

First Wave
07.40 hrs

Second Wave
08.50 hrs

36 Fighters

54 High-
Level
Bombers

Haleiwa

45 Fighters

81 Dive
Bombers

54
Dive
Bombers

Wheeler Field

Kaneohe

O A H U

40
Torpedo
Bombers

Pearl Harbor

50 High-
Level
Bombers

Ewa

Ford Island

Battleship Row
Navy Yard Dry Docks

Hickham Field

Bellows Field

Honolulu

The attack on Pearl Harbor, 7 December 1941

Map 16: Pacific Onslaught

Some hours before the Pearl Harbor attack, at dawn on 8 December 1941 (the other side of the International Dateline), Japanese troops landed in Thailand (by arrangement with the Thai government) and in Malaya. While outnumbered by the defenders, the Japanese proved adept at speedy manoeuvre in the jungle, and repeatedly outflanked the British defensive positions. Japanese aircraft were greatly superior to those the British had – and when Force Z, the Royal Navy's two largest units in the area, HMS *Repulse* and *Prince of Wales*, attempted to intervene without aircover, they were sunk by air attack. A new era of naval warfare had begun: without air cover the mightiest of battleships was in peril.

In the last months of 1941, the US had begun deploying B-17 Flying Fortress bombers to the Philippines as a deterrent to the Japanese. The Americans had decided in 1940 that in the event of war they would both defend the Philippines and use them as a base to attack Japanese communications. The perception of this by the Imperial Japanese Navy had been a major influence on the decision to launch a pre-emptive strike against the US as well as move against the possessions of the European imperial powers. When news of Pearl Harbor reached the Philippines, those B-17s that were already in place were readied for action, but were still caught unawares, standing in vulnerable positions on their airfields, when Japanese aircraft from Formosa attacked, although it was 12 hours since the Pearl Harbor attack. With the main strike force of B-17s destroyed, the Japanese proceeded to land on a number of the Philippine Islands. The American commander, General MacArthur, failed to stop them on the beaches, and elected rather late to base his defence on strongholds in the Bataan peninsula. Hemmed in there by the Japanese, and with inadequate supplies, the Americans and Filipinos put up a tough fight that forced the Japanese to send in more forces than they planned, but there was no possibility of relief, with the Pacific Fleet out of action after Pearl Harbor. They surrendered on 9 April (MacArthur had been withdrawn to Australia by Roosevelt in March – pledging as he went, 'I shall return'), followed by the fortress of Corregidor on 6 May. Some 14,000 of the 70,000 survivors were to die on the infamous 60-mile (96 km) Bataan Death March to prison camps.

Elsewhere, the Japanese carried all before them. US bases on Guam and Wake fell (though Wake repelled the first assault). Hong Kong fell on Christmas Day. British Borneo fell a few days later. In Malaya, British and Commonwealth forces fell back to Singapore. Pre-war cost-cutting (including by Churchill) meant Singapore was not the fortress stronghold some assumed that it was. Its guns were designed to defend against sea attack – as in Malaya, the jungle had been assumed to be a barrier to an enemy, but the Japanese found a way through. With a massively swollen population, Singapore had not the resources to endure a siege when the Japanese gained control of the water supply. On 15 February, General Percival surrendered to General Yamashita on behalf of his 62,000 (mainly British, Indian and Australian) troops in the most humiliating defeat the British Empire had ever suffered.

The second phase of the Japanese advance saw their forces headed for the Netherlands East Indies (NEI) the resources of which – oil, rubber, non-ferrous metals and rice – were the major object of the whole enterprise. The 'Arcadia' Conference in Washington in December 1941 formed the scattered Allied forces into American-British-Dutch-Australian Command (ABDA) under General Wavell, with the task of keeping the Japanese from the oil wells. The three-pronged Japanese attack was directed towards the east (Celebes and eastern Java), the south (Sumatra, western Java and north Borneo) and east Borneo in the centre. From Mindanao, Jolo and Kuching, all taken in December, Vice-Admiral Kondo's forces landed in January at Tarakan, Manado, Balikpapan and Amboina. On they went to Bandjermasin, Makassar, Bali and Timor in February, quickly breaching the Allied line of defence, the 'Malay barrier'.

The Allies had neither the forces nor the organisation to slow down the advance: the ABDA naval forces under the Dutch Admiral Doorman were brushed aside at the Battle of the Lombok Strait on 19–20 February. ABDA was dissolved on Wavell's suggestion: his responsibilities were far too scattered. An Allied fleet was still at sea, and on 27 February it attempted to intercept an invasion fleet heading for Java. The Battle of Java Sea was the largest naval engagement since Jutland. Admirals Takagi and Nishimura's Japanese naval forces were superior in firepower, equipment and tactics. In particular, in the 24-inch 'Long Lance' torpedo they possessed a powerful weapon. Doorman's five cruisers and nine destroyers lacked aircraft and all his cruisers were lost (and Doorman himself). The Japanese landings on Java were not delayed, and resistance by British, Dutch and Australians troops could not prevent them taking Surabaya, Batavia and Bandung. The Indonesians themselves felt no loyalty to their colonial overlords and where they fought, did so without conviction. On 8 March the NEI surrendered, and the local population welcomed the promise of the Co-prosperity Sphere and liberation from the Dutch. Landings at Lae and Salamua on Australian-controlled Papua-New Guinea, and on the Admiralty Islands followed later that month.

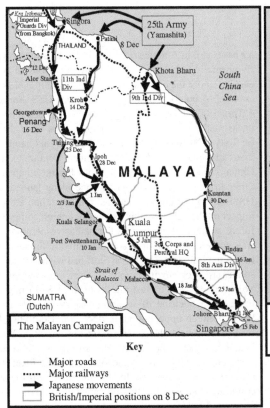

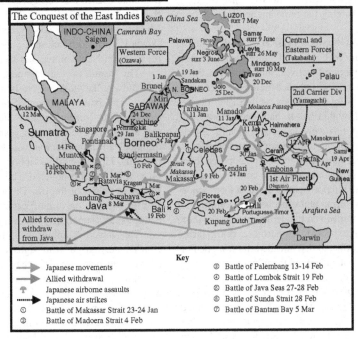

Map 17: Japan Triumphant

Moving through Thailand, the Japanese attacked the British colony of Burma in February 1942 (refer to Map 41). Burma was important for guarding the flank of forces in Malaya, and the Burma Road was the only remaining Allied supply route to China. Rangoon was the main port for supplies for China. Wavell believed it could be held, but the British, Indian and Burmese forces ('Burcorps') were outflanked and forced to fall back. Japanese forces took Rangoon on 7 March. The arrival of two Chinese armies under the American General Stilwell in March made little difference to Japanese progress, and the withdrawal northward became a rout. General Alexander, the new commander of Burcorps, was forced to order a general retreat to Assam across roadless hills in the face of Japanese skill in jungle fighting, and air superiority. By 30 April, Lashio, the Burmese terminus of the road to China, was in Japanese hands. When the monsoon season arrived in late May, the Japanese were in full possession of Burma, which served as the western edge of their defensive perimeter. As in the NEI, many Burmese welcomed their presence, and much of the Burmese armed forces joined the Japanese-sponsored Burmese Independence Army led by Aung San. The First Air Fleet inflicted more humiliations on the British, moving into the Indian Ocean to bomb Ceylon, sinking the carrier HMS *Hermes* (9 April) and other ships and forcing the remnants to seek safety in East African waters.

In the six months between Pearl Harbor and the fall of Corregidor, Japan had achieved unmitigated success in achieving its strategic objectives, and Japanese forces were now deployed on the intended defensive perimeter from Burma to the Solomon Islands, with all the desired resources contained within it. It had been done with remarkable speed, at relatively low cost. Japan's aircraft and ships, together with the training and experience of its fighting men, were far superior to those who opposed them. However, though these victories served to confirm Japanese assumptions about the inferior fighting spirit of their opponents, the fighting in Burma and especially the Philippines had lasted longer, and involved the deployment of far more troops, than had been expected. Furthermore, Pearl Harbor had had the opposite effect to that intended: far from demoralising the Americans, it had united them in a quest for total victory. It was clear even in May 1942 that they were building communications with Australia with a view to using it as a base for counter-attack. This needed to be prevented.

Moreover, there had already been evidence of their determination to strike a blow in return for Pearl Harbor, which seriously unbalanced Japanese strategic planning and led them to disaster. Japan was far out of range of any air bases still in American control. The risky solution was to fly normally land-based medium bombers from an aircraft carrier. Under the command of Colonel Doolittle, a famous aviator, 16 bombers were launched from USS *Hornet* on 1 April 1942. It was a one-way mission (they could not land back on the carriers) and although bombs were dropped on Tokyo, Nagoya, Kobe, Yokosuka and Yokohama, little material damage was done. The bombers went on to land in China – though some crews fell into Japanese hands (and three airmen were executed) and one plane landed in the USSR and the crew was interned. This raid had a decisive impact on the debate within the Japanese high command on future strategy. Wide though the defensive perimeter now was, there had been an attack that directly threatened the life of the Emperor. The Naval Staff had wished to advance southwards, occupying more of New Guinea and the Solomons to isolate Australia from the US. Firmly committed to a doctrine of securing victory by one decisive battle between opposing battle fleets, the Combined Fleet wished to provoke the American fleet by attacking Midway Island, a detached part of the Hawaii group. The resulting destruction of what remained of the Pacific Fleet would mean the Americans could not interfere with Japanese conquests and would, it was predicted, lead them to seek a negotiated peace that recognised the new order in Asia and the Pacific. Since *Hornet* had penetrated through the Midway gap, the Staff now agreed with Yamamoto that the 'keyhole', had to be closed. They would launch an attack on southern New Guinea, but would then turn to Midway.

The result of the Japanese determination to close the Midway 'keyhole' was to be two landmark defeats for Japan. The battles of Coral Sea and Midway are often described as 'turning points' in the Pacific War. That war still had three ferocious years to run, but the battles did establish how the war was to unfold. From Midway onwards, Japan would be fighting a defensive war to hold on to what it had conquered. The balance of naval strength shifted in favour of the US. The great strike weapon of the Pacific War was the aircraft carrier and Midway decisively ended Japan's superiority in naval aviation.

The Japanese approached the new campaigns with confidence, indeed with signs of 'victory disease' – of over-confidence. Certainly they made two cardinal errors in under-estimating their enemy and over-complicating their own plans. Their plans began to go awry as a consequence of poor signals security. The American code-breakers were able to inform the Commander-in-Chief of the Pacific Fleet, Admiral Nimitz, in advance of the attack on Port Moresby and he took a gamble and despatched two of his four carriers to intercept.

Key

——— Japanese gains by 1 Jan 1942	——▶ 1st Air Fleet operations Jan-Mar 1942	·····▶ US air strikes
········· Japanese gains by 16 Feb 1942	·····▶ 1st Air Fleet operations Apr 1942	▨ British Empire
▬▬▬ Japanese perimeter 16 June 1942	– –▶ Ozawa sortie Apr 1942	▨ Dutch Empire
Davao Staging bases in Japanese advance	——▶ Allied naval movements	▨ Japanese territory
➤ Major Japanese movements	·····▶ Japanese air strikes	▨ US territory

Map 18: Turning Points in the Pacific

Forewarned by signals intelligence, Nimitz was able to maximise the effectiveness of his few strike units. Carriers *Yorktown* and *Lexington* were sent to the Coral Sea to attack Japanese forces covering the attack on Port Moresby. They came up against the light carrier *Shoho* and the veterans of Pearl Harbor, *Zuikaku* and *Shokaku*, Japan's two most modern carriers.

The battle opened well for the Americans when on 7 May, *Shoho* was fortuitously caught by bombers and sunk. On 8 May, the two carrier forces located each other, and there followed the first ever naval battle when the two opposing fleets never came in sight of each other. Fighting at a distance of 175 miles (280 km), their aircraft delivered punishing attacks. *Shokaku* was heavily damaged, and *Zuikaku* suffered such losses to her air group that both were to miss the battle of Midway. *Yorktown* was damaged and *Lexington* was set on fire by a leak in aviation fuel, and poor damage control techniques led to her abandonment and loss. On balance, and in the short term, the Americans could less afford to lose *Lexington* than the Japanese could the *Shoho*, especially with *Yorktown* apparently also out of action for 90 days. However, the earlier Japanese failure to destroy the repair facilities at Pearl Harbor meant that she was repaired in 48 hours, ready for action at Midway. The Japanese transports heading for Port Moresby turned back, and the Army now had to assault the town by the tortuous land route. The American line of communication to Australia remained open. Perhaps most significantly, the Combined Fleet now had to fight its decisive battle without one third of its main strike force.

The Midway plan was fundamentally weakened by two other factors as well. Yamamoto planned a diversionary attack on the American Aleutian Islands. This was a pointless over-elaboration, even if intelligence had not indicated that this was just a diversion, as the Americans were in no position to divide their weak Pacific forces. The deployment for the Midway attack further dispersed Japanese forces, placing the carrier strike force apart from the main battle fleet and their protecting guns. Despite the way their own actions had revolutionised naval warfare, Japanese admirals still saw battleships as the main weapon, and were using the precious carriers almost as bait to draw the Americans towards their big guns. Most significantly, the Japanese lost the element of surprise. Radio security for the operation, codenamed MI, was rigorous, but one of the cryptanalysts at Pearl Harbor played a hunch. He had Midway send an uncoded message that they were short of drinking water. Decrypts then showed a Japanese signal referring to the target of operation MI, saying it was short

of water. They also showed the date of the operation. US Task Forces 16 (*Enterprise* and *Hornet*) and 17 (*Yorktown*) could therefore be deployed in readiness.

The battle still however, hinged on contingencies and fortune. The odds were heavily stacked in the Japanese favour, even if they were hamstrung by strategic confusion as to whether the prime objective was the occupation of Midway or bringing the US fleet to battle. The Japanese had four carriers to the American three, with 272 aircraft to 180 American. Their aircrews were battle-hardened and equipped with superior aircraft. Midway had land-based bombers, which played a key role in the battle, though in combat none could withstand the Zero fighter.

Aircraft from Midway spotted the Japanese on 3 June. Next day bombers attacked, with little result, but sufficient to convince Nagumo that he needed to neutralise US forces there. The first Japanese raid caused great damage, but a return attack by the Americans persuaded him to launch another – even though his planes were arming with torpedoes to attack US ships should they be sighted. At 7 a.m. *Hornet* and *Enterprise* launched their own bombers, followed by *Yorktown* at 8 a.m. Nagumo's reconnaissance aircraft reported US ships, but not until 8.20 was a carrier identified and Nagumo warned that the strike was on the way. The planes from *Hornet* and *Enterprise* arrived when the aircraft that had returned from the second strike on Midway were crowded on the Japanese carriers' decks, at their most vulnerable, refuelling and rearming. By 9.36 the Zeroes had destroyed virtually all the slow and obsolete US torpedo-bombers. A Japanese change of course meant the dive-bombers had not located their target. By 10 a.m., having found their target by good guesswork, *Yorktown*'s torpedo-bombers had met the same fate. It was then that the battle turned. With the Zeroes at sea-level to deal with the low-flying torpedo-bombers, one of *Enterprise*'s dive-bomber groups finally arrived after a long diversion. Thirty-seven Dauntless dive-bombers swooped down on the carriers, their decks packed with refuelling aircraft. Within five minutes *Akagi*, *Kaga* and *Soryu* were ablaze. They were abandoned and soon sank. *Hiryu* avoided destruction and launched a counter-strike which damaged *Yorktown*. Her turn came at 5 p.m., when she was set on fire in turn by bombers from *Enterprise*. Japan's magnificent First Air Fleet was no more. *Yorktown* had to be abandoned and sunk, but the balance of naval strength in the Pacific had irrevocably been altered. Japan would find it impossible to match the US in building replacement carriers, and the loss of the experienced aircrews was equally devastating.

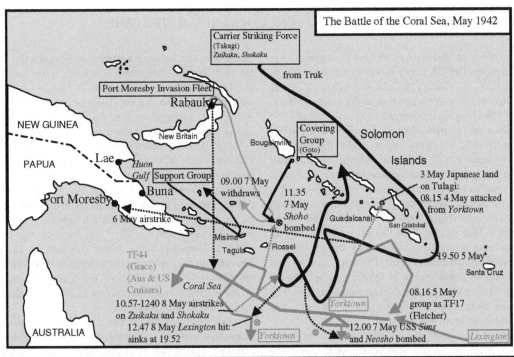

The Battle of the Coral Sea, May 1942

Carrier Striking Force
(Takagi)
Zuikaku, Shokaku

from Truk

Port Moresby Invasion Fleet

Rabaul

NEW GUINEA

New Britain

Covering
Group
(Goto)

Solomon

Bougainville

Islands

PAPUA

Lae

*Huon
Gulf*

Support Group

09.00 7 May
withdraws

3 May Japanese land
on Tulagi:
08.15 4 May attacked
from *Yorktown*

Buna

Port Moresby

11.35
7 May
Shoho
bombed

Guadalcanal

San Cristobal

6 May airstrike

Misima

Tagula

Rossel

TF44
(Grace)
(Aus & US
Cruisers)

Coral Sea

19.50 5 May

Santa Cruz

08.16 5 May
group as TF17
(Fletcher)

Yorktown

10.57–1240 8 May airstrikes
on *Zuikaku* and *Shokaku*

12.47 8 May *Lexington* hit:
sinks at 19.52

AUSTRALIA

Yorktown

12.00 7 May USS *Sims*
and *Neosho* bombed

Lexington

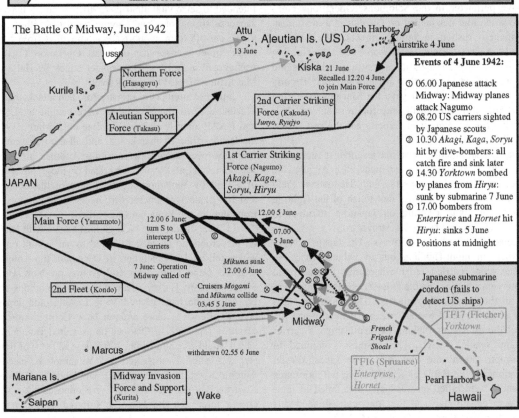

The Battle of Midway, June 1942

Attu

Aleutian Is. (US)

Dutch Harbor

airstrike 4 June

USSR

13 June

Kiska

21 June
Recalled 12.20 4 June
to join Main Force

Events of 4 June 1942:

Kurile Is.

Northern Force
(Hasaguyu)

① 06.00 Japanese attack
Midway: Midway planes
attack Nagumo

Aleutian Support
Force (Takasu)

2nd Carrier Striking
Force (Kakuda)
Junyo, Ryujyo

② 08.20 US carriers sighted
by Japanese scouts

③ 10.30 *Akagi, Kaga, Soryu*
hit by dive-bombers: all
catch fire and sink later

JAPAN

1st Carrier Striking
Force (Nagumo)
*Akagi, Kaga,
Soryu, Hiryu*

④ 14.30 *Yorktown* bombed
by planes from *Hiryu*:
sunk by submarine 7 June

Main Force (Yamamoto)

12.00 6 June:
turn S to
intercept US
carriers

12.00 5 June

07.00
5 June

⑤ 17.00 bombers from
Enterprise and *Hornet* hit
Hiryu: sinks 5 June

⑥ Positions at midnight

7 June: Operation
Midway called off

Mikuma sunk
12.00 6 June

2nd Fleet (Kondo)

Cruisers *Mogami*
and *Mikuma* collide
03.45 5 June

Midway

Japanese submarine
cordon (fails to
detect US ships)

TF17 (Fletcher)
Yorktown

French
Frigate
Shoals

Marcus

withdrawn 02.55 6 June

TF16 (Spruance)
*Enterprise,
Hornet*

Mariana Is.

Midway Invasion
Force and Support
(Kurita)

Wake

Pearl Harbor

Saipan

Hawaii

Map 19: The Solomons and New Guinea Campaigns

The defeat at Midway had not cost the Japanese any territory. The US began in the weeks following to develop its strategy to take the offensive. There was disagreement in Washington as to the point of attack. The Navy had long regarded Japan as its major enemy, and saw its own role as paramount in avenging Pearl Harbor. However, in 1942 it was not able to deploy the warships, transports, landing craft nor troops to launch an offensive in the direction it wished: across the central Pacific directly towards Japan. The commander of the growing US forces in Australia, MacArthur, wished to attack through New Guinea and to make good his promise to return to the Philippines. This strategy had the advantage of shorter distances between amphibious operations, though it would still require massive naval support. The result was the first of a number of compromises in Pacific strategy, shaped more by inter-service politics than strategic wisdom. The Southern Pacific command was divided in two, with one half commanded by an admiral, 'Bull' Halsey.

Halsey's first task was to penetrate the Japanese defensive perimeter in the Solomons. Operations commenced when Marines landed on Guadalcanal in August. The Japanese rushed in reinforcements. The Marines captured the vital airfield, Henderson Field. The fighting on the jungle-covered, malarial and swamp-ridden island then concentrated around this airfield and the 'Bloody Ridge' that overlooked it. It gave the Marines their first taste of the professionalism and commitment of their enemy and set the pattern of ferocity for the rest of the Pacific War.

Guadalcanal pitted the rival navies against each other as well. Off Savo Island on the night of 8 August, the Japanese sank four US cruisers. With Henderson Field giving the US air superiority at day, much of the fighting took place at night, centring on Japanese attempts to reinforce their troops by fast destroyer runs – what the Americans called the 'Tokyo Express'. The Japanese Navy was expert in night-fighting, but to balance that, the American ships carried radar where the Japanese did not. Four fierce battles and many lesser engagements were fought in the months that followed. The Americans lost *Hornet* at the Battle of Santa Cruz, but generally had the better of the exchanges, sinking two battleships, a carrier and many smaller vessels. The Japanese continued to run missions down 'the Slot' and were successful on 30 November in the Battle of Tassafaronga, but thousands of Japanese were killed on transports that failed in their attempts to get through and the Americans dubbed this sea-lane 'Ironbottom Sound' because of all the ships sunk there. Eventually, by January 1943, worn down by disease and combat and starved of supplies by growing US control

of the seas, the Japanese withdrew to Bougainville. It was the first reversal of Japanese conquests, a baptism of fire for the Americans: proof for them of how tough the task would be, but also for the Japanese an indication how wrong were assumptions they had made about American lack of martial rigour and capacity to take casualties.

The Japanese persisted in the attempt to take Papua. The land route to Port Moresby was by the Kokoda trail over the Owen Stanley mountains. The Australians fought a fighting retreat over the mountains, with such success that the Japanese finally ran out of momentum. It was then their turn to be pushed back in harsh fighting in an uncompromising environment. They fell back to the landing places at Buna and Gona, where they dug in. The siege was difficult to supply over the Kokoda trail, and Gona did not fall until 9 December, with Buna not following until 2 January 1943. The Japanese lost 12,000 dead, the Allies 2,850, most of them Australian.

This victory ended the threat to Australia, and enabled MacArthur to plan his advance towards the Philippines. He intended to seize vital airstrips to give air cover, bypassing Japanese strongholds and leaving them to 'wither on the vine', cut off from support and bombarded from the air. After more inter-service disputes, Operation Cartwheel was agreed in April 1943: a pincer attack by Halsey and MacArthur directed towards Rabaul.

Japanese attempts to prepare for such attacks received a setback when reinforcements were caught by USAAF and RAAF aircraft *en route* for Lae on 3 March 1943 in the Battle of the Bismarck Sea, and all the transports and four destroyer escorts were sunk. Another air success was achieved on 18 April. American cryptographers learnt of a visit by Yamamoto to the forces in the Solomons, and his plane was intercepted by P-38 Lightnings over Bougainville and Yamamoto was killed.

In June, the drive up New Guinea began, with landings on the Trobriand Islands, followed by an assault on Lae, which fell on 16 September. In December the Americans attacked Cape Gloucester and Arawe on New Britain. Simultaneously, Halsey advanced up the Solomons chain. By August he had reached Vella Lavella, and Japanese counter-offensives there and on New Georgia were successfully repulsed. In October he assaulted Bougainville, which would take him within 200 miles (320 km) of Rabaul. He was strongly opposed by Yamamoto's successor, Admiral Koga, in Operation RO. The landings at Empress Augusta Bay on 1 November were opposed by a strong cruiser force, but the Japanese suffered heavy losses in aircraft and ships. By 21 November the Americans were well-established on Bougainville and the pincers were tightening on Rabaul.

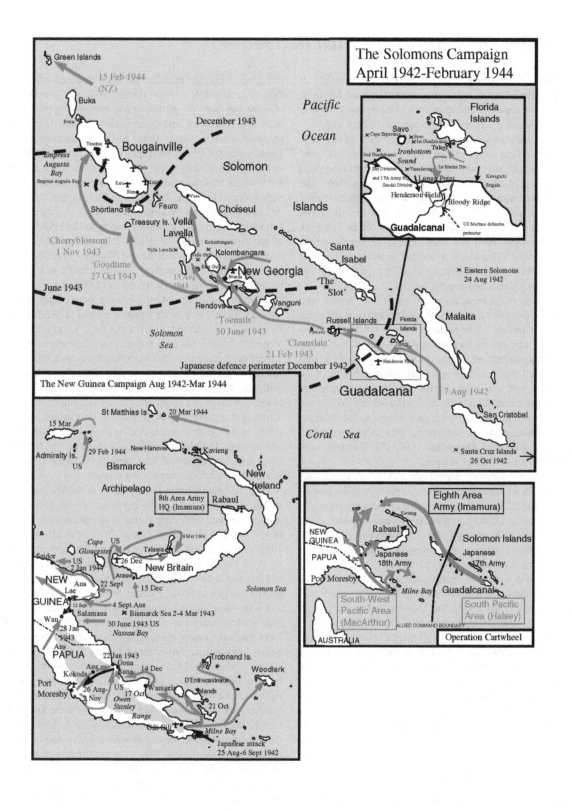

Map 20: The Battle of the Atlantic 1940–43

The *Kriegsmarine*'s principal task was to strike at Britain's most vulnerable point: the need for food, raw materials and munitions to be supplied by sea. Surface warships, disguised commerce raiders and submarines were deployed from September 1939 in this task.

While they achieved some successes in 1939–41, and received much attention from the British, the surface ships had only a small impact on Britain's maritime trade. The pocket-battleship *Admiral Scheer* had a successful raiding cruise in early 1941, and *Bismarck* sank HMS *Hood*, but surface raiding virtually ceased after the British sank *Bismarck* soon afterwards. *Bismarck*'s sister *Tirpitz* and the battle-cruiser *Scharnhorst* remained a threat to convoys to the USSR – though actually most damage to them was caused by U-boats and aircraft.

It was the submarine which made the impact, and U-boat crews came the closest of all Axis forces to defeating Britain. Germany's submarine force was small at the outbreak of war, but the menace was clear. The British began convoying immediately, though lack of escort vessels limited how much they could be protected. Magnetic mines took a heavy toll until the British developed de-gaussing. The U-boat campaign really took off after the occupation of Norway and France, which gave access to the Atlantic. The RAF's attacks on submarine pens were ineffectual. Between June and December 1940, the Germans sank almost 3 million tons of shipping.

Admiral Dönitz, commanding U-boat operations, pressed for an increase in building, especially of the longer-range Type IX, and for more cooperation from the *Luftwaffe*, but neither of Dönitz's requirements were fully met. Even so, and able to deploy only about 20 boats per month, with new wolfpack tactics concentrating boats against convoys, surface attacks at night that could not be detected by ASDIC (sonar) and with vital information on convoys provided by the signals intelligence service, *B-Dienst*, which was reading Admiralty codes, the U-boats took a heavy toll: 875 Allied vessels were sunk in 1941 (3,295,000 tons).

However, the balance was shifting: the British acquired 50 old destroyers from the US in exchange for use of British bases in September 1940, and more importantly, the Canadian Navy was deployed on convoy duty. The British also realised the importance of aircraft, though the RAF was very reluctant to allow any to be diverted from strategic bombing. The US Navy began assisting with convoys as far as Iceland, although it was unclear whether they should fire on U-boats until Roosevelt ordered to 'shoot on sight' on 11 September after USS *Greer* was attacked. Convoy protection was therefore greatly increased, and escorts were equipped with better radar and anti-submarine equipment. Also crucial was the decryption of German signals. An

intact naval Enigma machine had been obtained when the British captured *U-110* in March 1941, and techniques steadily improved for extracting and interpreting the information in 'real-time' and disseminating it quickly enough to route convoys away from wolfpack concentrations. There were still times when the flow was interrupted, but this information was to be the Allies' main asset against the U-boats until the end of 1942. However, convoys were very vulnerable to the wolfpacks in the 'air gap' in mid-Atlantic not covered by land-based aircraft. As their anti-submarine techniques improved, and with the introduction of the first escort carrier, HMS *Audacity*, in September, sinkings decreased towards the end of 1941 – only 26 Allied ships were sunk in December, aided by transfer of U-boats to the Mediterranean by Hitler, against Dönitz's wishes.

However, during 1942 the balance swung back to the U-boats. Twenty new boats a month entered service. When the Americans entered the war, it put the US Navy fully on a combat footing, but poor anti-submarine measures in the US coastal region meant that from January to June, 492 ships were sunk off the US east coast. Dönitz then switched his wolfpacks to the 'air gap', and sent the longer-range U-boats to the Caribbean and south Atlantic; by November, 42 were active in the north and 39 elsewhere. That month, Allied losses in the Atlantic reached their peak at 729,000 tons; altogether in 1942 losses were 1,664 ships of which 1,160 (over 6 million tons) had been sunk by U-boats, bringing Britain's oil and food supplies dangerously low.

Dönitz became commander-in-chief of the *Kriegsmarine* in January 1943, and U-boat construction was given priority. After winter weather curtailed operations, the Battle of the Atlantic reached its climax from February to May 1943. A total of 108 ships were sunk in February and 107 up to 20 March, as changes in Enigma reduced the supply of Ultra intelligence. However, improvements on the Allied side then began to tip the balance. Sufficient escort carriers and long-range aircraft became available to cover the air gap. Vessels became available after the Torch landings to form specialist escort groups. Escorts were equipped with better, centimetric, radar for detecting U-boats on the surface and forward-firing depth charge weapons. In the last ten days of March only ten Allied ships were lost: Allied losses were halved in April (partly helped by bad weather) and 15 U-boats were sunk. Thirty were lost next month, and on 23 May Dönitz withdrew the U-boats from the Atlantic. Aircraft began to take a heavy toll of submarines on the surface as they traversed the Bay of Biscay, and most of the important *Milchkuh* supply submarines were destroyed. The submarine threat remained, but was never again to be the potent menace to Britain's survival that it had been.

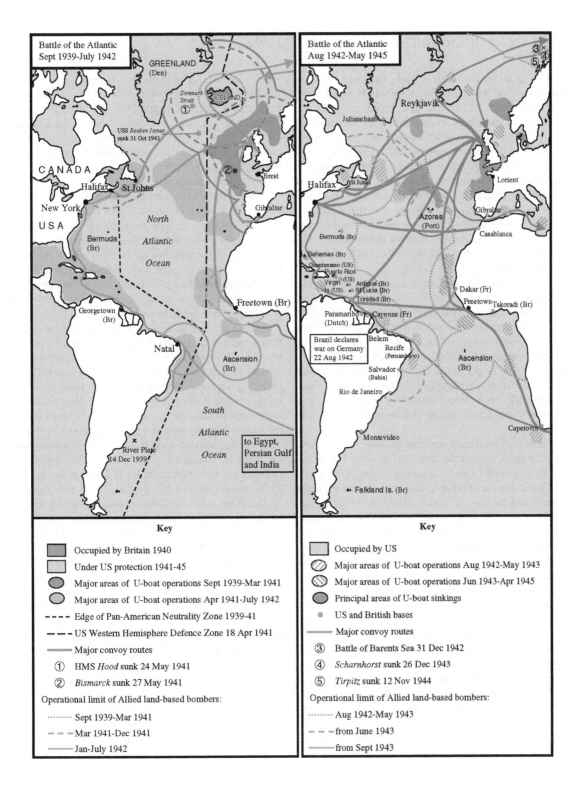

**Battle of the Atlantic
Sept 1939-July 1942**

GREENLAND
(Den)

Denmark Strait ①⊗

ICELAND

USS *Reuben James*
sunk 31 Oct 1941

②⊗

Brest

CANADA

Halifax
St Johns

New York

USA

Bermuda
(Br)

*North
Atlantic
Ocean*

Gibraltar

Georgetown
(Br)

Freetown (Br)

Natal

Ascension
(Br)

*South
Atlantic
Ocean*

River Plate
14 Dec 1939

to Egypt,
Persian Gulf
and India

**Battle of the Atlantic
Aug 1942-May 1945**

③×
④
⑤

Reykjavik

Julianehaab

Halifax
St Johns

Lorient

Azores
(Port)

Gibraltar

Bermuda (Br)

Casablanca

Bahamas (Br)
Guantanamo (US)
Puerto Rico (US)
Virgin Is (US)
Antigua (Br)
St Lucia (Br)
Trinidad (Br)

Dakar (Fr)

Freetown Takoradi (Br)

Paramaribo
(Dutch)

Cayenne (Fr)

Brazil declares
war on Germany
22 Aug 1942

Belem
Recife
(Pernambuco)

Ascension
(Br)

Salvador
(Bahia)

Rio de Janeiro

Capetown

Montevideo

Falkland Is. (Br)

Key

- ⬛ Occupied by Britain 1940
- ⬜ Under US protection 1941-45
- ⬭ Major areas of U-boat operations Sept 1939-Mar 1941
- ⬭ Major areas of U-boat operations Apr 1941-July 1942
- - - - - Edge of Pan-American Neutrality Zone 1939-41
- — — — US Western Hemisphere Defence Zone 18 Apr 1941
- ——— Major convoy routes
- ① HMS *Hood* sunk 24 May 1941
- ② *Bismarck* sunk 27 May 1941

Operational limit of Allied land-based bombers:

- ·········· Sept 1939-Mar 1941
- — — — Mar 1941-Dec 1941
- ——— Jan-July 1942

Key

- ⬜ Occupied by US
- ⬭ Major areas of U-boat operations Aug 1942-May 1943
- ⬭ Major areas of U-boat operations Jun 1943-Apr 1945
- ⬭ Principal areas of U-boat sinkings
- • US and British bases
- ——— Major convoy routes
- ③ Battle of Barents Sea 31 Dec 1942
- ④ *Scharnhorst* sunk 26 Dec 1943
- ⑤ *Tirpitz* sunk 12 Nov 1944

Operational limit of Allied land-based bombers:

- ·········· Aug 1942-May 1943
- — — — from June 1943
- ——— from Sept 1943

Map 21: The Soviet–German War 1942

Spring in Russia brings a thaw that turns roads to oceans of mud. Both sides paused to make good their losses. Hitler was determined to finish the destruction of the USSR, undeterred by the fact that the Red Army was rebuilding its strength and re-equipping with tanks from factories relocated to the Urals – and was doing so faster than the *Wehrmacht*. Stalin expected a resumption of the drive towards Moscow, but on 5 April, Hitler set the south as the target of the summer's Operation Blue: across the Don, to the Volga and down through the Caucasus mountains to the oil wells at Maikop and Baku. This would relieve Germany of dependence on oil from Ploesti, and, by denying it to the Soviets, finish them as a fighting force.

Blue opened with spectacular success as soon as the roads were hard enough, on 8 May. Manstein captured 170,000 in the Crimea, though Sevastopol held out until 4 July. The Soviets counter-attacked towards Khar'kov, but once again were encircled by armoured thrusts, leaving 239,000 prisoners in German hands. On 28 June two Army Groups, South (Bock) and A (List) struck and forced the Soviets into rapid retreat, despite Stalin's orders to stand and fight. The open steppes offered no defence lines and the panzers sped across the corridor from the Donets river to the Don.

Hitler then launched Operation Brunswick on 23 July. Army Group A crossed the Don, having taken Rostov on 24 July, and headed rapidly across the steppe to Maikop. The Caucasus passes beckoned, and beyond them the main oil-wells and the port of Tuapse. However, the going got tougher as they entered the foothills of the Caucasus and to Hitler's anger came to a halt. He fired his army chief of staff, Halder, and replaced List with himself.

The German forces were headed for disaster. In the Caucasus they had 300-mile (480 km) long supply lines. To protect the flank of the southern advance, Army Group B had been directed to take Stalingrad. This city was turned by the Soviets into a stoutly-defended stronghold, and Hitler became obsessed with taking it (Stalin was equally obsessed that his name city would not fall). Supported by Hoth's 4th Panzer Army, von Paulus's 6th Army attacked Stalingrad on 19 August. By 23 August, the *Luftwaffe* had reduced much of the city to rubble. Stalin was determined that his 'no step backward' order of 28 July would be applied here. Under Zhukov's overall command, Chuikov commanded the 62nd Army in Stalingrad itself, grouped around the three factories that

were to be the focus of terrible fighting. The Germans were resisted street by street. Forces were commanded from underground and fought from cellar to cellar. Slowly the Germans pushed the Soviet perimeter back against the river, across which Chuikov received supplies and sent out his wounded. By 21 September 6th Army surrounded the Tractor, Barricades and Red October factories and overlooked the landing stage.

After a pause to regroup, the street battles recommenced in October. The front stabilised on 18 October; at places it was just 300 yards from the river. Split in two, and having lost the Red October factory, Chuikov's forces, told by him to resist like there was nothing the other side of the Volga, fought on. Paulus's men were equally exhausted, and Hitler's obsession had pulled him into a fatal error. The original objective – a strong defensive line to protect the main thrust into the Caucasus – had been compromised. The Don front was held by Hungarian and Italian armies. It was against them that a counter-offensive, Operation Uranus, was launched by Zhukov on 19 November. By 23 November, the two pincers of his attack had met at Kalach, encircling Paulus in Stalingrad. Hitler refused to allow a breakout while the Soviet line was still shallow. Paulus was to be supplied from the air, while Manstein broke through the Soviets from the west. His panzers began the attempt on 12 December, making good progress, but Soviet attacks on the Italians threatened their flanks. The 6th Panzer Division got to within 35 miles (55 km) of the city, but Paulus made little move to try and link up with them. By 24 December, Manstein's forces could go no further, and had to retreat. With them went Army Group A, unable to hold the Caucasus salient with such an exposed flank.

In Stalingrad, the Red Army now advanced, capturing by 10 January the airstrips to which the *Luftwaffe* flew in supplies. On that day, the Soviets began the largest artillery barrage in history – 7,000 guns. Hitler promoted Paulus to Field-Marshal on 30 January – hoping he would make an honourable end and commit suicide: but on that day his headquarters was overrun and he surrendered. When the last fighters gave in on 2 February, 90,000 soldiers, plus 20,000 wounded were captured by the Soviets. Few of them were to survive. Twenty-two divisions had been wiped out at Stalingrad and the Kremlin celebrated at achieving its first unequivocal and decisive victory against the German invaders – invaders, however, who still occupied territory where 45 per cent of the Soviet population lived. The turn of the tide was still to come.

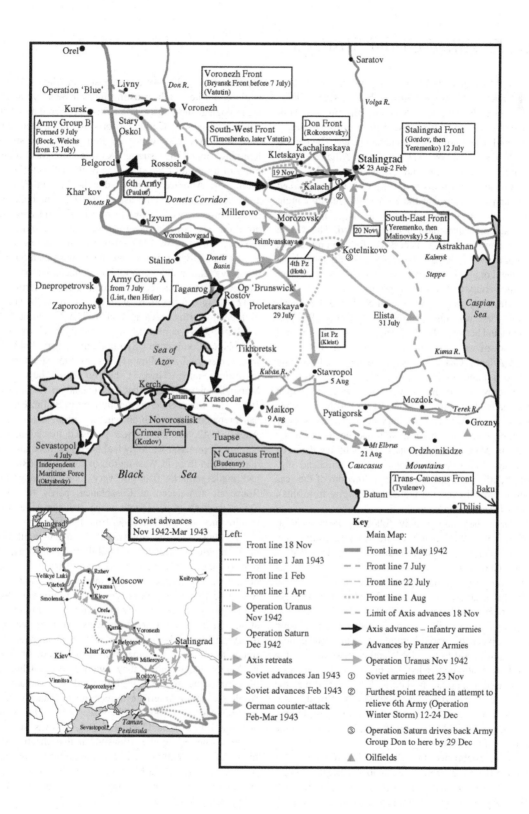

Operation 'Blue'

Army Group B
Formed 9 July
(Bock, Weichs
from 13 July)

Voronezh Front
(Bryansk Front before 7 July)
(Vatutin)

South-West Front
(Timoshenko, later Vatutin)

Don Front
(Rokossovsky)

Stalingrad Front
(Gordov, then
Yeremenko) 12 July

6th Army
(Paulus)

Donets Corridor

19 Nov

Kalach

South-East Front
(Yeremenko, then
Malinovsky) 5 Aug

20 Nov

4th Pz
(Hoth)

Army Group A
from 7 July
(List, then Hitler)

Op 'Brunswick'

Proletarskaya
29 July

1st Pz
(Kleist)

Elista
31 July

Crimea Front
(Kozlov)

N Caucasus Front
(Budenny)

Independent
Maritime Force
(Oktyabrsky)

Trans-Caucasus Front
(Tyulenev)

Soviet advances
Nov 1942-Mar 1943

Left:
━━━ Front line 18 Nov
······ Front line 1 Jan 1943
──── Front line 1 Feb
······ Front line 1 Apr
➡ Operation Uranus
    Nov 1942
➡ Operation Saturn
    Dec 1942
➡ Axis retreats
➡ Soviet advances Jan 1943
➡ Soviet advances Feb 1943
➡ German counter-attack
    Feb-Mar 1943

Key

Main Map:
━━━ Front line 1 May 1942
--- Front line 7 July
─── Front line 22 July
····· Front line 1 Aug
--- Limit of Axis advances 18 Nov
➡ Axis advances – infantry armies
➡ Advances by Panzer Armies
➡ Operation Uranus Nov 1942
① Soviet armies meet 23 Nov
② Furthest point reached in attempt to
    relieve 6th Army (Operation
    Winter Storm) 12-24 Dec
③ Operation Saturn drives back Army
    Group Don to here by 29 Dec
▲ Oilfields

Map 22: Allied Grand Strategy

On 1 January 1942 in Washington the United Nations declaration affirmed that the signatories – China, the US, the USSR and Britain, and later 22 others – would collectively use their resources to defeat the Axis and would not make a separate peace. The central core of the United Nations was the 'Grand Alliance' of the 'Big Three' – the US, UK and USSR. It was a less than perfect alliance, full of mistrust. Suspicion was reinforced by geography to mean that the Soviets essentially fought a separate war against Germany, and they only joined the war against Japan days before it ended. The Grand Alliance, however, was a necessary, functioning entity, and without it the defeat of the Axis would have been impossible. For all the tensions, the alliance stayed together to gain the victory that was its purpose.

It effectively began when Churchill and Roosevelt had their first wartime meeting, in Placentia Bay off Newfoundland between 9 and 12 August 1941. They agreed a vague set of war aims (though the US was not yet at war), the Atlantic Charter, issued a warning to Japan and agreed to a three-power supply conference in Moscow. Privately, they agreed that if war came with both Japan and Germany, they would first defeat the stronger enemy, Germany. Anglo-American military contacts had already been taking place and this principle had been set out by planners in March (ABC-1 plan). The Charter declared that the signatories had no territorial ambitions, and supported liberation, self-government and freedom of the seas (though Churchill excepted the British Empire from this). The Soviets acceded to it later.

In December, immediately following Pearl Harbor, Churchill flew to Washington for the 'Arcadia' conference, while his Foreign Secretary, Anthony Eden, travelled to Moscow. Churchill and Roosevelt confirmed the focus would be on Germany; the strategy in the Pacific would be to hold the Japanese but not take the offensive. The US Atlantic fleet would not be moved to the Pacific. The strategy in Europe would be the British one of 'closing the ring' – blockade, aerial bombardment and subversion, accompanied by aid to the USSR and campaigning in the Middle East. Stalin demanded that his pre-1941 conquests be recognised as part of the USSR: Eden stalled and the issue was to be a divisive one between the British (who wished to concede so as to dampen Stalin's suspicions) and the Americans (who thought it would compromise the moral aims of the war).

Arcadia established the Combined Chiefs of Staff Committee (CCS) to coordinate Anglo-American strategy. Its deliberations revealed deep disagreements as to how the war should be fought. The Americans wished to engage the Germans where they were strongest, and where a decisive battle could be fought, trusting in their own strength and technological superiority. The British preferred an attrition strategy, dispersing German efforts by hitting them where they were weakest, while the Red Army and strategic bombing sapped their strength so that there was no possibility of a repeat of the stalemate of the 1914–18 Western Front. The Americans proposed a landing in France in 1942, followed by a major assault in 1943. The bulk of the force, however, would have to be British, and they could not do it. The Americans agreed in April to a build-up of forces in the UK in 1942 ('Bolero') for an invasion in 1943 ('Round-Up'). Roosevelt, faced with clamour from the Navy and public opinion to concentrate on Japan, wanted American forces in action against Germany in 1942. He agreed therefore, with British plans for landings in French North Africa ('Torch'). The US Joint Chiefs of Staff (JCS) continued to press their views at the Casablanca Conference ('Symbol') in January 1943. They were persuaded to allow forces in the Mediterranean to invade Sicily ('Husky'), but no action beyond that. Marshall acknowledged that this meant no Round-Up in 1943. This was a great disappointment to Stalin; Churchill had prepared him for Torch when he went to Moscow in August 1942, but the Soviets persisted in claiming that Foreign Commissar Molotov had been promised an immediate second front in Washington in June 1942 (Roosevelt had made remarks that got very close to a promise). Roosevelt announced at Casablanca, partly to assuage Soviet fears about a separate peace, that the Allies would require unconditional surrender from the Axis.

In May 1943, the Big Two again met without Stalin, in Washington ('Trident'). Churchill pressed for exploitation of the North African victory. The JCS insisted on a firm commitment to the invasion of France (now 'Overlord') on 1 May 1944. Some of Eisenhower's forces in the Mediterranean were withdrawn to Britain in preparation, but he was allowed to proceed with the remainder to try and get Italy out of the war; the Americans continued to regard this campaign as a side-show. At Quebec in August ('Quadrant') they again rejected Churchill's plea for concentration on Italy and the Balkans. An Anglo-Canadian-American agreement on sharing atomic research was made (this was kept secret from the Soviets), and South-East Asia Command (SEAC) was set up to facilitate moving to the offensive in that theatre. When the Big Three finally met, in Teheran in November, Stalin was essentially the arbiter between the two strategic conceptions for action in Europe, and he put his weight behind Overlord.

Churchill's plan for Operation Jupiter: Anglo-Soviet invasion of Norway: rejected Oct 1942

US Troops occupy Iceland July 1941

US 8th Air Force flies to Britain spring-summer 1942

US troop build-up in Britain, 1942-43: Operation Bolero

Operation Round-Up

Operation Gymnast, later Torch

Churchill conference with Stalin August 1942

Operation Velvet: offer of RAF squadrons to Caucasus front: rejected Nov 1942

Churchill's 'Mediterranean Strategy'

ICELAND

North Cape   Barents Sea
Petsamo
Murmansk

Arkhangelsk

FINLAND

U S S R

NORWAY

SWEDEN

Leningrad

Demyansk   • Kuibyshev

• Moscow

DENMARK   REICHS-
KOMMISSARIAT
OSTLAND

Smolensk

Voronezh

GREAT   EIRE
BRITAIN

NETH.
London
BELG.

Berlin   • Minsk

• Khar'kov   Stalingrad

• Kiev

19 Aug 1942
Dieppe
Brest   Paris   Zone
OCCUPIED FRANCE   Interdit
Vichy
VICHY FRANCE   Jura   SWITZ.

GENERAL
GOVERNMENT   REICHSKOMMISSARIAT
UKRAINE   Zaporozhye   Rostov
Odessa

GERMANY   SLOVAKIA

Vienna   'Ljubljana Gap'
Budapest   HUNGARY   ROMANIA   • Ploesti
Lower
Genua   Zagreb   Bucharest
CROATIA   Belgrade
Split   SERBIA   BULGARIA
Genoa   ITALY   Sofia
ALBANIA   Ital.

Sevastopol

Black Sea   Batum

Caucasus Mts   • Tbilisi

Caspian
Sea   Baku

PORTUGAL   SPAIN
Gibraltar (Br)

Safi   Casablanca   Oran   Algiers
ALGERIA   TUNISIA
Bone   Tunis
MOROCCO
FRENCH   NORTH   AFRICA
(Vichy)

Toulon   Corsica
Sardinia
• Rome   Naples
Kosovo
Macedonia   GREECE
Athens   Dodecanese Is. (Ital.)
Sicily   MALTA (Br.)
Crete

TURKEY

IRAN
(Sov-Br
Occup.)

SYRIA
(Free Fr.)

LEBANON
(Free Fr.)
CYPRUS   PALESTINE
(Br.)   TRANS-
JORDAN
(Br.)

IRAQ
(Br. Occup.)

Tripoli   Benghazi   Tobruk
LIBYA (Ital.)   El Agheila

Alexandria
El Alamein   Cairo
E G Y P T

Key

German Reich	Occupied and regained by Finland	① Salonika
Incorporated into Reich	Occupied by *Panzerarmee Afrika*	② Thrace
Axis allies and satellites	German sector of Croatia	③ Demotika
Axis ally not at war with USSR	Italian sector of Croatia	④ Eupen and Malmedy
Occupied by Germany	Allies	⑤ Bialystok
Occupied by Italy	Occupied by Allies	⑥ Transnistria
Regained by Romania	‑ ► Allied strategic options	⑦ Baranyan Triangle
Annexed by Romania	► US troop deployments	⑧ Prekmurje and Medjumurje
Annexed by Hungary	‑ ‑► US air force deployment	⑨ Bessarabia (Moldavia)
Annexed by Bulgaria	► Dieppe Raid	⑩ Lower Styria and Upper Carniola
Annexed by Italy		

Map 23: The War in North Africa 1942

The start of 1942 found Rommel back where he had started from in March 1941. However, the same problem that had afflicted him after his advance the previous year – logistical overstretch – was now a British problem. He was back near the source of his supplies, Tripoli, while the British were a long way from theirs, and Benghazi was too damaged to serve and was in range of Rommel's dive-bombers. The British once again needed to transfer troops elsewhere: not to Greece this time, but to their crumbling position in the Far East. When Rommel launched a counter-attack, therefore, the British were pushed back in their turn, as far as the Gazala–Bir Hacheim line, which they had fortified. The battle of Gazala was one of the toughest of the Desert War. The British had learnt much about desert fighting, but Rommel's boldness again paid off as he led a thrust deep into the British position. Meanwhile the Free French on the flank were beaten at Bir Hacheim by German and Italian units, which then swept on to help Rommel in 'the cauldron'. On 14 June Auchinleck withdrew to a better position at Alam Halfa, where the impassable Qattara Depression protects the flank.

Tobruk was once again left as a fortress behind the enemy lines – but this time it fell quickly, on 21 June, the defences having been neglected since the breakout the previous November. Churchill, in Washington, was deeply distressed, but received in recompense a promise of supplies of the new American Sherman tank from Roosevelt. Churchill desperately needed a victory, and travelled to the Middle East in August to shake things up. Auchinleck was replaced with Alexander, and to command the 8th Army, Churchill brought General Montgomery out from England, a man with a reputation for tough fighting and efficiency. He also had a way with the troops, and from the beginning the morale of the 8th Army stiffened. It needed to, for Rommel launched a probing offensive on 31 August. This time they held firm.

Montgomery began meticulously to build up his forces; he resisted Churchillian urgings to attack until he was fully ready. Desert Air Force attacks on convoys to Tripoli had inflicted severe losses of fuel on Rommel, and the material balance, with a flow of new material coming in to Egypt via the Cape route, shifted decisively in the British favour. Montgomery had 11 divisions to Rommel's ten, with 1,030 tanks (including the 250 Shermans) and 500 guns. Six of Rommel's divisions were Italian, and their morale was low from past defeats. He decided to 'corset' these units with German ones to try and prevent the Italian parts of the line being points of weakness.

Montgomery was intent on destroying *Panzerarmee Afrika*, rather than just pushing them back, and fought the battle of Alamein as a grinding infantry/artillery battle, rather than one of mobile tank warfare, which he saw the Germans did much better than the British. After a week of heavy fighting, 8th Army drove two 'corridors' through the enemy, reducing German tank strength to 35. Rommel was refused permission to retreat by Hitler, and reinforced the corridor on the coastal road, but Montgomery knew from Ultra that he was doing so and attacked through the southern corridor. By the afternoon of 4 November, 7th and 10th Armoured Divisions had destroyed the Italian Ariete Division and was in *Panzerarmee Afrika*'s rear. Rommel ordered a full-scale retreat. Montgomery pursued slowly, hamstrung by the weather, but also determined not to give *Afrika Korps* the chance of using their mobility to reverse the result of El Alamein. His forces nearly caught them at Fuka, and the Desert Air Force harried them all the way back to Tripoli. 8th Army losses at Alamein were 13,500 killed or wounded: about 25 per cent of its infantry. Rommel had only 80 tanks left, and had lost 40,000 killed, wounded or taken captive.

On 8 November Operation Torch had begun. Contacts were made with sympathetic Frenchmen in North Africa prior to the landings, but led to nothing and there was some opposition when the troops went ashore at Algiers, Oran and Casablanca. The French would not follow Giraud, whom the Allies had wished to take charge, but Admiral Darlan, Vichy commander-in-chief, was in Algiers, and he changed sides and ordered an armistice on 8 November. The Allies swiftly took possession of the coasts of Morocco and Algeria, though creating a political problem for themselves in doing a deal with a man so recently a collaborator with the Nazis.

Hitler's response was typically swift. The Allies had landed too far west, allowing him to despatch reinforcements to Tunisia, including the first batch of the new Tiger tank. He occupied the southern part of France on 11 November (failing, though, to capture the French fleet at Toulon), and from there the 334th, Hermann Göring and 10th Panzer Divisions headed to Tunis and Bizerta, arriving from 16 November and forming 5th Panzer Army. Allied hopes after the landings and the victory at Alamein that North Africa would easily fall into their hands were replaced with the prospect of a hard campaign.

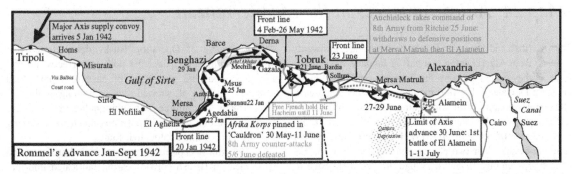

Rommel's Advance Jan–Sept 1942

Major Axis supply convoy arrives 5 Jan 1942

Front line 4 Feb–26 May 1942

Front line 23 June

Auchinleck takes command of 8th Army from Ritchie 25 June: withdraws to defensive positions at Mersa Matruh then El Alamein

Tripoli

Homs

Misurata

Via Balbia Coast road

Sirte

El Nofilia

Gulf of Sirte

Benghazi 29 Jan

Barce

Derna

Jebel Akhdar Mechili

Gazala

Tobruk 21 June Bardia

Sollum

Alexandria

Mersa Matruh

El Alamein

Cairo

Suez Canal

Suez

Msus 25 Jan

Antelat

Saunnu 22 Jan

Mersa Brega

Agedabia 22 Jan

El Agheila

Front line 20 Jan 1942

Afrika Korps pinned in 'Cauldron' 30 May–11 June 8th Army counter-attacks 5/6 June defeated

Free French hold Bir Hacheim until 11 June

27–29 June

Limit of Axis advance 30 June: 1st battle of El Alamein 1–11 July

Qattara Depression

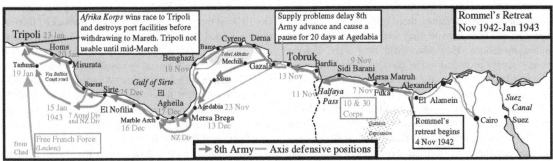

Rommel's Retreat Nov 1942–Jan 1943

Afrika Korps wins race to Tripoli and destroys port facilities before withdrawing to Mareth. Tripoli not usable until mid-March

Supply problems delay 8th Army advance and cause a pause for 20 days at Agedabia

Tripoli 23 Jan

Homs 20 Jan

Tarhuna 19 Jan

Misurata

Via Balbia Coast road

Buerat

Sirte 25 Dec

El Nofilia

15 Jan 1943 7 Armd Div and NZ Div

Marble Arch 16 Dec

Gulf of Sirte

El Agheila 17 Dec

Agedabia 23 Nov

Mersa Brega 13 Dec

NZ Div

from Chad

Free French Force (Leclerc)

Cyrene Derna

Barce

Benghazi 19 Nov

Jebel Akhdar Mechili

Gazala

Msus

Tobruk 13 Nov

Bardia

11 Nov

Halfaya Pass

10 & 30 Corps

9 Nov

Sidi Barani

Mersa Matruh

7 Nov Fuka

El Alamein

Alexandria

Cairo Suez

Suez Canal

Qattara Depression

Rommel's retreat begins 4 Nov 1942

→ 8th Army — Axis defensive positions

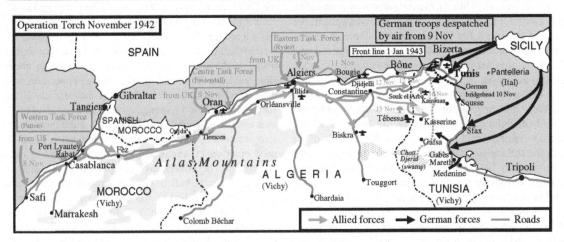

Operation Torch November 1942

German troops despatched by air from 9 Nov

SPAIN

Eastern Task Force (Ryder)

from UK

8 Nov

Front line 1 Jan 1943

Bizerta

SICILY

Centre Task Force (Fredendall)

from UK 8 Nov

Algiers 11 Nov

Bougie

Bône

Djidjelli 12 Nov

Tunis

Pantelleria (Ital)

Tangier

Gibraltar

Oran

Orléansville

Blida

Constantine

Souk el Arba

Kairouan

German bridgehead 10 Nov

Sousse

Western Task Force (Patton)

SPANISH MOROCCO

Oujda

Tlemcen

15 Nov

Tébessa

Kasserine

Sfax

from US

8 Nov

Port Lyautey Rabat

Fez

Atlas Mountains

ALGERIA (Vichy)

Biskra

Gafsa

Chott Djerid (swamp)

Gabès

Mareth

Medenine

Tripoli

Casablanca

Safi

MOROCCO (Vichy)

Marrakesh

Colomb Béchar

Ghardaia

Touggort

TUNISIA (Vichy)

→ Allied forces → German forces — Roads

Map 24: Allied Advances in the Mediterranean

British and American forces' easy advances eastwards from Algeria came to a halt in January 1943, when they came up against the Germans established in the Eastern Dorsale of the Atlas mountains. Further south-east, Rommel, retreating from Montgomery, had established the *Afrika Korps* on the Mareth defensive line. With von Arnim, commander of 5th Panzer Army, he conceived a typical counter-attack: their two panzer divisions drove at the US 2nd Corps and by 19 February had pressed them back to Kasserine Pass in the Western Dorsale. However, the British and American forces then held the Germans in the passes, and from then on, they were only able to mount spoiling operations. How successful they were, despite growing supply problems – the convoys from Italy were decimated by Allied airpower – is shown by the fact that Montgomery only turned Rommel out of the Mareth line by 31 March, and that it took until May to finally defeat them. However, the time the Axis gained by their efforts has to be offset against the fact that though Hitler's attention was elsewhere, he insisted Arnim fight to the end (Rommel was called home), meaning that even when defeat was inevitable little effort was made to withdraw the troops to fight elsewhere. By 13 May, the Axis force of 11 divisions was squeezed into Cape Bon and finally surrendered: 275,000 troops were taken prisoner, the largest capitulation of Axis troops yet.

The delayed conclusion to the Tunisian campaign limited Allied options for 1943. Round-Up in 1943 was already doubtful because of shortages of landing craft and the slow pace of build-up in Britain, with the Battle of the Atlantic still raging. The choice was either to begin no new campaigns in 1943, leaving Allied ground forces largely inactive and giving no relief to the Soviets, or to attempt further advances in the Mediterranean.

Churchill had always intended this. He believed Italy to be the weak link in the Axis – the 'soft underbelly'. Italian weakness certainly offered political opportunities. The general staff was doubtfully loyal to Mussolini, and the Italian people felt no real enmity to Britain, and traditionally had a high regard for the US. Since Italians were the occupying forces for much of the Balkans, an Italian surrender offered enticing prospects. Hitler saw this danger clearly, for it would give the Allies a position on the flank of Germany's eastern front and would threaten vital resources, especially oil. He offered Mussolini five more divisions to supplement those that had managed to get out of Tunisia, but the *Duce* refused. Hitler prepared plans (Operation Alaric) for the occupation of Italy in the event of Allied attack, but in fact expected that the blow would fall on Sardinia, Corsica, or, where he feared it most, Greece.

The course of Operation Husky demonstrated that while Churchill anticipated the politics correctly, he was mistaken about the possibility of easy or rapid Allied advances. Instead it showed the continuing ability of the Germans to reinforce with high-quality troops and to re-form in strong defensive positions much more rapidly than the Allies could deploy their forces.

Successful deception measures – including Operation Mincemeat (a British corpse bearing fabricated information) – meant that Husky achieved complete surprise. On 10 July the Allied forces of eight divisions (180,000 troops) landed from the sea either side of Cape Passero, accompanied by two airborne divisions. However, the first Anglo-American attempt at opposed amphibious landings was less than a complete success. Airborne troops particularly suffered, when they were shot at by nervous Allied gunners, and dropped in the sea by mistake. Valuable lessons were pointed up regarding shore bombardment and coordination of operations.

There were 12 Axis divisions on the island, but only the 15th Panzergrenadier Division and the Hermann Göring Panzer Division were of high quality. Alexander assigned the aggressive American General Patton to capture the western half of the island, Montgomery the eastern. Patton made rapid progress, but Montgomery, advancing either side of Mount Etna, encountered serious opposition, and the rugged terrain in Sicily favoured the defence. Hitler sent two divisions to strengthen the defence, and it was only a series of amphibious 'hooks' that undid their defensive positions – and even then Axis evacuation began in good order on 11 August, taking with them most of their equipment. The Americans finally entered Messina on 17 August, but the bulk of German forces had escaped, and were now in a position to oppose the next Allied advance.

The landings in Sicily had, however, been the final straw for Mussolini's opponents. On 25 July the Fascist Grand Council demanded his resignation, and when he visited the King, he was arrested. Marshal Badoglio became Prime Minister, and entered secret negotiations with the Allies. The result was a mess. The Allies drove a hard bargain, and on 3 September the Italians agreed to terms that were effectively unconditional surrender. They had hoped for an Allied landing north of Rome to forestall a German response, but instead the landings were in the far south – and though it had been agreed that the Italian surrender would be kept secret so that they could prepare for a German intervention, Eisenhower revealed it just after Allied forces made their landing at Salerno on 8 September. It was the Germans who arrived in Rome, not the Allies.

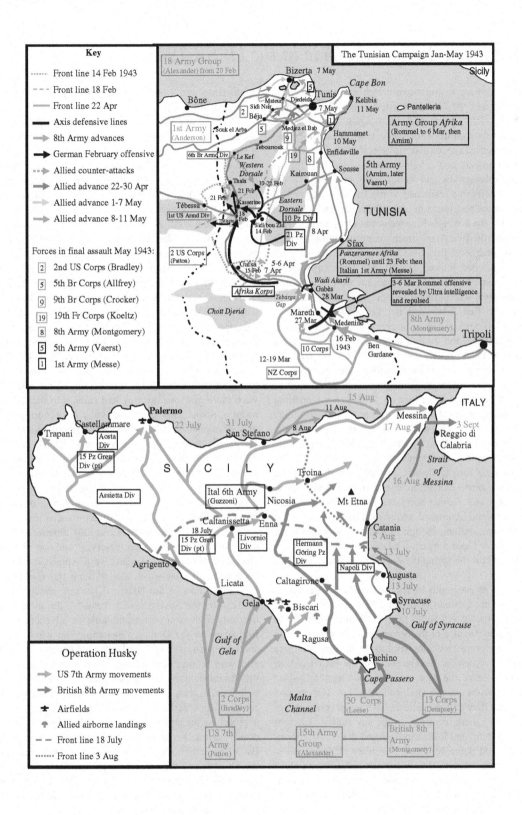

Key

...... Front line 14 Feb 1943
- - - Front line 18 Feb
——— Front line 22 Apr
——— Axis defensive lines
➤ 8th Army advances
➤ German February offensive
┅┅➤ Allied counter-attacks
➤ Allied advance 22-30 Apr
➤ Allied advance 1-7 May
➤ Allied advance 8-11 May

Forces in final assault May 1943:
[2] 2nd US Corps (Bradley)
[5] 5th Br Corps (Allfrey)
[9] 9th Br Corps (Crocker)
[19] 19th Fr Corps (Koeltz)
[8] 8th Army (Montgomery)
[5] 5th Army (Vaerst)
[1] 1st Army (Messe)

The Tunisian Campaign Jan–May 1943

Sicily

18 Army Group (Alexander) from 20 Feb

Bizerta 7 May
[5]
Cape Bon
Bône
Mateur
Djedeida
Sidi Nsir
[2] Béja
Souk el Arba
[5]
6th Br Armd Div
Medjez el Bab
[9]
Le Kef
Teboursouk
Western Dorsale
[19]
Thala 19-22 Feb
21 Feb
21 Feb
Kasserine
18 Feb
Tébessa
1st US Armd Div
Thélepte
Sidi bou Zid 14 Feb
Eastern Dorsale
[10 Pz Div]
[21 Pz Div]
Gafsa 5-6 Apr
15 Feb 7 Apr
2 US Corps (Patton)
Afrika Korps
Tebarga Gap
Chott Djerid

Tunis
7 May
[1]
Kelibia 11 May
Pantelleria
Hammamet 10 May
Enfidaville
Kairouan
Sousse

Army Group *Afrika* (Rommel to 6 Mar, then Arnim)

5th Army (Arnim, later Vaerst)

TUNISIA

8 Apr
Sfax

Panzerarmee Afrika (Rommel) until 23 Feb: then Italian 1st Army (Messe)

3-6 Mar Rommel offensive revealed by Ultra intelligence and repulsed

Wadi Akarit
Gabès 28 Mar
Mareth 27 Mar
Medenine
16 Feb 1943
Ben Gardane
12-19 Mar
[10 Corps]
NZ Corps

8th Army (Montgomery)
Tripoli

---

15 Aug
ITALY
Messina
17 Aug
3 Sept
Reggio di Calabria
11 Aug
8 Aug
31 July
San Stefano
Castellammare
Palermo
22 July
Trapani
Aosta Div
15 Pz Gren Div (pt)
Assietta Div
Troina
Strait of Messina
16 Aug
▲ Mt Etna
S I C I L Y
Ital 6th Army (Guzzoni)
Nicosia
Caltanissetta
18 July
15 Pz Gren Div (pt)
Enna
Livornio Div
Hermann Göring Pz Div
Catania
5 Aug
13 July
Napoli Div
Augusta
13 July
Agrigento
Licata
Caltagirone
Syracuse
10 July
Gela
Biscari
Ragusa
Gulf of Syracuse
Gulf of Gela
Pachino
Cape Passero

Operation Husky

➤ US 7th Army movements
➤ British 8th Army movements
✈ Airfields
♟ Allied airborne landings
- - - Front line 18 July
...... Front line 3 Aug

2 Corps (Bradley)
Malta Channel
30 Corps (Leese)
13 Corps (Dempsey)
US 7th Army (Patton)
15th Army Group (Alexander)
British 8th Army (Montgomery)

Map 25: The Turn of the Tide in the USSR 1943

Germany's disastrous overstretch into the Caucasus had cost the *Ostheer* (eastern army) 20 divisions. The Red Army had once again succeeded in holding out through disastrous defeats in the summer and had then achieved spectacular victories in the winter. Young battle-experienced and tough commanders like Zhukov, Chuikov, Rokossovsky and Konev were emerging. To the traditional defensive resilience of the Russian soldier had been added the best medium tank of the war, the T-34, and from the US the 4-wheel-drive jeeps and Dodge trucks that were to give the Red Army much greater mobility, even in the worst conditions, than the *Ostheer*. In the planning for Uranus, Stalin had showed himself able temporarily to put aside his titanic suspicions and to accept views contradictory to his own, when argued forcibly by Vassilievsky and Zhukov. The Red Army had not yet, however, held up against the *Wehrmacht* in a summer campaign. The great test, and arguably the turning point of the Second World War, was to come in July 1943. As in 1942, in fact, the *Stavka* had overplayed its hand in following up its winter success. In the wake of Stalingrad, Soviet forces had re-taken Rostov and Khar'kov by 12 February, opening a gap between Army Groups South and Centre (as they were renamed on that day). The effort exhausted the Voronezh and South-West Fronts, which had been heavily engaged all winter. Manstein's panzers encircled Popov's forces heading for the Dniepr, pushed them back to the Donets, and, joined by reinforcements rushed from France, re-took Khar'kov. Further north, the Soviets opened a land route to besieged Leningrad, and pushed back the Germans in the Vyazma salient, though failing to reach Smolensk (Army Group Centre made a planned withdrawal from Rzhev), but now the spring thaw – the *rasputitsa* – brought a pause.

Despite its enormous losses the Red Army was growing in strength. German plans for 1943 were designed to disrupt that growth: as Hitler said, to 'light a bonfire' and disrupt the confidence of the Soviet high command. Stalin and Zhukov were not sure (rightly) that their soldiers were yet the match for the Germans on the battlefield, so preferred to leave the first move to the Germans, while planning assaults on the Orel and Khar'kov (Operations Kutusov and Rumyantsev) salients. The Soviet commanders in their own salient, centring on the key railway junction at Kursk, Vatutin and Rokossovsky, used the civilian population to build defensive lines 100 miles (160 km) deep. Aware of this, and with Hitler very nervous, German plans were postponed repeatedly to build up their own strength, in particular to equip with the new Panther heavy tank. Finally, on 5 July, Operation Citadel was launched, with 2,700 tanks and 1,800 aircraft, initiating the largest tank battle in history.

The aim of Citadel was another encirclement, by breaking into the salient from north and south. Initial penetration was made, and Model's 9th Army came close to a breakthrough, but the Soviet defences exacted a heavy toll, and progress slowed, even though the Germans threw in their reserves. Zhukov and Vassilievsky, in overall command, sent in their reserves from the Bryansk Front and the Steppe Front and Zhukov launched Operation Kutusov against Orel. In the south, over a thousand tanks were engaged in the battle near Prokhorovka between Rotmistrov's 5th Guards Army and Hoth's 4th Panzer Army – which included SS panzer divisions with the fearsome Tiger tank. The Germans nearly reached their objective at Oboyan, but were held, and the story was the same in the north. On 13 July, Hitler decided Citadel should be shut down, needing to move divisions to Italy to face the Anglo-American forces that had broken from their beach-heads in Sicily on 12 July. Both sides had suffered heavy losses in tanks – more than half the Soviet tanks were destroyed. German losses were more grievous, as they had eaten into their strategic reserve. Soviet tank production was far outstripping that of their opponents, which was barely covering losses.

In the face of the opportunity to launch a summer offensive, the *Stavka* was hesitant. Stalin began to assert himself once more over Zhukov and Vassilievsky, banning encirclements – the Red Army had failed to complete a single one since Stalingrad – and ordering broad front advances based on pulverising direct assaults instead. First attacks failed against Model's skilful defence, but they drew in the last German reserves and on 3 August Operation Rumyantsev began. By 8 August it had taken Belgorod and punched a hole through the German line, in the direction of the Dniepr. Khar'kov was once again re-taken by the Soviets on 23 August – the most fought-over city in the war – and simultaneous advances took the Red Army to the Donets, threatening the whole German southern position, which still extended beyond the Crimea, and with it their control of the resource-rich areas of the Ukraine. On 31 August, Hitler sanctioned some withdrawals, but Soviet breakthroughs prevented these being at all orderly. By 8 September the Red Army was approaching the Dniepr and Kiev. Further north, Sokolovsky drove against the Smolensk line of Army Group Centre. By 30 September, the Soviets held five bridgeheads over the Dniepr, and the German front had been forced back 150 miles (240 km) and more importantly had no natural defensive position in the south. There would be no respite for them when winter came.

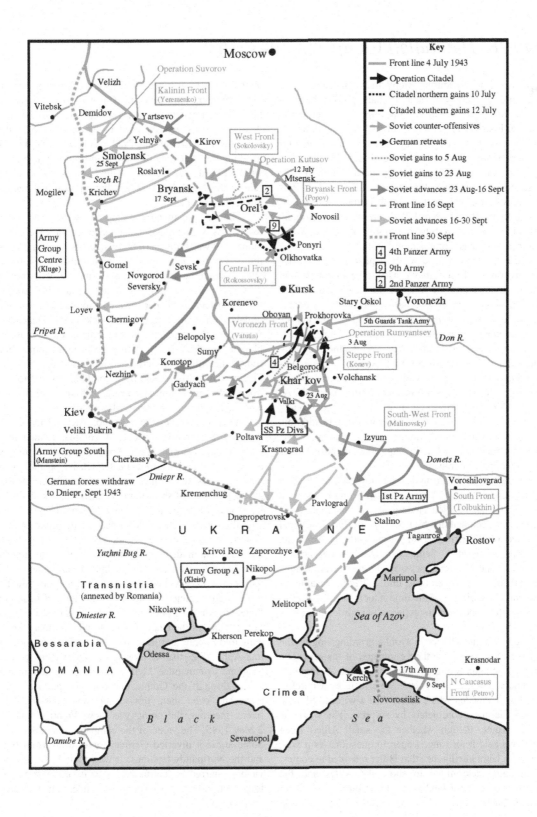

Key

———	Front line 4 July 1943
►►►	Operation Citadel
·····►	Citadel northern gains 10 July
- - -►	Citadel southern gains 12 July
⇨	Soviet counter-offensives
—►	German retreats
········	Soviet gains to 5 Aug
— — —	Soviet gains to 23 Aug
➤	Soviet advances 23 Aug–16 Sept
— — —	Front line 16 Sept
⇨	Soviet advances 16–30 Sept
·······	Front line 30 Sept
4	4th Panzer Army
9	9th Army
2	2nd Panzer Army

Moscow

Velizh

Vitebsk

Demidov

Yartsevo

Operation Suvorov

Kalinin Front
(Yeremenko)

Yelnya

Kirov

West Front
(Sokolovsky)

Smolensk
25 Sept

Roslavl

Operation Kutusov

12 July
Mtsensk

Sozh R.

Krichev

Bryansk
17 Sept

2

Orel

Bryansk Front
(Popov)

Mogilev

9

Novosil

Army
Group
Centre
(Kluge)

Gomel

Sevsk

Ponyri
Olkhovatka

Novgorod
Seversky

Central Front
(Rokossovsky)

Loyev

Chernigov

Kursk

Pripet R.

Korenevo

Stary Oskol

Voronezh

Belopolye

Oboyan

Prokhorovka

5th Guards Tank Army

Sumy

Voronezh Front
(Vatutin)

Operation Rumyantsev
3 Aug

Don R.

Konotop

4

Belgorod

Steppe Front
(Konev)

Nezhin

Gadyach

Khar'kov

Volchansk

Valki

23 Aug

Kiev

SS Pz Divs

South-West Front
(Malinovsky)

Veliki Bukrin

Poltava

Izyum

Army Group South
(Manstein)

Cherkassy

Krasnograd

Donets R.

German forces withdraw
to Dniepr, Sept 1943

Dniepr R.

Voroshilovgrad

Kremenchug

Pavlograd

1st Pz Army

South Front
(Tolbukhin)

Dnepropetrovsk

Stalino

U   K   R   A   I   N   E

Taganrog

Rostov

Yuzhni Bug R.

Krivoi Rog

Zaporozhye

Mariupol

Army Group A
(Kleist)

Nikopol

Transnistria
(annexed by Romania)

Melitopol

Sea of Azov

Dniester R.

Nikolayev

B e s s a r a b i a

Kherson

Perekop

Krasnodar

Odessa

17th Army

R O M A N I A

Kerch

9 Sept

N Caucasus
Front (Petrov)

Crimea

Novorossiisk

B   l   a   c   k   *S   e   a*

Danube R.

Sevastopol

Map 26: The Italian Campaign 1943–45

After finally securing Sicily in August, the Allies moved quickly to land in Italy proper. Lack of landing craft, and the need for air cover determined for Eisenhower that his landings had to be in the far south. The consequences for the Italians were disastrous. The German response as usual was rapid and effective. Mussolini was rescued and set up in the north in the 'Italian Social Republic'. Italians were disarmed in Italy and the Balkans, and on the Greek islands, where they resisted, their officers were killed. Fresh divisions under Rommel were deployed to the north of Rome, while Kesselring was given command in the south.

Once Germany was able to deploy into defensive positions south of Rome, Italy ceased to be an opportunity for a quick entry into the heart of the Reich and became instead a wasteful diversion. Italian terrain favoured the defence: a central mountainous spine, and narrow coastal plains – sometimes as little as 20 miles (32 km) wide – crossed by rivers and steep valleys, while the mountain slopes offered positions where small numbers of defenders could dominate the coastal roads and took a great deal of effort to shift, being well-protected from air attack. As a result, Allied superiority in material resources and in airpower was of less use than in other theatres. In addition, Hitler deployed high-quality troops from the central reserve, and Kesselring was skilful in organising defensive lines and conducting withdrawals.

Montgomery's 8th Army landed in Reggio di Calabria on 3 September, followed by the 1st Airborne Division at Taranto. The main Allied landing was at Salerno, where the 5th Army, commanded by US General Mark Clark and composed of the British 10th Corps and the American 6th Corps, landed on 9 September. The landing site was predictable, and counter-attacks by German forces almost pushed them off the beach-head, until halted by naval bombardment. Kesselring used the time it took for the Allies to overcome this opposition to prepare a winter defensive line north of Naples.

The best Allied chance to avoid a grinding slog up the length of Italy was to use their command of the seas. The attempt, Operation Shingle, which took place at Anzio on 22 January 1944, was however described by Churchill as landing a stranded whale rather than a wildcat. Shingle took the Germans completely by surprise. The way was open to Rome, though whether the small Allied force could have held it for long is open to question. As it was, advised by Ultra intelligence that Hitler intended to contest the landings (determined to show the Allies and the German people that a landing could be thrown back into the sea), General Lucas chose to consolidate his position on the beach-head instead of driving for Rome or extending his perimeter. This gave the Germans time to surround him, so that when the attempt was made to break out it failed. Lucas was replaced by Truscott, who held the Germans at bay, but the final result was that far from breaking the stalemate of the Italian front, Shingle created an extra burden as the main Allied armies had to work to relieve the beach-head, rather than, as was intended, the other way around.

The key to an advance up the west coast towards Rome was Monte Cassino. The sixth-century Benedictine monastery was built there because of its impregnable position: qualities that remained undiminished 1,400 years later. The commander of the German 10th Army was a lay Benedictine and would not deploy his troops in the monastery itself, but their positions were no less formidable for that. Successive attacks were launched by Americans, New Zealanders and Indians, but they were all bloodily repulsed. B-17 bombers reduced the monastery to ruins. The rubble this created merely aided the defence. Finally, the fourth attack, by a combination of Moroccan troops adept at mountain warfare, and the Polish II Corps, won the heights at Cassino in May 1944.

After the success at Cassino, Alexander, who had replaced Eisenhower in overall command, intended to encircle the German 10th Army south of Rome, and prevent it falling back to its next defensive position. Clark, however, was determined to be the liberator of Rome ahead of the British, whom he distrusted, and diverted his troops from the job of encirclement. They linked up with the forces in Anzio, who had finally broken out, and American troops entered Rome on 4 June 1944, but the Germans had made a good retreat, and were able to establish themselves on the Gothic line. This condemned the Allies to another winter of hard campaigning in Italy. Their forces were depleted for the Dragoon landings in southern France in August 1944. The ambition was to strike for one of the 'gaps' at the head of the Adriatic, but there were no amphibious craft available for this, and it was not until mid-April 1945 that Clark's forces (Alexander was now Supreme Commander, Mediterranean) were able to batter a way through the Gothic line onto the plain of the Po river, and even then, this region was criss-crossed by rivers, meaning the going was slow. Fighting ended on 2 May 1945. The value of the campaign remains debated. Some argue it diverted German forces away from France and the Normandy landings. It was, though, an expensive victory, marred by confusion as to its ultimate purpose, fought on exhausting terrain. The underbelly had proved anything but soft.

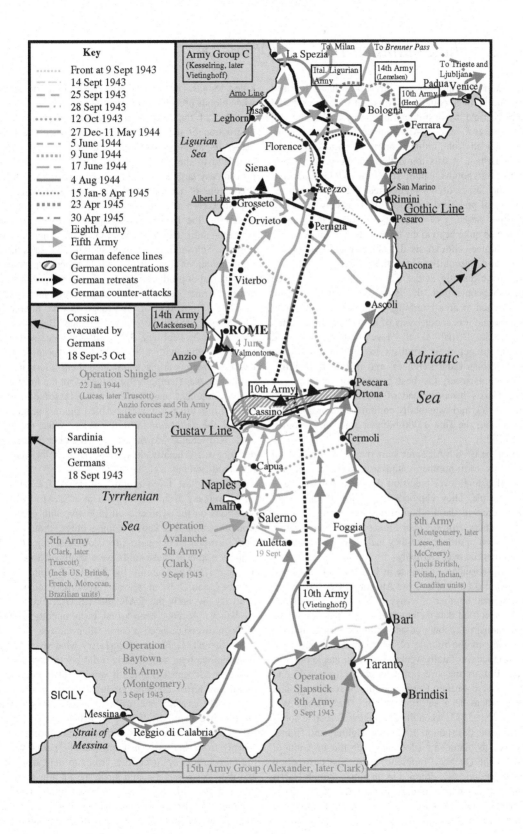

Key

- .... Front at 9 Sept 1943
- – – – 14 Sept 1943
- — — 25 Sept 1943
- – · – 28 Sept 1943
- ·········· 12 Oct 1943
- ——— 27 Dec–11 May 1944
- – – – 5 June 1944
- ·········· 9 June 1944
- — — 17 June 1944
- ——— 4 Aug 1944
- ·········· 15 Jan–8 Apr 1945
- ▪▪▪▪ 23 Apr 1945
- – · – 30 Apr 1945
- ⟶ Eighth Army
- ⟶ Fifth Army
- ━━ German defence lines
- ⬭ German concentrations
- ······> German retreats
- ⟶ German counter-attacks

Army Group C
(Kesselring, later
Vietinghoff)

La Spezia   To Milan   To *Brenner Pass*
To Trieste and
Ljubljana

Ital. Ligurian
Army

14th Army
(Lemelsen)

Padua   Venice

10th Army
(Herr)

Arno Line   Pisa   Bologna   Ferrara
Leghorn

*Ligurian
Sea*

Florence

Siena   Ravenna
San Marino
Arezzo   Rimini   **Gothic Line**
Albert Line   Grosseto   Pesaro
Orvieto   Perugia

Ancona

Viterbo   Ascoli

Corsica
evacuated by
Germans
18 Sept–3 Oct

14th Army
(Mackensen)

ROME
4 June
Valmontone

Adriatic

Anzio

Sea

Operation Shingle
22 Jan 1944
(Lucas, later Truscott)

Anzio forces and 5th Army
make contact 25 May

10th Army

Pescara
Ortona

Cassino

Gustav Line

Sardinia
evacuated by
Germans
18 Sept 1943

Termoli

Tyrrhenian

Capua

Sea   Operation
Avalanche   Naples
5th Army
(Clark)   Amalfi   Salerno   Foggia
9 Sept 1943
Auletta
19 Sept

5th Army
(Clark, later
Truscott)
(Incls US, British,
French, Moroccan,
Brazilian units)

8th Army
(Montgomery, later
Leese, then
McCreery)
(Incls British,
Polish, Indian,
Canadian units)

10th Army
(Vietinghoff)

Operation
Baytown
8th Army
(Montgomery)
3 Sept 1943

Operation
Slapstick
8th Army
9 Sept 1943

Bari

Taranto

Brindisi

SICILY

Messina

*Strait of
Messina*   Reggio di Calabria

15th Army Group (Alexander, later Clark)

Map 27: The Combined Bomber Offensive

In Britain and the US, air strategists had theorised that the bomber could win wars before armies could take the field, by destroying an enemy's economy and morale. However, after RAF Bomber Command's campaign expanded from military or naval targets after the Battle of Britain, it was found that bombers were rarely dropping their bombs within five miles (8 km) of their targets, and losses of the unescorted aircraft were high. The dream of precise destruction of the enemy economy, by selective targeting of oil plants, factories and railway yards, proved quite beyond the technology available.

The bomber enthusiasts did not change their views, however, and Churchill needed their efforts as the only way to strike directly at the Reich as well as persuade the British people that 'the Blitz' was being avenged. They switched to area-bombing, arguing that damage to civilian morale was another way of disrupting the German economy. The British slowly developed methods and equipment to get their bombers to the target, and to confuse German radar defences, and in late 1942 introduced the Lancaster, the best bomber of the war. Air Marshal Harris became head of Bomber Command in February 1942, and was totally committed to area bombing, launching the first 1,000-bomber raid, on Cologne, in May 1942.

When the US 8th Air Force started to arrive in England in 1942, its own bomber enthusiasts were determined to show that high-level precision day-time bombing was indeed possible. They claimed their Norden bomb-sight enabled a crew to 'land a bomb in a pickle-barrel'. Their first experiences, in raids over France from August 1942, increased their optimism, but they had a nasty shock when raids commenced over Germany.

The Casablanca Conference in January 1943 accepted a plan by the commander of 8th Air Force, General Eaker, for a combined bomber offensive (CBO). The Casablanca Directive specified that the aim was the destruction of the German industrial, economic and military system and the undermining of the morale of the German people until their resistance was fatally weakened. The strategic purpose of the CBO in the eyes of Churchill, Roosevelt and Marshall was to weaken German ability to resist a ground invasion, not to be a substitute for it. The strategy was refined in June 1943, when the Pointblank Directive set as the priority the destruction of German fighters and fighter production, to obtain air supremacy for the invasion of France. At the Quebec Conference in August destruction of German morale was dropped as an aim – though Harris continued with area bombing, particularly of the Ruhr and Berlin – and in August, 1943, incendiary bombing of Hamburg caused a new phenomenon, the firestorm, which killed 45,000. The USAAF area-bombed too, on occasions when clouds prevented any attempt at precision.

One of the reasons for the switch in emphasis to destruction of the Luftwaffe was that when the USAAF began its missions over the heavily-defended industrial heartland of the Reich, the unescorted B-17s and B-24s proved easy targets for fighters, vectored in by their radar. Predictions of accuracy had also been exaggerated. Eaker persisted, even after the loss of 147 out of 376 aircraft in a raid on the ball-bearing plant at Schweinfurt on 17 August – until 'Black Week' in October, which included a return to Schweinfurt, involved such heavy losses that daylight operations were suspended. The Germans responded by dispersal of production and with Albert Speer's reorganisation German output actually dramatically increased.

The introduction of long-range escorts, notably P-51 Mustangs, changed the situation. In the 'Big Week' raids from 19 to 25 February, 3,000 8th Air Force sorties were flown, together with 500 by 15th Air Force from Italy. Big RAF night raids accompanied them. German fighter production was (temporarily) reduced, but the most important development was the enormous losses of Luftwaffe pilots. From this point on, the Allied fighters progressively cleared the Luftwaffe from the skies. What might have made a difference was the Me262 jet fighter, but its introduction was crucially delayed by Hitler's insistence that it be modified into a fighter-bomber.

By the last three months of 1944, the Allies had air supremacy over Germany. The USAAF focused its attentions on the synthetic oil industry, with great effect. Bomber Command kept bombing cities, though the Air Staff favoured moving to precision bombing. At Soviet request, some of these raids were designed to ease their advance: Berlin was hit by 1,000 US bombers on 3 February, and Dresden was pulverised between 13 and 15 February by both the RAF and USAAF. Up to 60,000 are believed to have been killed, in an operation which is still controversial, since it came when the war was clearly about to end. Debate continues on what overall impact strategic bombing had. Clearly it did not deliver all that its strongest advocates claimed it would, either in destroying morale by terror bombing or in precision destruction of targets. The casualty rate for bomber crews was very high. On the other hand, by late 1944, it had caused great dislocation to German transportation, and production fell sharply from then on. Most importantly, perhaps, it drew the Luftwaffe away from other fronts to defend the Reich, and then destroyed it – and since the 88 mm anti-aircraft gun that was deployed in huge quantities against the bombers was also the best anti-tank gun of the war, it could be said that it diverted key weapons from the battlefield.

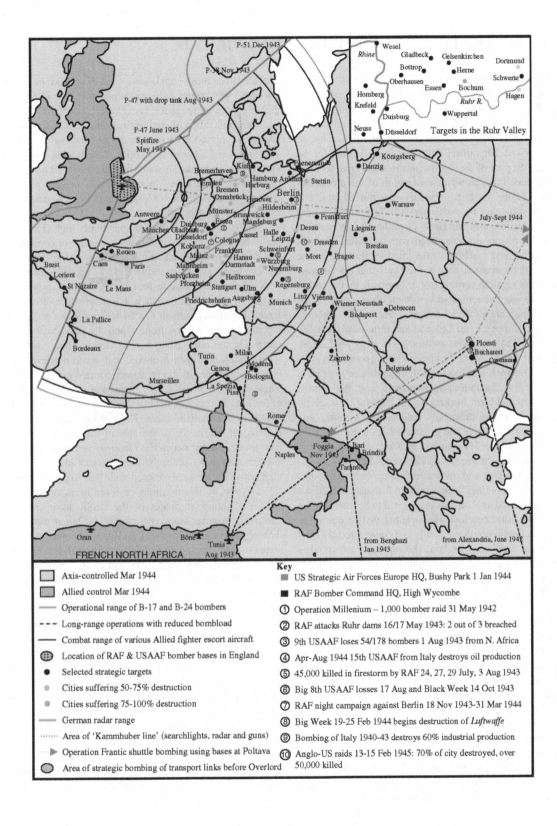

Targets in the Ruhr Valley

Key

Axis-controlled Mar 1944

Allied control Mar 1944

Operational range of B-17 and B-24 bombers

Long-range operations with reduced bombload

Combat range of various Allied fighter escort aircraft

Location of RAF & USAAF bomber bases in England

Selected strategic targets

Cities suffering 50-75% destruction

Cities suffering 75-100% destruction

German radar range

Area of 'Kammhuber line' (searchlights, radar and guns)

Operation Frantic shuttle bombing using bases at Poltava

Area of strategic bombing of transport links before Overlord

US Strategic Air Forces Europe HQ, Bushy Park 1 Jan 1944

RAF Bomber Command HQ, High Wycombe

① Operation Millenium – 1,000 bomber raid 31 May 1942

② RAF attacks Ruhr dams 16/17 May 1943: 2 out of 3 breached

③ 9th USAAF loses 54/178 bombers 1 Aug 1943 from N. Africa

④ Apr-Aug 1944 15th USAAF from Italy destroys oil production

⑤ 45,000 killed in firestorm by RAF 24, 27, 29 July, 3 Aug 1943

⑥ Big 8th USAAF losses 17 Aug and Black Week 14 Oct 1943

⑦ RAF night campaign against Berlin 18 Nov 1943-31 Mar 1944

⑧ Big Week 19-25 Feb 1944 begins destruction of *Luftwaffe*

⑨ Bombing of Italy 1940-43 destroys 60% industrial production

⑩ Anglo-US raids 13-15 Feb 1945: 70% of city destroyed, over 50,000 killed

Map 28: The USSR in the 'Great Patriotic War'

Germany conquered an area containing 40 per cent of the USSR's population, 60 per cent of Soviet arms production, 63 per cent of its coal, 60 per cent of its pigs. Little had been done to plan for relocation, on the grounds that it was 'defeatist' so evacuation had to be improvised. The railway network was inadequate for the task, and the pace of the German advance too rapid to allow it to be done fully. However, one eighth of the productive capacity of the western provinces was moved, and this made the difference for Soviet survival. The priorities were arms production, iron and steel: 17 of the 64 steelworks in the Donets region were evacuated, with their workforces. It was chaotic, and machinery was piled by the side of the railways in unprepared sites in the Urals, but Soviet arms production began to surpass that of Germany by the end of 1941. The margins remained very tight during 1942, when further vital areas were over-run. The small amounts coming in through Lend-Lease at that time were therefore important. The focus was ruthlessly on arms production. Consumer needs were ignored. Food production was harder to relocate, and food was strictly rationed to provide sufficient for the industrial workforce and Red Army. Dependants and farm workers had to fend for themselves; with the workforce drastically reduced (by a third), and shortages of machinery and livestock, life on the collective farms was harsh. The burden of food production was largely carried by women, the elderly and children.

Fuel, transport and mineral ores were the vital bottlenecks. New coal mines were opened in Karaganda, Kuzbass and Pechora, and new sources of ores had to be found, as the major ones had been lost. Harsh military-style discipline and improvisation pulled the railway system through. New lines to the east had to be laid. The supply of locomotives from the US was vital: Soviet production of them virtually ceased.

These massive problems were handled by the State Defence Council (GKO), though this committee rarely met formally. Stalin was an excellent chairman with a great memory and an ability to penetrate to the heart of a problem. He was capricious, but showed during the war a readiness to employ experts and weigh up different views. GKO's appointees (such as Kaganovich for railways, Shvernik for factory location) were given wide dictatorial powers to deal with the bottlenecks, and addressed them successfully, but with ruthless disregard of the suffering of the Soviet people.

Foreign observers had predicted that the Soviet regime's hold on its people would be so poor that they would not be motivated to fight. The regime resorted to nationalistic themes and slogans and downplayed ideology. Assisted by the brutal attitude of the German occupiers, which soon alienated even those populations, such as the Ukrainians or Latvians, who might have welcomed them as liberators, this theme was to prove remarkably successful. There was some relaxation of conformity – the Russian Orthodox Church supported resistance to the invader, and in return churches were allowed to re-open. Tsarist-style uniforms and the Guards designation for successful units were reinstated; indeed even party officials began wearing uniforms. However, the NKVD secret police maintained an iron grip on the population.

Soviet casualty rates were appallingly high. This was partly because of the no-holds-barred nature of combat on this front: the USSR was not a signatory of the Hague or Geneva Conventions, and after Hitler's 'commissar order', both sides showed little respect for the rights of prisoners-of-war. Of 5.8 million Soviets who were prisoners-of-war, at least 3.3 million perished. The GUlag continued, and penal battalions were formed from which the only escape was death. On the other hand, behind German lines, soldiers whose units had been over-run, and others escaping the genocidal policies of the occupiers, formed partisan units. These harried German supply routes and forces resting out of the line. To maintain control, NKVD officers were parachuted in to command them. The partisans' actual impact is debated: except for in the area of the Pripet marshes, tank-proof country which the Germans never managed to subdue, they were probably only a minor nuisance until their activities were coordinated with Red Army advances.

In spite of its enormous reserves of manpower, by 1944 the human resources of the USSR were severely stretched. Women were conscripted in larger numbers than anywhere else (800,000), and uniquely were put into combat units – including fighter squadrons in the Red Air Force. Women made up 53 per cent of the workforce by the end of the war – and were a much higher proportion in agriculture. The Soviet people showed remarkable tenacity and resilience in what they called the Great Patriotic War. The price paid for victory was enormous. As many as 27 million died, but when forced labour deportations are factored in, together with hundreds of thousands who died as a result of the regime's own atrocities, the figure is much higher, with the great burden of it falling on Ukraine and Byelorussia. Thirty per cent of the national wealth was destroyed: over 1,700 cities and 70,000 villages were devastated. There was to be no respite. As the war ended, the regime tightened its grip, particularly in liberated territories the Germans had occupied, treating with suspicion anyone who had been outside their control and making clear to the Soviet peoples that the privations would continue.

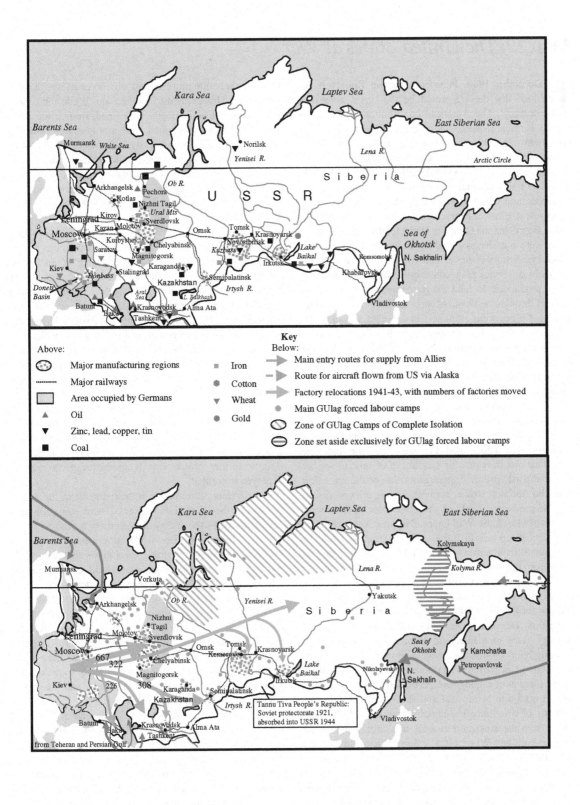

Above:

- (⊙) Major manufacturing regions
- .... Major railways
- ▨ Area occupied by Germans
- ▲ Oil
- ▼ Zinc, lead, copper, tin
- ■ Coal

- ▪ Iron
- ⬤ Cotton
- ▼ Wheat
- ● Gold

Key

Below:

- ➜ Main entry routes for supply from Allies
- ⇢ Route for aircraft flown from US via Alaska
- ➜ Factory relocations 1941-43, with numbers of factories moved
- • Main GUlag forced labour camps
- ▨ Zone of GUlag Camps of Complete Isolation
- ⬭ Zone set aside exclusively for GUlag forced labour camps

Map 29: The United States at War

In December 1940, President Franklin Roosevelt had pledged that the US would be the 'great arsenal of democracy'. The American contribution to the Allied victory is often, indeed, seen in terms of the production of armaments. The US produced 86,000 tanks, over 300,000 aircraft and 6,755 naval vessels; comparative figures for the whole of the Axis were 55,500, 157,000 and 1,400. To achieve this productivity required the mobilisation of resources, and labour. Roosevelt created a large number of government agencies to manage this, among them the War Labor Board and the Office of War Mobilization. However, these were not always coordinated, and while there were statutory controls of prices and wages, there was never a full national service plan, conscription of labour or nationalised production. Instead, the government and its agencies worked through the business corporations, many of whose leading figures were employed in the new agencies. The spectacular feats of production were therefore carried out largely by private industry: the Kaiser shipyards building Liberty merchant ships or Ford's Willow Run plant building bombers. Corporations were given tax incentives and their investment was underwritten by the government.

Aware that companies were making large profits, there was some worker discontent, though this was mostly controlled by 'no-strike' agreements made by the American Federation of Labor and the Congress for Industrial Organizations in return for guarantees of union membership and participation in the organisation of the war effort. This did not stop strikes entirely; a long miners' dispute in 1943 produced a backlash in Congress, with the passage in July 1943 of the War Labor Disputes Act, giving the President the power to break such strikes. This reflected the growth of a conservative political mood in Congress away from the previous more liberal New Deal period.

The growth of productivity had indeed ended many of the problems the New Deal had confronted and meant that the war for the US, unlike other belligerents, was a time of prosperity. Demands from allies and from the US's own military were insatiable, and companies expanded their working hours around the clock. With millions in uniform, this required an expanded workforce, and groups previously on the margins of employment, particularly black Americans, gained access to better-paid and skilled jobs. Established patterns of discrimination initially kept them from benefiting from the expansion in areas like aircraft production or ship-building. When black union leaders threatened a march on Washington in protest in June 1941, Roosevelt issued Executive Order 8802 prohibiting discrimination in companies receiving government contracts. While reluctant to do so, employers and unions found they had to accept black workers into more skilled jobs, so great was the need for labour. This applied to women too. While their social roles were not permanently re-defined, women too found access to better employment, and a propaganda campaign drew in women who previously had not been in the workforce, principally middle-aged, middle-class women.

These developments brought a sizeable migration. Blacks left the segregated South for the north and west. Under the *bracero* arrangement, 200,000 Mexicans came north, principally for farm work, though there was also a movement of Hispanic Americans into the cities. Newcomers swelled the populations of production centres like Detroit and Los Angeles, putting strain on housing, education and medical facilities. The influx of ethnically diverse groups led to racial conflict. In Los Angeles, tensions between servicemen and Hispanics produced 'zoot-suit riots' (the zoot-suit was the distinctive costume of young Hispanics). Racial tensions developed around military camps. Training camps were put in the South, because land was cheap, and blacks from outside the South, unwilling to conform to local segregation customs, were involved in a number of incidents. The armed forces remained segregated throughout the war. Blacks were used in combat reluctantly by the Army – again under the impetus of manpower shortages. Under pressure from Eleanor Roosevelt and others, a black military flying school was set up at Tuskegee, but it took further efforts for its graduates to be actually deployed in combat.

Americans were united in their support of the war, as a result of the Pearl Harbor attack. There was no need to stir up hatred of the enemy, though there was some propaganda to that effect. But while Americans distinguished between Nazis and Germans, their views of the Japanese were more racially-oriented. One result of this was the internment of 112,000 Japanese-Americans who lived on the west coast. Regardless of whether they were US citizens, their loyalty was regarded as unreliable, and a combination of fear, prejudice and local economics saw their removal by the military and the War Relocation Authority, with the President's approval. They were placed in camps inland, often in conditions of squalor. The Supreme Court endorsed the internments and many were not released until the end of the war.

While the US contribution is often seen in production terms, it should not be forgotten that by the end of the war the US had 16 million men and women in uniform, and had the largest navy, merchant fleet and strategic bombing force. It was also in possession of the atomic bomb, the product of the Manhattan Project, the pinnacle of achievement of the American industrial and scientific effort.

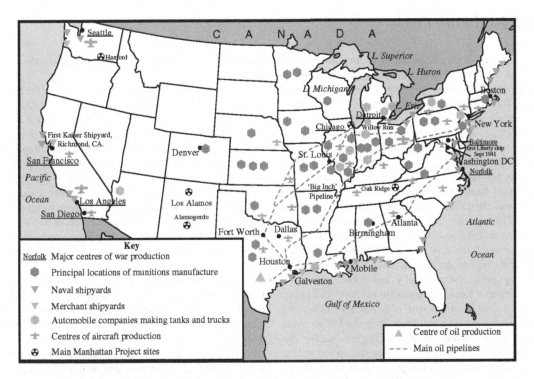

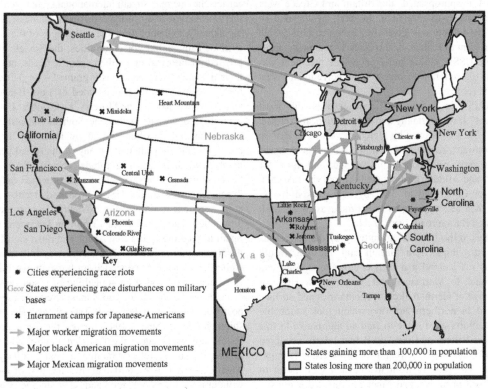

Map 30: Lend-Lease

Lend-Lease was a response to Churchill's pleas in late 1940 that Britain was bankrupt and could no longer afford to pay for munitions and other supplies essential for its fight against Germany. Many Americans were sceptical about such claims, in view of the size of the British Empire, and were still resentful of the failure to repay debts from the First World War. By the end of 1940 President Roosevelt still wished to avoid full involvement in the war, but believed a British victory was vital to US security. With Britain showing signs of resilience, and with his own re-election successfully achieved, Roosevelt argued that the US was like a householder whose neighbour's house was on fire, who would lend his firehose in the emergency and leave until later any discussion of recompense for damage to the hose. Loans and debts would be avoided by getting 'rid of the silly, foolish old dollar sign'. On 29 December Roosevelt argued to the American public that the US should be the 'arsenal of democracy'. Isolationist opponents claimed such aid would drag the US into war. The proposal was bitterly debated in Congress, but the idea of aiding the Allies short of war appealed to the public. The Lend-Lease Act was passed by Congress on 11 March. $7 billion was appropriated, and Britain and Greece were declared qualified to receive it. In total, by the end of the war, $50 billion was given in foreign aid, of which $31 billion went to Britain; of the other 37 recipients, most went to the USSR, China and France. The president was given wide discretion as to who would receive it, and what they should receive.

Churchill was to describe Lend-Lease as 'this most unsordid act'. It was certainly a massive logistical exercise. The bulk of it was shipped by merchant vessels to Britain and then onward. Aircraft were flown across the Atlantic by civilian ferry pilots, including women, and those for the USSR and Middle East crossed Africa via Takoradi. Supplies for China had to enter by over-worked Indian ports and then be shipped over the Himalayas by air until the Ledo and Burma roads were usable.

Supplies to the USSR went initially by the dangerous Arctic route. Ships from Britain and the US would rendezvous off Iceland and sail as close to the ice cap as they could, to Murmansk and Arkhangelsk. This put them in range of German aircraft, submarines and surface ships based in northern Norway, which took a terrible toll. Great efforts were made to find an alternative to this costly route. Britain and the USSR had jointly occupied Iran in 1941, fearing the strength of pro-German sympathies there. The railway from the Persian Gulf ports to the USSR was primitive, and American railroad engineers were sent to improve it: an increasing flow went by this route from 1943. Supplies were also sent across the Pacific to Siberia.

Despite Churchill's words, Lend-Lease was not entirely selfless. It was linked to concerted efforts by the Americans to reform the world economic system to avoid the problems that had followed the First World War and in particular prevent a repeat of the Great Depression. Repayment was exacted in concessions to open up American access to imperial trading blocs: this was clear in the 1941–42 Anglo-American negotiations for a Master Lend-Lease Agreement, and subsequently in monetary agreements made at the Bretton Woods conference in 1944 and at conferences on post-war civil aviation and economic issues. Dependent on Lend-Lease, the British had no choice but to acquiesce.

Lend-Lease to the USSR served a different purpose. It was a sensitive issue in the US, and Roosevelt waited four months after Barbarossa before declaring the USSR a recipient. For Roosevelt, quite apart from the contribution it would make to victory – which was clearly tiny in the crucial battles of 1941–42, before much aid could arrive – it was a political action designed to draw the suspicious Soviets into the mainstream international system, to convince them of American sincerity and trustworthiness, and also, incidentally, to demonstrate the advantages of the capitalist system. Thus, unlike for other allies, the Soviets were not pressed for information on their specific needs, but instead their demands were generously granted – in particular in the first Supply Protocol negotiated by Lord Beaverbrook and Averell Harriman in Moscow in October 1941. This backfired somewhat, in that the Soviets endlessly carped about shortfalls – often caused by losses in the Arctic convoys – and they alienated many of the Allied personnel involved by their lack of gratitude. They would argue that the amounts were small: Lend-Lease provided only about 7 per cent of what the USSR produced itself – but the point was that it allowed the Soviets to concentrate their production. The US supplied 13 million felt boots, enough Spam to feed the whole Red Army, and most significantly, the trucks that meant the Red Army was fully motorised while the *Wehrmacht* depended on horse-drawn transport.

Lend-Lease ended on something of a sour note, with disputes over payment for goods that were to be used in the post-war period, and President Truman abruptly stopped shipments on 15 August 1945, the day the war ended. That should not overshadow the fact that Lend-Lease was an immensely successful programme, a vital corollary to the American productive effort that dwarfed that of the Axis; without it the munitions, food and other supplies would not have reached the places where they made the difference.

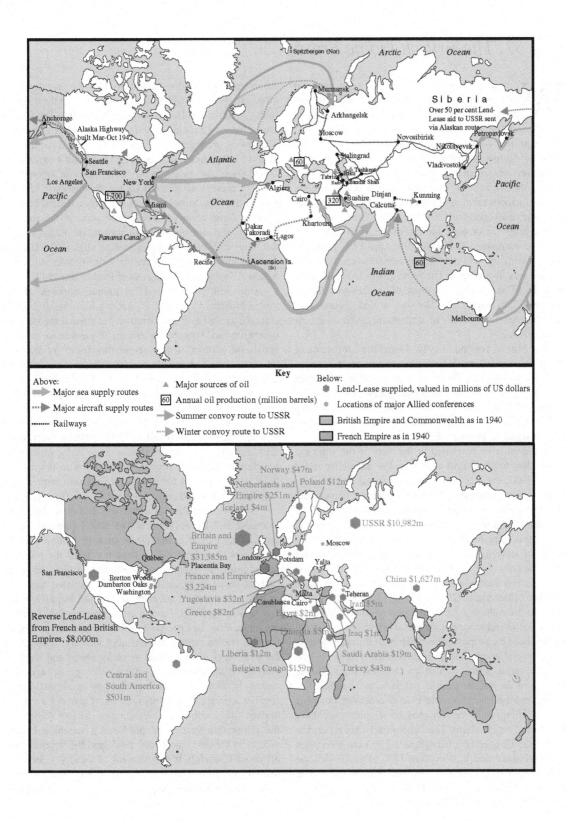

Map 31: The British Home Front

While its pre-war government had been prepared to appease Hitler to avoid war, Britain did not enter the war entirely unprepared. The appeasement period had given time for some rearmament, and most importantly for work to be completed on some vital technological developments, particularly radar. Aircraft production was increased from 1934 and contingency arrangements made to deal with aerial bombardment. Shadow factories capable of conversion to military production were built alongside civilian ones from 1936 and 27 new arms works were built between 1936 and 1939. Limited conscription was introduced in April 1939. However, Britain's army was still not fully mobilised when war broke out, and was ill-equipped. The retreat from Dunkirk saved the bulk of the Army, but most of its heavy weapons had been left behind. As Britain's armed forces were expanded, American supply of aircraft and tanks in particular was vital.

The blitz of London in 1940–41 and the later attack of V1 'flying bombs' and V2 missiles caused great damage, but failed to cause a collapse of morale – if anything they strengthened it – and in fact greater proportional damage was caused in the raids on smaller cities such as Coventry or Plymouth, and in the 'Baedeker' raids on cities of cultural significance that were lightly defended.

Children were evacuated at the start of the war, and though they began to drift back after the main blitz ended in May 1941, this was part of a major social phenomenon of the war: the erosion of Britain's traditional class structure, and also of the equally strong regional divisions of the nation. Measures to maintain morale emphasised that the war was being fought for a better future, and the mobilisation of women, the centralised management of labour under the control of the Minister of Labour, former union leader Ernest Bevin, and the unsettling arrival of large numbers of American GIs (including 130,000 blacks) all added to a developing public opinion in favour of measures of social and economic reform. This was shown in the popularity of the proposals for a national insurance system in the Beveridge report and for educational reform.

The major parties agreed an electoral truce for the duration of the war, though discontent with the conduct of the war and the desire for social change produced a number of by-election results that rejected government candidates in favour of independents. The Labour Party had refused to serve under Chamberlain, but agreed to join a coalition when Churchill succeeded him in May 1940 after the debacle in Norway. Churchill was determined that Britain would destroy Nazi Germany. Thus, 48 hours after the Germans reached the Channel, the Emergency Powers Act signalled the intention to mobilise the country fully for the war effort: all people, property and resources were to be at the disposal of the government. The effort was directed by a Production Executive, coordinating the efforts of the supply ministries, and setting priorities. The National Service Act at the end of 1941 conscripted all men aged 18–50 and women aged 20–30 (later also raised to 50) for military or labour purposes. Labour was directed by the Production Executive and by Bevin's Ministry. Given Britain's dependence on imports, strict controls over consumption in the form of rationing, and measures to boost agricultural output, such as the 'Dig for Victory' campaign, were vital as the U-boats took an increasing toll in the Atlantic. Britain still came within six weeks of running out of food in late 1942.

Churchill gave himself a unique position at the centre of Britain's war effort, naming himself Minister of Defence as well as Prime Minister. He chaired the Defence Committee and was able to indulge his passion for military and naval matters, sometimes to the despair of the professionals like General Brooke, the Chief of the Imperial General Staff from the end of 1941. This did mean, however, that Churchill was able to infuse his government with his own energy and determination. By no means all his strategic decisions were good ones, and in the years of setbacks between 1940 and 1942 he suffered much criticism, especially within the Conservative Party, which only reluctantly accepted him as its leader. For the British public, however, and for world opinion (most importantly, American), Churchill personified the British fighting spirit.

Britain ended the war exhausted. Rationing had been extensive and Britain's assets had been liquidated before the advent of Lend-Lease. Destruction by bombing would take years to make good, as Britain entered the post-war period with the intention of continuing to play the world role its status as victor implied. This included regaining control of its empire, an exercise that would prove costly and ultimately futile. For the British population, faced in the future with the uncertainties that these issues presented, the war was to represent a defining moment: particularly the year when Britain stood virtually alone, and Dunkirk and the Blitz formed a potent mythology of a Britain united. In fact, while the war did not throw up internal conflict as in some other belligerents, it generated a determination for reform and a rejection of the past (especially the Depression years) that produced a sweeping Labour victory in the election of June 1945, and the removal from office of Churchill at his moment of victory – an event that caused astonishment elsewhere in the world, but was reflective of the underlying social change, even discontent, that the war fostered in Britain.

Outer
Hebrides

Wick

Moray Firth

Inverness

Aberdeen

Inner

Hebrides

Dundee
Perth

Glasgow
Firth of Forth
Edinburgh

North

Sea

Firth
of
Clyde
Kilmarnock

Northern Ireland
(part of UK)

Belfast

Solway Firth

Newcastle
South Shields
Sunderland
Hartlepool

Isle of Man
Enemy aliens
interned on Man
1940: after vetting
many released by
1945

Barrow

Middlesbrough

York

EIRE
(Neutral)

Irish

Sea

Liverpool

Leeds
Hull

Manchester
Grimsby
Sheffield

Lincoln

Stoke
Nottingham
King's Lynn
Great Yarmouth
Norwich
Lowestoft

Derby
Burton
Leicester

Pembroke

Swansea
Cardiff

Cheltenham
Birmingham
Coventry

Bletchley
Colchester
Ipswich
Harwich
Felixtowe

V2 missile
launch sites in
Netherlands

Oxford

Weston-super-Mare
Bristol
Bath

Reading

London

Sheerness

Aldershot

Chatham
Canterbury

Dover

Atlantic Ocean

Exeter
Weymouth
Poole

Southampton
Portsmouth
Brighton
Newhaven

Plymouth

Torquay
Portland

Shoreham

Fowey
Dartmouth

Isle of Wight
Rendezvous point for
Overlord forces

Launch area
of V1 'flying
bombs'

Falmouth
Salcombe

Scilly Is.

English Channel

Alderney

Channel Is.
Occupied by Germany
June 1940-May 1945

Guernsey
Sark

Jersey

Shetland Is.

Orkney Is.

Scapa Flow

Wick

Key

Towns bombed by Germans

Major industrial areas

Direction of evacuation

Overlord 1st wave start points

Overlord 2nd wave start points

Naval bases

Shipbuilding centres

Code-breaking centres

Aircraft factories

Range of V1

Main concentration V1 strikes

Range of V2

Main concentration V2 strikes

Bath 1942 Baedeker raids

Map 32: The German Home Front

In 1936 Hitler inaugurated the Four Year Plan, directed by Göring, to make the German economy self-sufficient in key resources. To many outsiders, this was a 'guns not butter' policy of preparing Germany for war at the expense of civilian needs. Certainly, Hitler sought the militarisation of the German people for the Darwinian struggle that he saw as central to life. On the other hand, he was concerned to maintain popular support for the Nazi Party and acutely aware that the First World War had ended with a collapse of the German home front. Consequently, Germany entered the Second World War with an economy that was not fully mobilised for war, nor was there planning for a long-term struggle. Hitler was determined that he would achieve his radical re-shaping of Europe by war, but expected that the racial superiority of Germany would bring swift victory. The states which were brought under Germany's sway rectified its shortages in many key materials. Germany was self-sufficient only in coal and needed to import 85 per cent of its oil and 80 per cent of its iron. Trade agreements and then direct occupation provided food, nickel, textiles, copper, bauxite, iron ore from Hungary, Bulgaria, Greece and the USSR, and most importantly oil from Romania. Capital from 'occupation taxes' offset about 12 per cent of the cost of the war for Germany. Occupied Europe provided forced labour in vast quantities, though much of it was used so brutally as to compromise its economic utility. There were 4.2 million foreign workers in Germany in 1942, rising to 7.1 million in 1944. However, none of this exploitation was managed rationally, and little attempt was made to integrate the economy of occupied Europe properly.

Rationing was introduced early on, but the levels in the Reich remained high until late in the war, in comparison with Britain or the USSR. It was only when it became clear that the war was going to be a long struggle and when the Allies began to inflict damage with bombing, that the economy was properly organised for war. By then it was too late to reverse the harm done to the productive assets of the occupied states. Albert Speer became Minister for Armaments and Production in February 1942 and achieved a great surge in production, which reached a peak in autumn 1944. He finally transferred resources fully from civilian to war production, as already done in Britain, the USSR and the US. Belatedly, factory dispersal was carried out to protect from bombing. There were limits to what he could achieve. Nazi Germany was a mass of individual and institutional interests and he had to compete with others for resources and for the ear of Hitler. Traditionalist views on the role of women meant that they were not fully mobilised for war work as they were in the USSR or Britain. Intervention by Hitler crippled the German nuclear programme and the missile research by von Braun at Peenemünde up until 1943, and delayed the introduction of the jet fighter. German weaponry continued to be technologically advanced, but tended to be over-complicated for battlefield use and once again competing interests meant a proliferation of designs in use at the same time, which complicated maintenance and the supply of spares to front-line forces, which American and Soviet standardisation avoided. German productivity peaked in September 1944, but then declined steeply, as the flow of oil was interrupted by bombing and Soviet occupation of Romania. Programmes of extermination of Jews, Romanies, Sinti, dissidents, Slavs, homosexuals and the disabled diverted vital resources and the SS continued these activities even as the Reich disintegrated.

Resistance to Nazi rule did exist, but in small pockets and generally ineffectively against the power of the SS and Gestapo. The most notable example was the July Plot in 1944 when Count Stauffenberg and other traditionalist members of the officer corps narrowly failed to kill Hitler with a bomb in his East Prussian headquarters, the 'Wolf's Lair'. The military intelligence service (*Abwehr*) headed by Admiral Canaris was also a centre for opposition, but such resistance was somewhat handicapped by the refusal of the Allies to deal with them (especially suspicious of the *Abwehr*) or to compromise their requirement of unconditional surrender.

The majority of the German population put up with Nazi rule, and in comparison to 1918, Germany did not collapse in the face of enemy onslaught. Public morale was maintained by Goebbels' Propaganda Ministry. It was reinforced by the apparatus of oppression directed by the Reich Security Main Office (RSHA) set up by Himmler in 1939: the secret state police (Gestapo), the Nazi security service (SD) and the ever-present threat of the concentration camp, but the fact was that the social revolution carried out by Hitler – the creation of the *Volksgemeinschaft* ('national community') – had created a more egalitarian society for ethnic Germans: unemployment was non-existent and after defeating France, Hitler was immensely popular. The crusade against Bolshevism was not unpopular. After Stalingrad, Goebbels successfully called upon national myths of endurance, using the bombing, Allied demands for unconditional surrender and fears of Soviet barbarity to stiffen public resolve. Even in the last year, there were few acts of sabotage or resistance; though it should be noted that after the July Plot, Hitler gave Himmler and Goebbels and other Party loyalists greater power and the concentration camps bulged with more victims. Germans did fight on with a fatalistic efficiency until the end.

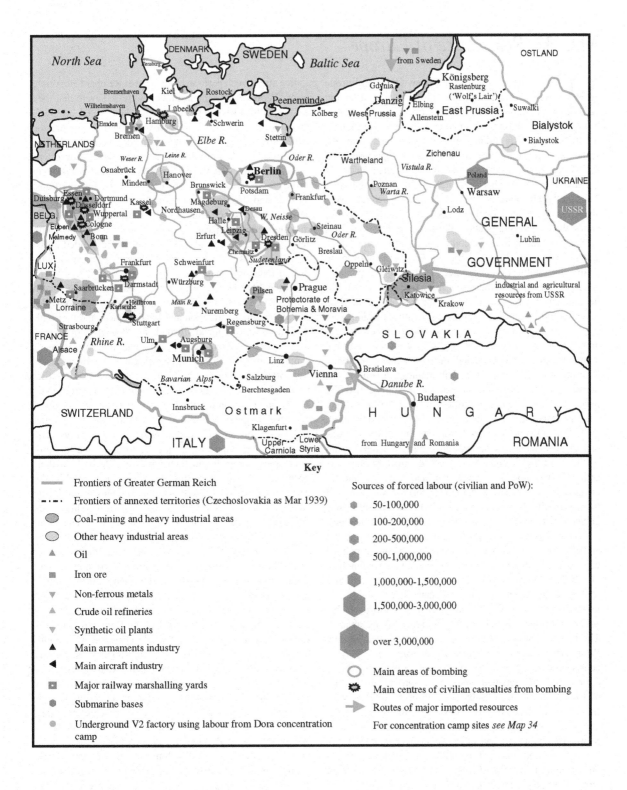

Key

Frontiers of Greater German Reich

Frontiers of annexed territories (Czechoslovakia as Mar 1939)

Coal-mining and heavy industrial areas

Other heavy industrial areas

Oil

Iron ore

Non-ferrous metals

Crude oil refineries

Synthetic oil plants

Main armaments industry

Main aircraft industry

Major railway marshalling yards

Submarine bases

Underground V2 factory using labour from Dora concentration camp

Sources of forced labour (civilian and PoW):

50-100,000

100-200,000

200-500,000

500-1,000,000

1,000,000-1,500,000

1,500,000-3,000,000

over 3,000,000

Main areas of bombing

Main centres of civilian casualties from bombing

Routes of major imported resources

For concentration camp sites *see Map 34*

Map 33: Resistance in Europe

Hitler's long-term plans for a 'New Order' in Europe were based on his racial ideology. His intention was to purge Europe of 'inferior' races to provide living-space for those he deemed racially pure. He thought it fitting that this should be achieved by war and conquest, as he saw life as a continual struggle for superiority and the worthiness of any nation was shown by their ability to prevail. However, the short-term needs of the war came first. Thus, although policies towards European peoples were shaped by Nazi racial ideologies, policies towards European states were more pragmatic. While native fascist parties often proved useful tools for control of vital territories, there was no concerted effort to impose a fascist ideology or to nazify the satellites or conquered territories, except those absorbed into the Reich. Local fascists could sometimes become an embarrassment because of their excessive zeal, which could disrupt the stability of countries which were important to Germany as supply routes or for resources – an example would be the Ustashi in Croatia, whose brutal activities greatly strengthened the resistance movement. Stability was more important than ideological conformity. German rule therefore impacted differently on the different parts of Europe they controlled, and provoked widely varying responses in terms of resistance or collaboration.

While a fiction was maintained that the New Order was one of cooperation and mutual advantage, the relationship between the Reich and the rest of occupied Europe was entirely exploitative. Resources and labour were ruthlessly directed towards the Reich, both to support the war effort and to maintain the standard of living in Germany, with disastrous effects for the economies even of Germany's erstwhile allies.

There has been much disagreement regarding the extent and effectiveness of resistance. A common picture is painted of widespread heroic resistance that tied down large numbers of German troops in occupation and anti-partisan duties, leading to the conclusion that resistance had a significant impact on eventual Allied victory. Churchill instructed his Special Operations Executive (SOE) to 'set Europe ablaze'. The reality, however, was that Europe was not set ablaze. With a few exceptions, German forces were not hugely or consistently discommoded by active armed resistance efforts, and they retained their ability through to the end of 1944 to crush major outbreaks with brutal efficiency, as shown in Warsaw, Slovakia and Vercors. Resistance movements were often politically divided, with uneasy relations between Communists and others in many countries, especially France and Greece. Their effectiveness often depended on proximity to sources of supply from the Allies. Difficult terrain like the mountains of Yugoslavia or the Pripet Marshes was essential if partisans were to operate effectively; in Western Europe, in particular, the geography was not helpful. German reprisals, such as the destruction of Lidice after Czech partisans assassinated Reinhard Heydrich, or of Oradour-sur-Glane in France, were so severe that they were an effective deterrent, except when Allied advances drew close. Then, resistance activities could greatly aid the Allied armies: as in France at the time of Overlord and when partisan activities were coordinated with Red Army offensives. Sometimes, however, as in Warsaw and Slovakia in 1944, these still meant crushing defeats for partisans. Warsaw had already seen an unsuccessful rising: in 1943 the Jewish Ghetto, faced with starvation, deportation and extermination, erupted in armed revolt, which was put down with ferocity. Other Jewish ghettoes in the east responded in the same way; in the west, where ghettoisation less frequently preceded deportation to the camps, it was rare.

Probably the most effective partisan resistance was in Yugoslavia. There, the terrain was favourable, they were part of the indigenous tradition and the occupiers and their collaborators were especially brutal. Tito brought Communist experience in covert activity, and had the advantage of supply from Allied forces in the Middle East and later Italy. Even in Yugoslavia, much effort was dissipated in conflict between Tito's partisans and Mihailovic's Četniks. The Allies came to regard Tito, despite his politics, as the more effective fighter, and eventually removed support from the četniks on the grounds that they were collaborators. The politics of resistance were thus far from straightforward. Some movements found themselves hostile both to their occupiers and to their so-called liberators: notably the *Armiya Kraiowa* (AK) in Poland, movements in the Baltic states and Ukrainians who looked back to the short-lived Ukrainian republic after the First World War. The latter were not fully suppressed by the Soviets until the 1950s.

More widespread than the kind of militant activity identified with the AK or Tito's partisans were non-militant actions like hiding downed Allied airmen, gathering intelligence, or civil disobedience such as a non-cooperation campaign in Norway, strikes in the Netherlands that assisted Operation Market-Garden, the Danish resistance's success in smuggling out the whole Danish Jewish population to Sweden, and deliberate inefficiency by railway workers across occupied Europe. Each country's resistance reflected their own particular interaction with the occupiers and the varied impact of the New Order, and drew on their own historical experience and culture. In some countries, resistance was class-based, where for instance the land-owning classes collaborated with neo-fascist regimes. In others, resisters were to be found from every class and ethnic group. Women were widely involved in resistance, and many were employed by SOE as agents: it was a fact that women were often treated with less suspicion by the occupiers and their contribution was significant to both militant and non-militant activities.

Key

![Major uprisings symbol]	Major uprisings
■	Uprisings in Jewish ghettoes
■	Uprisings in concentration camps
▲	Areas of Jewish partisan activity
◯	Main areas of Soviet partisan activity
◯	Main areas of Polish partisan activity
●	Areas controlled by Tito's partisans 1944
◯	Četnik areas 1944
•	Tito's headquarters 1944
●	Greek Communist resistance areas
●	Greek non-Communist resistance areas
X	Large-scale German reprisal massacres
×	Sites of major massacres by Ustashi
▲	Anti-Axis strikes
▲	Anti-Axis mass demonstrations
▼	Main areas of resistance sabotage
I	Sources of high quality intelligence
▣	SOE HQ
▣	SOE regional bases
◉	SOE missions
①	Anti-Mussolini partisans 1943-45
②	July Plot against Hitler 1944
③	Partisans kill Mussolini 28 Apr 1945
④	Raids on German heavy water plant 1942-43
	Axis-controlled Europe at greatest extent

Map 34: Nazi Genocide

From the start of Nazi rule in Germany, a principal objective was 'purification' of the population. Elements regarded as inferior or corrupting were to be forcibly removed: in addition to Jews, these ranged from political foes such as Communists, racial groups such as gypsies and Slavs, homosexuals, and the mentally and physically handicapped. The actual methods of doing this evolved in the years that followed, increasing in brutality to culminate in euthanasia, the extermination of gypsies and the 'Final Solution'.

In the early years of the Third Reich, Jews were segregated from the rest of the population, deprived of civil rights and stripped of their economic assets. In 1935, the Nuremberg Laws set a legal basis for anti-Semitism. Jewish businesses began to be expropriated, and in the *Kristallnacht* in November 1938, officially-orchestrated riots destroyed the Munich synagogue and Jewish stores, and resulted in 91 Jewish deaths and many arrests. The official approach to the issue at this time moved from containment within the Reich to deportation. While some left Europe, their numbers were limited by lack of interest by Britain, which wanted to limit Jewish migration to Palestine, and by the US, where Congress was concerned to maintain immigration limits because of anti-Semitism and fears of increasing unemployment. Most Jews expelled from the Reich therefore found themselves in countries such as Hungary, France and Poland, where they would once again fall under German control during the war.

There was as yet no policy of mass murder. The 'third solution' to deal with the large numbers of Jews in the conquered territories was ghettoisation, beginning in spring, 1940. The ghetto was a place of confinement in cities such as Warsaw, Lodz and Theresienstadt; resources were denied to them so that 2,000 died a month in Warsaw from starvation.

Some began to see extermination as the solution. Following in the wake of German forces in Operation Barbarossa were *Einsatzgruppen* (mixed SD, SS and Gestapo execution squads). Under the 'commissar order' any Communist officials were to be summarily executed – and it is clear that some ordinary units of the *Wehrmacht*, not just the SS, took the line that the Slav peoples of the USSR were *untermenschen* either to be worked to death in the Reich or summarily executed. The *Einsatzgruppen* developed mobile execution trucks, using poison gas, to go with mass shootings, focusing particularly on the Jewish populations of towns like Kiev, where 33,000 Jews were killed at Babi Yar. By early 1942 they had killed at least 500,000 people in Poland and the Ukraine.

This was the 'fourth solution'; but there tended to be too many witnesses, and for the fanatics, starvation and execution would take too long to wipe out the whole Jewish population. The final solution was genocide, begun under the auspices of Adolf Eichmann, the official at RSHA in charge of 'resettlement' (the common euphemism for deportations to death camps). The first death camp was at Chelmno, which killed over 1,000 Jews a day from 8 December 1941. In January 1942 15 senior government and SS officials met at the HQ of RSHA at Wannsee under Heydrich's chairmanship and agreed on the logistics of the final solution. It would be organised centrally like a military operation, with efficiency, secrecy and priority of resources. All Jews in occupied Europe were to be rounded up by local police, deported by train to distant camps, and gassed. The experiments of the *Einsatzgruppen* had now reached the point where this could be done on an industrial scale. At Birkenau, near the Auschwitz concentration camp in Poland, the able-bodied were separated out, to be worked to death, while the young, old and sick were gassed, using Zyklon-B (prussic acid), delivered in rooms disguised as showers. Operation Reinhard in March 1942 began the murder of Polish Jews at three camps, Belzec, Sobibor and Treblinka. By the end of 1943 all but a few Polish Jews had been killed.

Elsewhere in the Reich, the concentration camps also became places of death through deliberate neglect, producing disease and starvation, and also in macabre experiments on inmates. Likewise in other facilities, such as the Nordhausen underground factory (using labour from Dora-Mittelbau camp) making the V1 and V2 weapons, workers, who included political dissidents, Soviet prisoners-of-war and forced labour from outside the Reich, were subject to appalling conditions that killed them in large numbers.

About 10,000 Jewish communities around Europe were stripped of their populations. A few of the governments of occupied Europe resisted the demands of the SS, notably Bulgaria, Denmark, Finland and Hungary, though 400,000 Hungarian Jews were deported after the Germans occupied in March 1944. In other countries local authorities collaborated. By the time Birkenau had been over-run by the Soviets in November 1944, 2,225,000 had been killed there. Up to the last days of the war the SS had priority in transportation resources. As the Soviets advanced, so the inmates were marched westwards, over 100,000 dying on the way, and put to work or sent to the regular concentration camps such as Bergen-Belsen and Dachau.

Records of the genocide of the Jews and the mass murder of other 'undesirables' were incomplete or else destroyed in an attempt to hide Nazi guilt, so that any numbers can only be estimates: it is generally reckoned that 6 million Jews were murdered, together with over 3 million Soviet prisoners-of-war and forced labourers and up to 3 million other peoples.

ICELAND

GREAT
EIRE
BRITAIN
London
Alderney
100

Murmansk

Arkhangelsk

FINLAND
15

NORWAY
728

SWEDEN

USSR

Leningrad
1,000,000**
3,000,000** (PoWs)

Moscow

DENMARK
77

GERMANY
160,000 | 15,000

NETH.
500
106,000
BELG.
500
24,387
Drancy
Paris
200
700

1,000
1,000
Jungernhof
Riga

Einsatzgruppe A
248,468

80,000
2,500
Rumbuli

Smolensk

Meme
8,000
Kovno Kaunas
Ninth Fort
Ponar

135,000 1,000

Minsk

Einsatzgruppe B
71,555

Voronezh

Danzig
1,000
Stutthof

Bialystok
Neuengamme
Ravensbrück
Sachsenhausen
Berlin
Chelmno
Wannsee Oranienburg
Bergen-Belsen
Sachsenburg
Dora-Mittlebau
Buchenwald
Birkenau
Flossenburg
Theresienstadt
Grafeneck Mauthausen
6,500
Natzweiler
Dachau

Lodz
Warsaw
Treblinka
Majdanek
Belzec

4,000
Sobibor Zhitomir
3,000,000#
35,000# 3,000,000#
Lvov Bar

Maly Trostenets
30,000
2,600

Khar'kov
Drobitsky Yar

Kiev
Babi Yar

Einsatzgruppe C
105,988

Zaporozhye
Rostov

SLOVAKIA
217,000* 1,000
160,000 124,632
Balanovka
Edinet
200,000

Einsatzgruppe D
91,721

Odessa

Vienna
60,000
6,500

HUNGARY
Budapest
200,000
28,000

105,000

ROMANIA
40,000 36,000
Bucharest

Crimea
91,678
800

Sevastopol

FRANCE
83,000
15,000

SWITZ.

Bozen

Loborgrad
Jasenovac Zagreb
CROATIA
40,000
Split
28,000

Belgrade
SERBIA
10,000
12,000
Macedonia
1,000,000
Sofia

Black Sea

Fossoli

ITALY
8,000
1,000
Rome

Corsica

Naples

Sardinia

SPAIN

ALBANIA
200

BULGARIA
7,122
DEMOTIKA
SALONIKA
4,221 1,000

GREECE
65,000

TURKEY

Athens

Cos
120
Rhodes 1,700

CYPRUS
SYRIA
(Free Fr)

Tunis
Algiers
Oran
ALGERIA
TUNISIA

Sicily

MALTA (Br.)
LIBYA
562
↓
Crete 260

LEBANON
(Free Fr)

Key

Axis controlled on 1 Jan 1943	26,000 number of Jews murdered	①	Zemun
Allies/Allied controlled	26,000 number of gypsies murdered	②	Malines
■ Main concentration camps	* Figure for territory of pre-war Czechoslovakia	③	Westerbork
Camps built for 'Final Solution'	** Figure for territory of pre-1939 USSR	④	Gross Rosen
Euthanasia camps	# Figure for territory of pre-war Poland	⑤	Bratislava
● Major ghettoes	Einsat Einsatzgruppe and number murdered by Gruppe	⑥	Przemysl
▲ Mass murder sites	Drancy Holding areas prior to deportation eastwards	⑦	Krakow
15,000 large-scale murders of majority peoples		⑧	Tasmajden

Map 35: Central Pacific Advances

At the Casablanca Conference in January 1943, the US Navy's plan for a Central Pacific advance – Operation Granite – was approved by the CCS and by Churchill and Roosevelt. During early 1943 the Navy acquired the means to undertake this colossal task. No fleet had ever conducted prolonged operations over such huge distances (dotted only with tiny atolls). New fast battleships had entered service, and some of the victims of Pearl Harbor had been refitted, and while too slow to operate with the carrier task forces, were to play a vital role in the landings through off-shore bombardment. Most importantly, the new generation of aircraft carriers was now available: the small *Independence* class and the large *Essex* class. The latter were capable of carrying up to 100 aircraft. By October the Pacific Fleet had six of them. Moreover, it now had a fighter, the F6F Hellcat, that could out-perform the Zero. Problems with the American torpedo had been rectified. US industrial production was getting into full swing, and the Navy was beginning to put together the components of the 'fleet train' (oilers, floating dry-docks and other support vessels) that would enable the carrier task forces to operate over the vast Pacific, striking at the enemy and providing an air umbrella for the new fast attack transports and landing craft.

The campaign began with the attack on the Gilberts (Operation Galvanic), on the edge of Japanese conquered territory. Makin was easily captured on 21 November, but the Marines found Tarawa more difficult. It was defended by 5,000 Japanese, and poor surveying meant that landing craft stuck on the reef. They were pinned on the beach and took heavy casualties. When the battle ended on 23 November, the Marines had lost 1,000 dead; almost all the Japanese, some of whom made suicide charges at the American lines, were dead. Stark lessons were learnt on Tarawa about amphibious operations and the coordination of various arms of service, as well as the determination of the Japanese to fight for the smallest piece of territory. However, it was also concluded, since other Japanese forces did not intervene, that some Japanese island garrisons could be left to 'wither on the vine'. With the approval of the Cairo Conference in November, Nimitz pressed forward to the westernmost Marshalls, Eniwetok and Kwajalein. To cover the landings, the fast carriers in Task Force 58 (TF58) commanded by Vice-Admiral Mitscher, attacked the major Japanese naval base at Truk. In massive raids, 275 aircraft were destroyed and 39 merchant and warships sunk. Eniwetok fell on 21 February, after four days of determined defence.

Anxious not to be sidelined, MacArthur had increased the pace of his own offensives. The Quebec Conference in August decided that it would take too long to capture Rabaul; instead air attack was to 'neutralise' it and landings made up New Guinea towards the Moluccas and the Philippines. Fearing that the decision to go for the Marshalls would marginalise his campaign, MacArthur seized on reports that the Admiralty Islands were undefended, and in March 1944 they were taken, leaving Rabaul far in the rear. He did not stop there: in April his forces leapt 580 miles to Hollandia, bypassing 40,000 Japanese troops, thence to Biak in May, where the Japanese put up tough resistance till the end of June. It was therefore not until 30 July that he was able to seize the Vogelkop Peninsula as his final jumping off point for the Philippines.

By this time, in fact the two lines of advance were converging. The Japanese were uncertain how to respond. The Combined Fleet was deployed in May to win back Biak, but when the advance to the Marianas appeared imminent, it was diverted to the central Pacific to fight the fleet action it still cherished, equipped now with the giant battleships *Musashi* and *Yamato*.

Before it could get there, over 20,000 Americans were put ashore on Saipan, in landings as large as those in the Mediterranean. The 32,000 Japanese resisted strongly – following their usual pattern of not defending the beaches, but holding defensive strongholds inland, which the Americans had to capture at great cost. The nine Japanese carriers in First Mobile Fleet (Admiral Ozawa) were spotted by a US submarine, and Mitscher's 15 carriers turned to face them. The Japanese were able to attack first, but the Americans were now superior in numbers, in aircraft and in radar. The Americans called this Battle of the Philippine Sea the 'Marianas Turkey Shoot': 243 Japanese aircraft were lost to 29 American, and Japanese naval airpower was effectively destroyed. To round off the American victory, submarines sank two carriers, *Shokaku* and Ozawa's flagship, the brand new *Taiho*, Japan's largest carrier. TF58 then caught the First Mobile Fleet, sank the carrier *Hiyo* and damaged others.

Saipan was secured on 9 July, after many of the defenders, having run out of supplies, committed suicide. Tinian followed on 1 August, and Guam, after heavy bombardment, on 11 August. These victories changed the parameters of the Pacific war: the Combined Fleet no longer possessed a credible carrier strike force, while US possession of the Marianas put Japan in range of the massive new B-29 Superfortress strategic bomber, and also offered a base from which to attack the Philippines in concert with MacArthur's forces from the south. The pincers were closing on Japan.

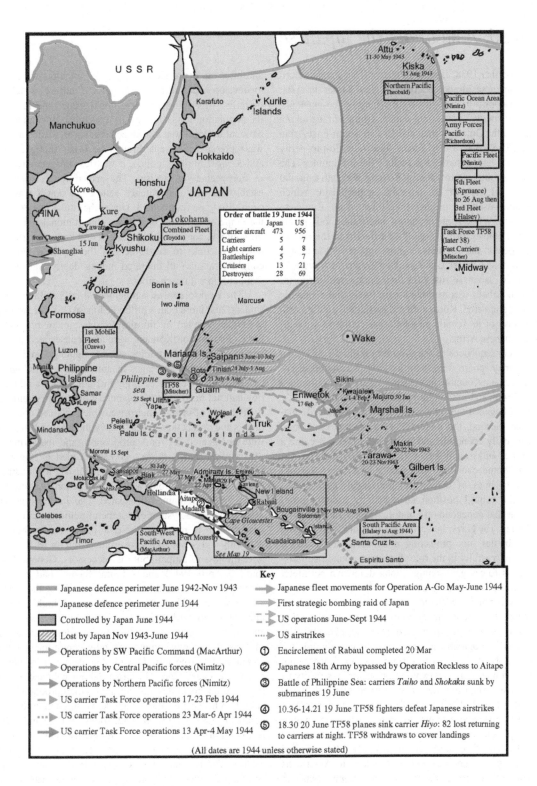

USSR

Manchukuo

Karafuto

Kurile Islands

Attu
11-30 May 1943

Kiska
15 Aug 1943

Northern Pacific (Theobald)

Hokkaido

Honshu

Korea

JAPAN

CHINA

Kure

Yawata

Yokohama

from Chengtu

15 Jun

Shanghai

Shikoku

Kyushu

Combined Fleet (Toyoda)

Order of battle 19 June 1944		
	Japan	US
Carrier aircraft	473	956
Carriers	5	7
Light carriers	4	8
Battleships	5	7
Cruisers	13	21
Destroyers	28	69

Okinawa

Bonin Is

Iwo Jima

Marcus

Formosa

1st Mobile Fleet (Ozawa)

Luzon

Manila

Philippine Islands

Mariana Is.

Saipan 15 June-10 July

Rota

Tinian 24 July-1 Aug

21 July-8 Aug

TF58 (Mitscher)

Guam

Wake

Bikini

Eniwetok
17 Feb

Kwajalein
1-4 Feb

Majuro 30 Jan

Marshall Is.

Philippine sea

23 Sept

Ulithi

Yap

Woleai

Truk

Jaluit

Samar

Leyte

Mindanao

Peleliu
15 Sept

Palau Is. C a r o l i n e   I s l a n d s

Morotai 15 Sept

Makin
20-22 Nov 1943

Tarawa
20-23 Nov 1943

Gilbert Is.

Sansapor

Biak

30 July

27 May

17 May

22 Apr

Admiralty Is.

Manus 29 Fe

Emirau

Kavieng

New Ireland

Moluccas Is.

Hollandia

Aitape

Madang

Cape Gloucester

Rabaul

Bougainville 1 Nov 1943-Aug 1945

Solomon

Is.

South Pacific Area (Halsey to Aug 1944)

Celebes

Timor

South-West Pacific Area (MacArthur)

Port Moresby

Guadalcanal

See Map 19

Santa Cruz Is.

Espiritu Santo

Pacific Ocean Area (Nimitz)

Army Forces Pacific (Richardson)

Pacific Fleet (Nimitz)

5th Fleet (Spruance) to 26 Aug then 3rd Fleet (Halsey)

Task Force TF58 (later 38) Fast Carriers (Mitscher)

Midway

Key

—— Japanese defence perimeter June 1942-Nov 1943

—— Japanese defence perimeter June 1944

▨ Controlled by Japan June 1944

▨ Lost by Japan Nov 1943-June 1944

➜ Operations by SW Pacific Command (MacArthur)

➜ Operations by Central Pacific forces (Nimitz)

➜ Operations by Northern Pacific forces (Nimitz)

– ➤ US carrier Task Force operations 17-23 Feb 1944

···➤ US carrier Task Force operations 23 Mar-6 Apr 1944

➜ US carrier Task Force operations 13 Apr-4 May 1944

➜ Japanese fleet movements for Operation A-Go May-June 1944

➜ First strategic bombing raid of Japan

- -➤ US operations June-Sept 1944

····➤ US airstrikes

① Encirclement of Rabaul completed 20 Mar

② Japanese 18th Army bypassed by Operation Reckless to Aitape

③ Battle of Philippine Sea: carriers *Taiho* and *Shokaku* sunk by submarines 19 June

④ 10.36-14.21 19 June TF58 fighters defeat Japanese airstrikes

⑤ 18.30 20 June TF58 planes sink carrier *Hiyo*: 82 lost returning to carriers at night. TF58 withdraws to cover landings

(All dates are 1944 unless otherwise stated)

Map 36: Asia under the Japanese

In November 1938, Japanese Premier Konoye announced the Japanese aimed to create a New Order in Asia: an economically self-sufficient sphere of 'co-existence and co-prosperity' containing Japan, China, Manchukuo, Korea, and the Dutch, French and British South-East Asian colonies. The scope of this 'Greater East Asia Co-prosperity Sphere' was later expanded to include the Philippines. The plan was an attempt to enlist pan-Asian and anti-colonial sentiment in support of Japanese imperialism, which represented itself as a liberating force from European imperialism. While some economic integration took place, in its exploitative form it was little different to the rule of the Europeans, and attempts to gain support for the idea at events like the Greater East Asia Conference in November 1943 failed. Japanese rule over their conquered territories was harsh: labour was exploited mercilessly and economic resources plundered. Korea suffered particularly badly, with exploitation of its female population as 'comfort women' for the Japanese Army.

The consequences of the failure to build a consensual co-prosperity sphere were twofold. First, it fostered resistance movements, notably in Vietnam, led by the Communist Ho Chi Minh, and in the Philippines, where there was little resentment against the Americans, who had promised independence. Second, the empire that Japan had conquered for principally economic and military purposes became a burden, not an asset. It was never coherently tied into the Japanese home economy, and proper protection was not afforded to lines of communication. Japan appeared to occupy the central position cherished by military strategists, but that depended on good maritime connections to its colonies. The Navy, however, was designed for fighting decisive battles, not protecting commerce, and it never adapted successfully to the role. The Army found itself dissipating its forces garrisoning a long defensive perimeter that could be breached by a bold naval strategy the same way *blitzkrieg* breached static land defences in Europe.

Within Japan, the armed forces were effectively ruling the country in an oligarchy headed by General Hideki Tojo. This led to a dogmatic pursuit of victory – though the Army and Navy had many differences on fundamental strategy – rather than the exploration of the possibility of compromises when the tide of war turned after the initial conquests of 1941–42. Pursuit of further expansion to protect these gains, and a failure to properly develop, exploit (beyond plundering) and defend the expanded empire led to disaster. The effects of these failures only fully impacted upon the Japanese people in late 1944 when the Americans began to inflict serious damage on the supply routes to Japan and opened their strategic bombing campaign.

Japanese society had been steadily militarised from the 1920s. As the armed forces gained greater power during and after the depression of 1930–32, attempts were made to develop a patriotic and disciplined culture, which had the effect of emphasising traditional values and preparing the population for sacrifices. In November 1940 an austere national uniform was introduced. However, while authority was repressive of dissent, through the *Tokko* 'thought police' and *Kempei* military police, it was less all-pervasive than in European-style fascism. The armed forces wished to establish a 'national defence state', but power was both centralised and fragmented. Under the titular leadership of the Emperor, who was in reality a constitutional figurehead, the supreme command, war cabinet and key ministries (the latter with links to the leaders of the *Zaibatsu* industrial conglomerations) all operated independently and often in competition with each other.

The workforce was supplemented by 3 million school students and more than a million Chinese and Korean workers either tempted by the promised wages or brought by force. Two million Koreans were also conscripted into the armed forces. Food rationing steadily tightened, and textile, rubber and leather shortages meant civilians found getting clothing and shoes increasingly difficult. Japan's mobilisation had not been properly planned, and industry remained in the hands of private enterprise, which retained control of profits and production. Japan's heavy industry and shipyards were not geared for mass production, and indiscriminate conscription meant skilled workers needed on the home front were used as infantry. Tojo established a Ministry of Munitions in 1943, but while some rationalisation took place, control remained dissipated. The Japanese government remained a system of competing elites and Tojo was unsuccessful in resolving the debilitating fissure between the Army and Navy. Tojo's government fell on 18 July 1944 after the loss of Saipan, but his successors, General Koiso (until 5 April 1945) and Admiral Suzuki had no more success in controlling the war effort or unifying the cabinet.

However, with patriotic appeals and higher wages, plus conscription of student labour, use of prisoners-of-war and women volunteers, production rose dramatically after Midway. Reluctantly compromising his commitment to traditional values, Tojo introduced the conscription of unmarried women aged below 25 into a 'labour volunteer corps'. By using up stockpiles and cutting civilian production, the aircraft industry produced a remarkable surge in production, producing 8,861 aircraft in 1942, 16,693 in 1943 and 28,180 in 1944. Earlier failure to plan for defence, however, meant that few of these were of the type needed: high-level interceptors. The real hardships came in 1945, when the fire-bombing of cities largely constructed of wood caused great devastation and progressively brought Japanese transportation and production to a standstill. Over 10 million city dwellers fled to the countryside for safety and food.

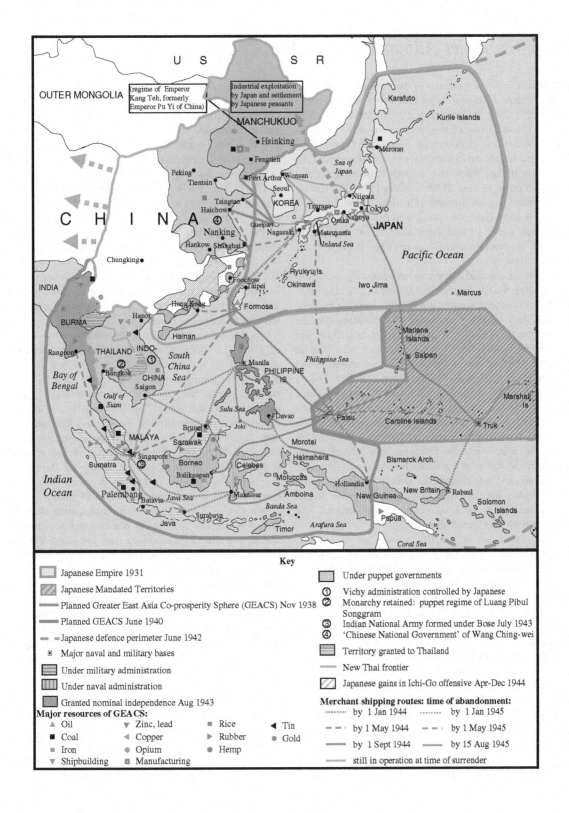

OUTER MONGOLIA

U S   S   R

(regime of Emperor Kang Teh, formerly Emperor Pu Yi of China)

Industrial exploitation by Japan and settlement by Japanese peasants

MANCHUKUO

Hsinking

Karafuto

Kurile Islands

Muroran

Fengtien

Peking

Tientsin

Port Arthur Wonsan

Seoul

Sea of Japan

Tsingtao

Haichow

KOREA

Tsuruga

Niigata

Tokyo

Nagoya

Osaka

Matsuyama

JAPAN

Nanking

Quelpart

Nagasaki

Hankow Shanghai

Inland Sea

C H I N A

④

Chungking

Pacific Ocean

INDIA

Foochow

Taipei

Ryukyu Is.

Okinawa

Iwo Jima

Marcus

Hong Kong

Formosa

BURMA

Hanoi

Hainan

Mariana Islands

Rangoon

THAILAND

INDO-

①

CHINA

②

Bangkok

Saigon

South China Sea

Manila

PHILIPPINE IS.

Philippine Sea

Saipan

Bay of Bengal

Gulf of Siam

Marshall Is

Sulu Sea

Davao

Palau

Caroline Islands

Truk

Brunei

Jolo

MALAYA

Sarawak

Morotai

Halmahera

Bismarck Arch.

Singapore

③

Sumatra

Borneo

Celebes

Moluccas

Balikpapan

Hollandia

New Britain

Rabaul

Palembang

Batavia

Java Sea

Makassar

Amboina

New Guinea

Solomon Islands

Indian Ocean

Surabaya

Banda Sea

Java

Timor

Arafura Sea

Papua

Coral Sea

Key

| | Japanese Empire 1931 |
| | Japanese Mandated Territories |

— Planned Greater East Asia Co-prosperity Sphere (GEACS) Nov 1938
— Planned GEACS June 1940
– – Japanese defence perimeter June 1942
☒ Major naval and military bases

	Under military administration
	Under naval administration
	Granted nominal independence Aug 1943

Major resources of GEACS:

▲ Oil	▼ Zinc, lead	■ Rice	◀ Tin
■ Coal	◀ Copper	▶ Rubber	● Gold
▦ Iron	● Opium	⬣ Hemp	
▼ Shipbuilding	☒ Manufacturing		

	Under puppet governments
①	Vichy administration controlled by Japanese
②	Monarchy retained: puppet regime of Luang Pibul Songgram
③	Indian National Army formed under Bose July 1943
④	'Chinese National Government' of Wang Ching-wei

| | Territory granted to Thailand |

— New Thai frontier

| | Japanese gains in Ichi-Go offensive Apr-Dec 1944 |

Merchant shipping routes: time of abandonment:

.... by 1 Jan 1944   .... by 1 Jan 1945
– – – by 1 May 1944   – – – by 1 May 1945
——— by 1 Sept 1944   ——— by 15 Aug 1945
——— still in operation at time of surrender

The offensive capabilities of the Red Army continued to grow. With increasing production, by autumn of 1943 it was able to deploy a mobile strategic reserve like the one that had earlier given the Germans their flexibility. Citadel and its aftermath meant the Germans no longer had such reserves and they were also faced with the weakening of their allies, growing attacks from the air, and the threat from the west: Hitler explained in a directive on 3 November that an invasion of France would bring the Allies close to Germany's vital centres, while Germany could still afford to lose large amounts of territory in the east. He would not therefore reinforce the east at the expense of the west.

However, the Red Army was not yet strong enough to attack along the length of its 2,000-mile (3,200 km) front, so for the next year it would advance in either the north or south as circumstances warranted, with the armour in the mobile reserve deployed to either as necessary. Hitler was determined to hold the Crimea, which had been hard to win and which he saw as vital to protect oil supplies from Ploesti. When Tolbukhin's 4th Ukrainian Front attacked on 27 October Hitler ordered the 17th Army there to hold fast. However, Soviet advances left 200,000 German troops cut off, and on 30 November Soviet landings on the Kerch peninsula threatened their survival. Simultaneously further north, the other Ukrainian Fronts made a bridgehead on Manstein's southern flank at Krivoi Rog and on 3 November 1st Ukrainian Front crossed the Dniepr to liberate Kiev. In the centre, Smolensk was recaptured and Soviet forces were now heading back on the route the Germans had taken in 1941 (and Napoleon in 1812).

The freeze set in late that winter, but in January, Soviet advances again threatened the position of Kleist and Manstein's forces, and Hitler reluctantly allowed Army Group A to give up the valuable mining districts of Nikopol and Krivoi Rog. Vatutin pressed Manstein west of Cherkassy, causing a redeployment of his panzer armies, which in turn left open the way for the 1st Ukrainian Front to advance south of Pripet. By 1 March it had crossed the pre-1939 frontier of Poland and was a hundred miles from the Carpathian Mountains. The siege of Leningrad was finally lifted on 27 January. Nearly a million Leningraders had starved to death in the 900-day ordeal. German forces were forced back: Model was appointed to command, but could only consolidate on Germany's sole prepared defensive line in the east, the Panther line from Narva to Lake Pskov – in the process causing the Finns to begin leaving the war (negotiations began on 28 July).

The Red Army's strength in reserves allowed the *Stavka* to maintain the pressure: six tank armies attacked Army Group South, which they outnumbered two to one in tanks and men. Zhukov replaced the wounded Vatutin himself and after heavy bombardment the Ukrainian Fronts opened great gaps in the German line, encircling 4th Panzer Army at Kamenets. Success was fastest against Army Group B, and by 15 April the Bug, Dniester and Prut rivers had been crossed and Odessa re-taken. Tolbukhin advanced against the isolated 17th Army, and on 9 May their last foothold in the Crimea, Sevastopol, was captured. Over 100,000 German and Romanian troops were lost. Altogether, in their winter and spring offensives, the Soviets had advanced 165 miles (260 km), taking a succession of potential defensive positions before the Germans could develop them, and recovering much of the Ukraine, the most productive territory of the Soviet Union.

Stalin had a number of strategic options in the summer of 1944. He appointed Timoshenko and Shtemenko to consider them, and they concluded that the first objective must be to destroy Army Group Centre: attacks to the north or south ran the risk of counter-attack against their flanks by that force. The Red Army now had better techniques for concentrating forces, and through April tanks and artillery were moved to the central sector for Operation Bagration. Diversions began in the north on 9 June. Then, on the third anniversary of Barbarossa, Bagration itself began. Some 166 divisions, with 2,700 tanks, were deployed against the 38 divisions of Army Group Centre. The Germans were anticipating an attack further north. The first Soviet breakthrough was towards Minsk, and two German armies were encircled. Within a week Army Group Centre lost nearly 200,000 men and 900 tanks. A great gap had been opened in the German eastern front. Hitler appointed his favourite 'fire-fighter', Model, to try to stabilise the situation. He could not prevent the rapid advance of Rotmistrov's tanks to Minsk. Forty thousand died trying to break out; those who remained surrendered on 11 July. The *Stavka* had already started planning for its next objectives, and by 10 July Vilnius had fallen and the first Soviet soldiers, from the 3rd Byelorussian Front, had entered German territory, in East Prussia. On 13 July Konev's 1st Ukrainian Front attacked the old fortress city of Lvov. It fell on 27 July and by the end of the first week in August, Soviet forces were on the Vistula south of Warsaw, and had crossed the Niemen and the Bug to the north of the Polish capital. These Soviet advances were to trigger one of the great tragedies of a tragic war.

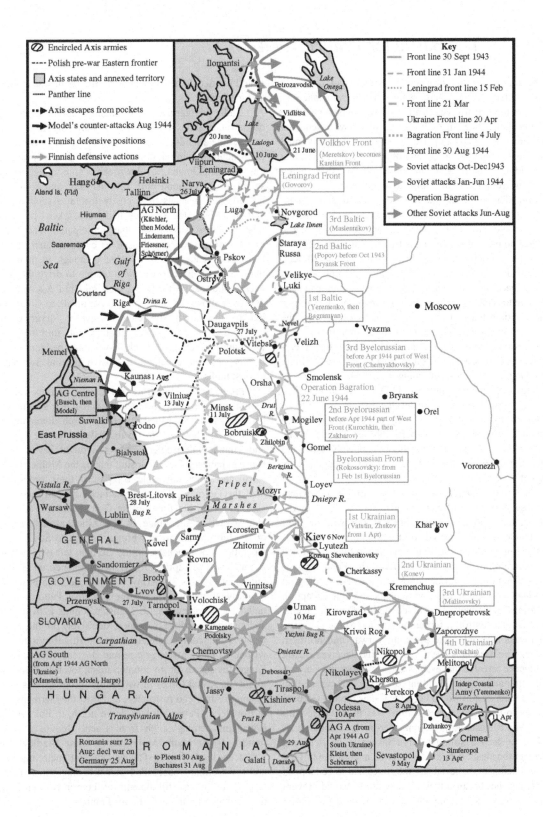

Encircled Axis armies

- Encircled Axis armies
- Polish pre-war Eastern frontier
- Axis states and annexed territory
- Panther line
- Axis escapes from pockets
- Model's counter-attacks Aug 1944
- Finnish defensive positions
- Finnish defensive actions

Key

- Front line 30 Sept 1943
- Front line 31 Jan 1944
- Leningrad front line 15 Feb
- Front line 21 Mar
- Ukraine Front line 20 Apr
- Bagration Front line 4 July
- Front line 30 Aug 1944
- Soviet attacks Oct-Dec 1943
- Soviet attacks Jan-Jun 1944
- Operation Bagration
- Other Soviet attacks Jun-Aug

Ilomantsi

Petrozavodsk

Lake Onega

Vidlitsa

Lake Ladoga

20 June   10 June   21 June

Volkhov Front
(Meretskov) becomes
Karelian Front

Viipuri
Helsinki
Hangö
Tallinn
Narva 26 July

Aland Is. (Fld)

Luga   Novgorod

Leningrad Front
(Govorov)

Leningrad

Baltic Sea

Hiiumaa

AG North
(Küchler,
then Model,
Lindemann,
Friessner,
Schörner)

Saaremaa

Pskov   Staraya Russa

Lake Ilmen

3rd Baltic
(Maslennikov)

Ostrov

2nd Baltic
(Popov) before Oct 1943
Bryansk Front

Velikye
Luki

Gulf of Riga

Courland

Riga   *Dvina R.*

Daugavpils   Nevel
27 July

1st Baltic
(Yeremenko, then
Bagramyan)

Moscow

Memel

Vitebsk   Velizh

Polotsk

Vyazma

3rd Byelorussian
before Apr 1944 part of West
Front (Chernyakhovsky)

Nieman R.

Kaunas 1 Aug

Orsha   Smolensk

Bryansk

AG Centre
(Busch, then
Model)

Vilnius
13 July

Operation Bagration
22 June 1944

Orel

Suwalki

Grodno

Minsk   *Drut R.*   Mogilev
11 July

2nd Byelorussian
before Apr 1944 part of West
Front (Kurochkin, then
Zakharov)

East Prussia

Bobruisk

Zhilobin   Gomel

Bialystok

Berezina R.

Byelorussian Front
(Rokossovsky): from
1 Feb 1st Byelorussian

Vistula R.

Brest-Litovsk   *Pripet*   Mozyr   Loyev
28 July

Pinsk   *Marshes*   *Dniepr R.*

Voronezh

Warsaw   *Bug R.*
Lublin

GENERAL

Korosten   Kiev 6 Nov
Kovel   Sarny
Zhitomir   Lyutezh

1st Ukrainian
(Vatutin, Zhukov
from 1 Apr)

Rovno   Korsun Shevchenkovsky

Khar'kov

GOVERNMENT

Sandomierz

Brody   Vinnitsa   Cherkassy

2nd Ukrainian
(Konev)

Lvov
27 July   Tarnopol

Przemysl   Volochisk

SLOVAKIA

Kamenets
Podolsky

Uman
10 Mar

Kirovgrad   Kremenchug

3rd Ukrainian
(Malinovsky)

Carpathian

Chernovtsy   *Yuzhni Bug R.*

Krivoi Rog   Dnepropetrovsk

Zaporozhye

4th Ukrainian
(Tolbukhin)

AG South
(from Apr 1944 AG North
Ukraine)
(Manstein, then Model, Harpe)

Dniester R.

Dubossary

Nikopol

Melitopol

Mountains

Nikolayev   Kherson   Perekop   8 Apr

**Indep Coastal
Army (Yeremenko)**

HUNGARY

Jassy   Tiraspol   *Prut R.*

Kishinev

Odessa
10 Apr   Dzhankoy   *Kerch*

11 Apr

Transylvanian Alps

Crimea

Simferopol
13 Apr

AG A (from
Apr 1944 AG
South Ukraine)
Kleist, then
Schörner)

Sevastopol
9 May

**Romania surr 23
Aug: decl war on
Germany 25 Aug**

R O M A N I A

29 Aug

to Ploesti 30 Aug,
Bucharest 31 Aug

Galati   *Danube*

Map 38: The Battle for France 1944

Planning for the invasion of France had begun in January, 1943. Thus, when British reluctance to commit themselves firmly to it was overcome at the Teheran Conference, the outline of the plan now codenamed Overlord was already in place. Eisenhower was appointed Supreme Commander at the end of 1943. British fears that the landings would be repulsed led to the plans being enlarged from three divisions to eight, including three airborne. This put back the date from May to June, 1944. As finally conceived, British, American and Canadian forces would land on five beaches, preceded by airborne landings to prevent the Germans from making too effective an early response, and by heavy naval bombardment, which had proved its worth in the Pacific. Normandy was chosen because it provided the necessary flat beaches. A key requirement was port facilities to supply the troops. It was anticipated that any port would be blocked by the Germans and would require up to three months to clear. Two artificial harbours, codenamed Mulberries, were therefore devised to be installed on the beachheads to facilitate unloading of supplies. Eisenhower set the date for the landings (Operation Neptune) – D-Day – for 5 June. The weather forecast, however, meant that operations had to be called off for that day, with many troops already sealed in their landing ships. The experts forecast a break in the weather for 6 June, and Eisenhower bravely gave the order to go, privately rating the chances of success as only fifty-fifty.

The main danger was perceived to be a German response before a sufficient lodgement had been made. The strategic bomber forces (against the will of their commanders) were diverted from bombing German cities to attacking railway junctions and the routes by which German reinforcements would arrive. The French resistance carried out similar activities in the weeks leading up to D-Day. This was in addition to major strategic deception operations, code-named Fortitude. Using German agents under British control, information was fed to the Germans that invasions would take place in Norway and northern France. The Germans were successfully deceived; Ultra intelligence revealed that even as late as August, the German high command was still holding forces back in expectation that the main assault would be in the Calais region. German strategy to defend against Overlord was in any case confused. Von Rundstedt, the commander-in-chief in the west, wished to keep a strong reserve inland to be deployed wherever the attack happened. Rommel, in command of the western defences, believed that the Allies had to be stopped on the beaches because their air superiority would prevent German reserves moving far to deal with them. Hitler would not decide between the two: the result was confused and ineffective.

Under Montgomery's command, Neptune began after dawn on 6 June. The Germans, believing the weather to preclude a landing, were caught by surprise. On four of the beaches, the initial objective was fairly easily attained. On the fifth, Omaha, the Americans came up against seasoned troops in good cliff-top positions, and could only get off their beaches by a costly frontal assault. By the end of D-Day, the beaches had been taken, but thereafter progress was slower than anticipated. The British and Canadians were supposed to capture Caen, but the German defence was formidable – though in their turn, the German panzer forces were unable to drive the Allies back to the sea. Further west, General Bradley's American 1st Army moved up the Cotentin peninsula to Cherbourg, but to the south struggled to get to dryer ground where their mobile forces could come into play. The low-lying ground and thick Normandy hedgerows, the *bocage*, proved excellent defensive ground for troops against tanks.

Progress was therefore very slow, and in the first month the size of the bridgehead was much smaller than had been planned. Allied airpower, which dominated the skies, began, however, to tip the balance, as the Typhoon and Thunderbolt fighter-bombers wrought havoc on the German panzers. Despite losing one of the Mulberries in a storm, the Allies were able to replenish their forces better than the Germans. The forces attacking Caen made very slow progress, but drew in the German forces, and were able to act as the hinge of the Allied armies. Finally, on 26 July the Americans broke through to St-Lô and in Operation Cobra penetrated the German left flank towards Avranches. The capture of Avranches opened up Brittany, but when Patton's 3rd Army was activated, the possibility of a drive to the Seine was more attractive. Patton's mobile units dashed ahead to Le Mans, reaching it in a week, and the battle began to swing decisively in the Allies' favour. Hitler compounded this by removing Rundstedt, who wished to make a strategic retreat. Instead Hitler ordered Kluge, his successor, to counter-attack towards Avranches, to cut the Allied forces in two. Initial progress was halted by tough American resistance, and then the Germans were in trouble, as Patton's forces drove north, to link with the Canadians coming south from Caen. Due to a certain timidity (some blame Montgomery, some Bradley) there was delay in closing the Falaise Gap and encircling them, and the Germans succeeded in extricating some of their forces – but it was still the end for them in Normandy and the turning point in the battle for France.

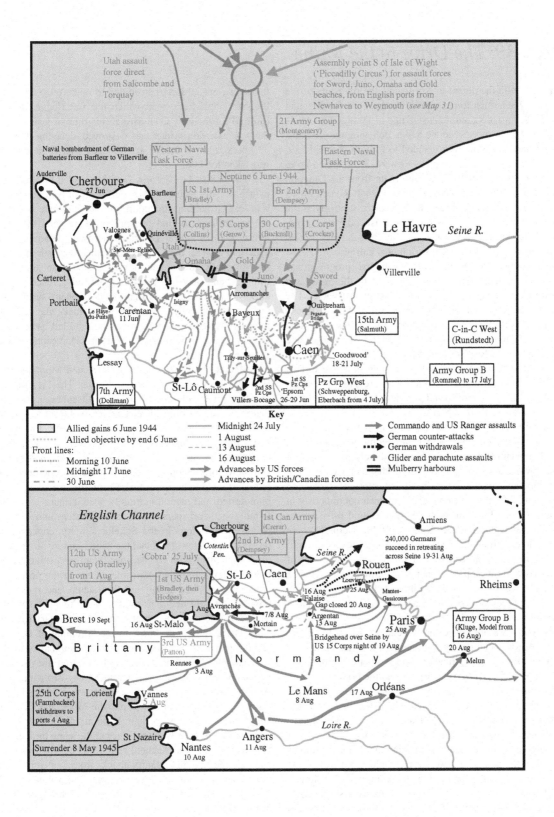

Upper map labels:

Utah assault force direct from Salcombe and Torquay

Assembly point S of Isle of Wight ('Piccadilly Circus') for assault forces for Sword, Juno, Omaha and Gold beaches, from English ports from Newhaven to Weymouth (*see Map 31*)

21 Army Group (Montgomery)

Western Naval Task Force

Eastern Naval Task Force

Neptune 6 June 1944

Naval bombardment of German batteries from Barfleur to Villerville

US 1st Army (Bradley)

Br 2nd Army (Dempsey)

7 Corps (Collins) | 5 Corps (Gerow) | 30 Corps (Bucknall) | 1 Corps (Crocker)

Anderville

Cherbourg 27 Jun

Barfleur

Le Havre — Seine R.

Valognes

Quinéville

Ste-Mère-Eglise

Utah

Omaha   Gold

Juno

Sword

Villerville

Carteret

Portbail

Le Haye-du-Puits

Carentan 11 Jun

Isigny

Arromanches

Bayeux

Ouistreham

Pegasus Bridge

15th Army (Salmuth)

C-in-C West (Rundstedt)

Lessay

Caen

'Goodwood' 18–21 July

Army Group B (Rommel) to 17 July

Tilly-sur-Seulles

7th Army (Dollman)

St-Lô Caumont

Villers-Bocage

2nd SS Pz Cps

1st SS Pz Cps

'Epsom' 26–29 Jun

Pz Grp West (Schweppenburg, Eberbach from 4 July)

Key

Allied gains 6 June 1944
Allied objective by end 6 June

Front lines:
Morning 10 June
Midnight 17 June
30 June

Midnight 24 July
1 August
13 August
16 August
Advances by US forces
Advances by British/Canadian forces

Commando and US Ranger assaults
German counter-attacks
German withdrawals
Glider and parachute assaults
Mulberry harbours

Lower map labels:

English Channel

1st Can Army (Crerar)

Cherbourg

2nd Br Army (Dempsey)

Cotentin Pen.

Amiens

240,000 Germans succeed in retreating across Seine 19–31 Aug

Seine R.

12th US Army Group (Bradley) from 1 Aug

'Cobra' 25 July

St-Lô

Caen

Rouen

Louviers

Rheims

1st US Army (Bradley, then Hodges)

16 Aug   25 Aug

16 Aug Falaise

Mantes-Gassicourt

Brest 19 Sept

16 Aug St-Malo

1 Aug Avranches

7/8 Aug

Gap closed 20 Aug

Argentan 13 Aug

Paris 25 Aug

Army Group B (Kluge, Model from 16 Aug)

B r i t t a n y

Mortain

N o r m a n d y

Bridgehead over Seine by US 15 Corps night of 19 Aug

20 Aug

3rd US Army (Patton)

Rennes 3 Aug

Le Mans 8 Aug

17 Aug Orléans

Melun

25th Corps (Farmbacker) withdraws to ports 4 Aug

Lorient

Vannes 5 Aug

Angers 11 Aug

Loire R.

St Nazaire

Surrender 8 May 1945

Nantes 10 Aug

Map 39: The Drive to the Rhine

With the defeat in Normandy, the remnants of the German forces rapidly headed east, for they had no prepared defensive line in France. The Allies followed them speedily to the Seine. Believing the Germans to be beaten, Eisenhower decided to forgo a planned halt, and ordered his armies to press forward. They linked up in the south with Allied forces coming up from the Dragoon landings that had taken place on the French Riviera on 15 August. Free French forces under Leclerc were given the honour of liberating Paris on 25 August, after the resistance had thwarted a German plan to burn the city. A few days later de Gaulle made his triumphal entrance.

However, the Allies' own triumphal progress was now under threat. The precipitate drive to the Seine and beyond stretched their supply lines past their capacity. The American 'Red Ball Express', a continual line of trucks from Normandy, fed the front line forces, but even that was not enough. Troops and machinery were exhausted and fuel stocks low. The Allies felt themselves to be on the verge of victory, however, and saw no reason to pause. This led them to overlook Ultra intelligence regarding German strength and intentions, and the next three months were to see serious Allied setbacks.

When he handed over command of Allied land forces to Eisenhower on 1 September, Montgomery argued that a bold concentrated stroke made immediately might reverse the slowing-down of Allied advances that had been brought by logistical problems and by the slowness of advancing on a broad front with troops that had been continuously in combat since June. He proposed that a rapid drive across the Lower Rhine into the Ruhr while the Germans were still reeling from the pace of the Allied advance might bring the war to an end by Christmas. It was a variant of a 'narrow front' approach that Eisenhower rejected when Patton advocated it during his drive to the Seine, but now he agreed, confronted otherwise with what looked like a grinding campaign to reach and then cross the Rhine. Montgomery's idea became Operation Market-Garden: Market was landings by paratroopers to take bridges at Veghel, Eindhoven, Nijmegen and Arnhem; Garden was the advance by British 30 Corps across the bridges to cross the Rhine at Arnhem.

The plan was fatally flawed. The Allies were showing signs of 'victory disease'. Human and signals intelligence were ignored when the operation was planned, for Montgomery was certain that no substantial German forces stood in the way. There were gross under-estimates of the time it would take for the Guards Armoured Division of 30 Corps to reach Arnhem, based on faulty assessment of the terrain. The US 82nd and 101st Airborne Divisions did their part, but 30 Corps struggled to make progress along the one single-track road which the waterlogged terrain (normal for the Low Countries at this time of year) forced them to use. Zon bridge was destroyed, delaying them by 33 hours, and the bridge at Nijmegen was contested and was taken too late.

The British 1st Airborne Division landed by glider and parachute a distance from Arnhem. Some of their equipment was lost on landing, including radios. Only one battalion got to Arnhem, to find one bridge blown, and the other intact. Two SS Panzer Divisions were recuperating in the area. They were short on equipment after their mauling in Normandy, but much heavier-armed than the paratroopers, and they had recently practised defence against airborne assault. The British held Arnhem bridge for days, but eventually those who could make it, including recently-arrived Polish paratroops were pulled back across the Rhine. Over 6,000 of 1st Airborne Division became captives.

Market-Garden has severely tarnished Montgomery's record and is generally seen as a disaster. The 1st Airborne Division effectively ceased to exist. Eisenhower resolved that in future he would advance on a broad front, no matter how long it would take. On the credit side, the Allies had captured valuable ground. However, the operation could only be justified if indeed it opened up the heart of Germany, for the concentration of forces for the operation left German forces on the flank of the Allied advance unmolested, and most importantly, the Germans were able to pull together disparate and scattered forces into strongly defensible positions in the Scheldt Estuary, concentrated on Walcheren. This meant that the Allied capture of Antwerp on 4 September with its facilities intact was valueless, as the Germans controlled maritime access to the port. This rendered the Allied supply situation acute, and made any broad front advance before the New Year impossible. Market-Garden was also the first German military triumph since D-Day and contributed to the stiffening of German resolve that came from standing with their backs to the Reich itself. Canadian forces only cleared the Scheldt Estuary in early November after an 85-day campaign, and Antwerp was not usable until 28 November. Hitler recognised the importance of Antwerp to the Allies, and it experienced more V2 attacks than London. American forces suffered one of their worst reverses at the same time, in the Huertgen Forest near Aachen, which was heavily defended and required slogging infantry attacks from September until December. The war in the west was by no means over: indeed, it was clear that the Western Allies still very much needed hammer blows in the east to ensure their victory.

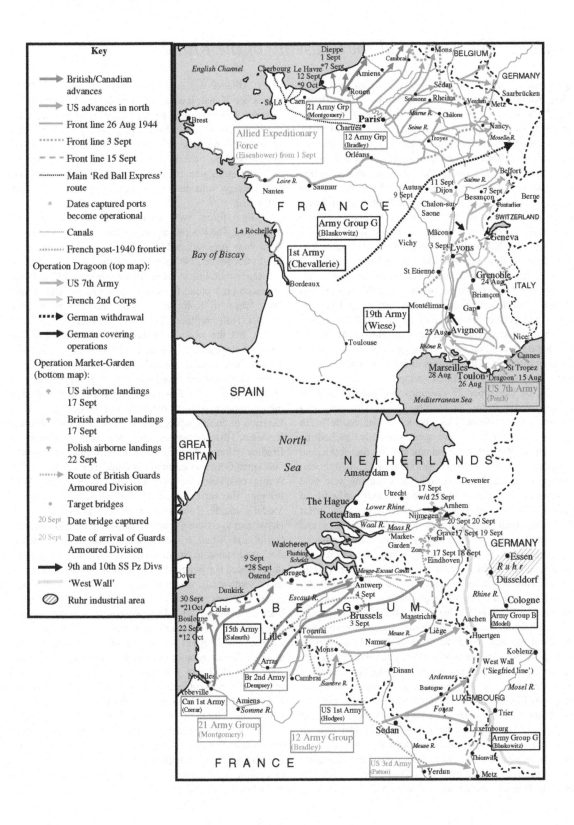

Map 40: The Bulge and the Crossing of the Rhine

Since September, perceiving the Allies had over-extended themselves, Hitler had been considering risking a counter-offensive, codenamed *Wacht am Rhein*. If German forces could repeat their feat of 1940, forcing their way through the Allied lines in the Ardennes and then up to Antwerp, he would strike a blow that would, he hoped, buy time, allowing the V2s to wreak destruction on London and Paris. It was an unrealistic notion, and opposed by Model and Rundstedt, but Hitler's control over German strategy was still complete. He marshalled all his remaining reserves for what was now called Operation Autumn Mist, believing that a victory would enable him to transfer them to the east while the Soviets were still a distance from Berlin. Initially, conditions worked in his favour. Allied forces were recuperating after the dash through France, Market-Garden and the long fight in the Huertgen Forest and Scheldt Estuary. Exhaustion combined with a certain complacency at Allied Supreme Headquarters. The fog that descended on the Ardennes gave perfect cover for the concentration of the panzers in the narrow forest roads and valleys and negated Allied air superiority.

On 16 December 25 divisions (11 panzer) in three armies overran resting or recently arrived US units on a 60-mile (95 km) front. The advance of Manteuffel's 5th Panzer Army in the centre went smoothly, backed by Dietrich in the north, Brandenburger in the south and Operation *Greif* – German infiltration units in American uniforms – in the Meuse region. The Germans were held at key points, however, by the courage and resilience of detached and isolated American units, particularly the 101st Airborne, rapidly deployed from Rheims to Bastogne, and 7th Armored at St Vith, and including non-combatant personnel such as cooks. Bastogne was the key to the roads leading into the Allied rear and the delay there proved crucial. Time was gained to reorganise and deploy 200,000 troops to hold the breakthrough and for the weather to improve sufficiently for the fighter-bombers to operate. German failure to capture fuel dumps meant their shortage of petrol stopped the drive short of the Meuse. Patton turned the front-line units of 3rd Army through 90 degrees across their line of march, to strike at the German flank from the south, and Montgomery, given command of US troops by Eisenhower, more conventionally struck with the 1st Army from the north. The bulge into the Allied line was steadily reduced and by early January Hitler ordered withdrawal. It had been the largest American land battle in the war, and had removed any complacency about an early end to the war. It meant the Yalta Conference would take place in February with a conviction on both sides that the

Grand Alliance was still a necessity as the job was by no means completed. It also, however, depleted the last of the German armoured and aircraft reserves in the west and diverted attention away from strengthening the West Wall, so that once the Allies had forced a way across the Rhine, there would be little to prevent a rapid advance into the Ruhr industrial area and the tanks and aircraft squandered in the Bulge were desperately needed against the Soviets in the east.

Allied forces were soon able to resume offensive operations. The Roermond and Colmar salients west of the West Wall were reduced in early February. Montgomery's Anglo-Canadian 21st Army Group had a tough fight in the Reichswald Forest. In February and March Eisenhower advanced on a broad front to close up on the Rhine itself from Wesel to Koblenz, and the Mosel from Koblenz to Trier. Hitler replaced Rundstedt with Kesselring on 10 March, but the advance of the eight Allied armies could not be held back. It began on 23 March with airborne assaults and massive air and ground bombardments. The Allies vastly outnumbered the *Westheer* – effectively 85 divisions against 26. Eisenhower's plans were modified by the fortuitous capture by spearheads of the US 9th Armored Division of an unguarded railway bridge over the Rhine at Remagen. Eisenhower switched the axis of advance to Bradley's front, while the British and Canadians pressing into north Germany covered his flank. The US 1st and 9th Armies completed the encirclement of the Ruhr on 1 April, bringing the surrender of 317,000 German soldiers and Model's suicide. Eisenhower wrote to Stalin on 28 March. He wished to ensure a properly organised junction between Soviet and Allied armies, reducing the risk of 'friendly fire', and stated to Stalin that Berlin had lost its primary importance. He believed the German government would move southwards, and was concerned, with Bradley, that fanatical Nazis would seek to hold out in a 'National Redoubt' in the Bavarian Alps. Stalin agreed, though possibly worried that Eisenhower's new line of advance towards Leipzig and Dresden would still take him well into the assigned Soviet zone of occupation; certainly, he immediately ordered Zhukov and Konev to strike at Berlin, and a few days later complained to Roosevelt that a secret deal had been done by the Allies that meant the Germans were letting them through in return for easy armistice terms. There was no such deal – though it was true that the destruction of Army Group B left a gap in the front that the Allies moved through rapidly – by 7 April they were halfway to the Elbe and a junction with their Soviet allies in the heart of the Reich.

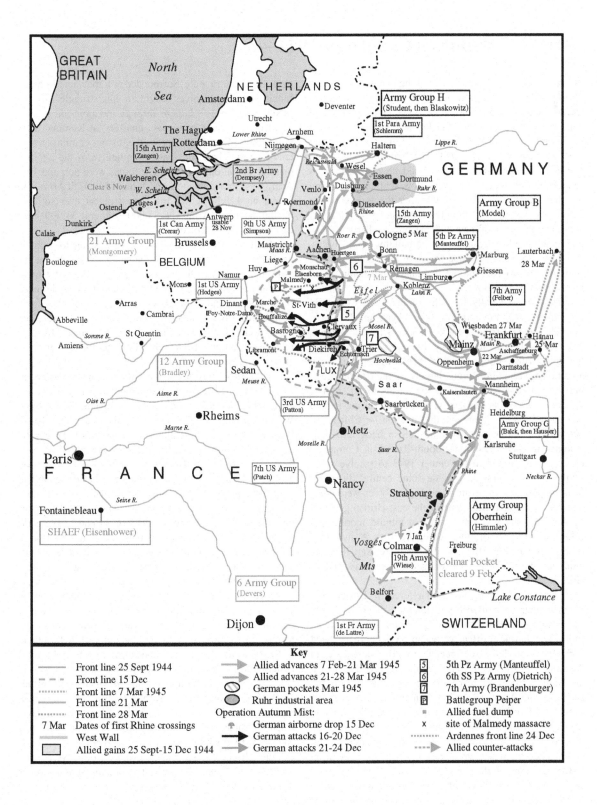

Key

——————	Front line 25 Sept 1944
– – – –	Front line 15 Dec
··········	Front line 7 Mar 1945
——————	Front line 21 Mar
··········	Front line 28 Mar
7 Mar	Dates of first Rhine crossings
	West Wall
	Allied gains 25 Sept–15 Dec 1944

➤	Allied advances 7 Feb–21 Mar 1945
➤	Allied advances 21–28 Mar 1945
◫	German pockets Mar 1945
	Ruhr industrial area

Operation Autumn Mist:

♣	German airborne drop 15 Dec
➤	German attacks 16–20 Dec
➤	German attacks 21–24 Dec

5	5th Pz Army (Manteuffel)
6	6th SS Pz Army (Dietrich)
7	7th Army (Brandenburger)
P	Battlegroup Peiper
▪	Allied fuel dump
x	site of Malmedy massacre
··········	Ardennes front line 24 Dec
➤	Allied counter-attacks

Map 41: The Burma Campaign 1942–45

Burma was to be the theatre of the longest continuous British campaign, from 1941 to 1945 – fought in varying terrain of jungle, mountains, plains and wide rivers. By May 1942, the Japanese occupied almost the entirety of this British colony, and granted it nominal independence in August 1943. The British, having been forced back into Assam, had to build up resources from scratch, and the process was very slow, with priority given to other theatres. Unrest in India after the failure of the Cripps mission in 1942 to agree a timetable for independence and the arrest of many Indian Congress Party leaders, including Gandhi, also impeded the building up of forces, and gave the Japanese scope to create an Indian National Army out of troops captured in Malaya and commanded by Subhas Chandra Bose.

The British finally took the offensive in Arakan in December 1942, attempting to take Akyab and Donbaik, but failed, and guerrilla operations under Brigadier Wingate (the 'Chindits') achieved only limited success, though boosting British morale in India. The British retained the ambition to recapture Burma, largely by the coastal route, but through 1943 did not have the means to do so. The American view was that any campaign in Burma should be directed towards improving the situation for China, and not part of a strategy to put the British back into their colonies in South-East Asia. South-East Asia Command (SEAC) was formed in November 1943 to resolve some of these issues, and did provide some central direction. More importantly, the British and Indian forces were commanded by General Slim, one of the best British generals of the war, who was slowly able to rebuild morale and forge an offensive fighting force, the 14th Army. Most of his soldiers were Indians, though there were Kerens, Ghurkas, West Africans and other ethnicities, as well as British.

The Japanese reorganised their forces in Burma, and planned their own offensive to interdict the new supply routes to China and ultimately to disrupt British rule in India. The Japanese offensive began on 3 February 1944 with Operation Ha-Go, designed to hold British reserves in Arakan. Improved tactics and supply enabled the British and Indian forces to resist the Japanese assault in the Battle of the Admin Box. US General Stilwell sent his irregular 'Merrill's Marauders' behind Japanese lines around Myitkyina, matched by operations by the Chindits on the central front. However, the main Japanese assault commanded by Mitaguchi opened on 7 March, Operation U-Go; the start of the invasion of India. They achieved some surprise, but 14th Army's new tactics and improved morale meant that they held their positions on the crucial

roads that led into India. Surrounded at Imphal and Kohima, Indian and British forces fought an epic struggle with the Japanese and Bose's Indians through the monsoon season. The troops were at very close quarters: at Kohima, there was fighting for months across the district commissioner's tennis court. The Allies were supplied from the air in a massive operation; the Japanese forces were not, and 14th Army was finally able to force Mitaguchi's 15th Army into retreat on 4 July. It was the largest defeat ever suffered by the Japanese Army: of 85,000 soldiers, 53,000 were casualties (30,000 killed).

Further north, the Allied offensive was able to continue unaffected by U-Go, but the Japanese held out against Stilwell at Myitkyina for two months until 1 August, though the Chinese captured the airfield in May allowing despatch of supplies to and from China. Chinese forces also drove southwards from Yunnan to open the Burma Road, but the Ichi-Go offensive in China (Map 42) caused Jiang to remove his support from Stilwell's plans for further operations into Burma.

The British pressed forward their advance: by October, 14th Army had crossed the Chindwin river and was approaching Mandalay and Meiktila. The Chinese captured Wanting in January 1945, re-opening the Ledo Road. Tough fighting in the swamps and river country of the coastal region in January and February (the 'Chaung War'), led to the capture by the British and Indians of Meiktila on 4 March. An amphibious landing directed at Rangoon had long been planned; this finally took place as Operation Dracula on 3 May, and Rangoon was entered by 4th Corps on 6 May, 1945, effectively bringing an end to the campaign, though the Japanese forces remaining in Burma did not surrender until 28 August. It had always been something of a side-show for the Americans and Chinese, but for the British it was a vital campaign if they were to regain control of their empire and some of their prestige as an imperial power. For some Indians it was a war of national defence against the Japanese, who had shown themselves to be unsympathetic liberators, while for others in Bose's army, it was the opportunity to free India from British rule – the latter were decimated as a fighting force at Kohima and Imphal. The British planned further amphibious operations to regain Malaya and to attack Sumatra, but they had not come anywhere near fruition when the Japanese surrendered, and it was that event that enabled the British to re-enter their other South-East Asian colonies. Ironically, disarmed Japanese troops were to be used in the months following to maintain internal order as the British struggled to re-assert their authority against people that no longer held them in any kind of awe.

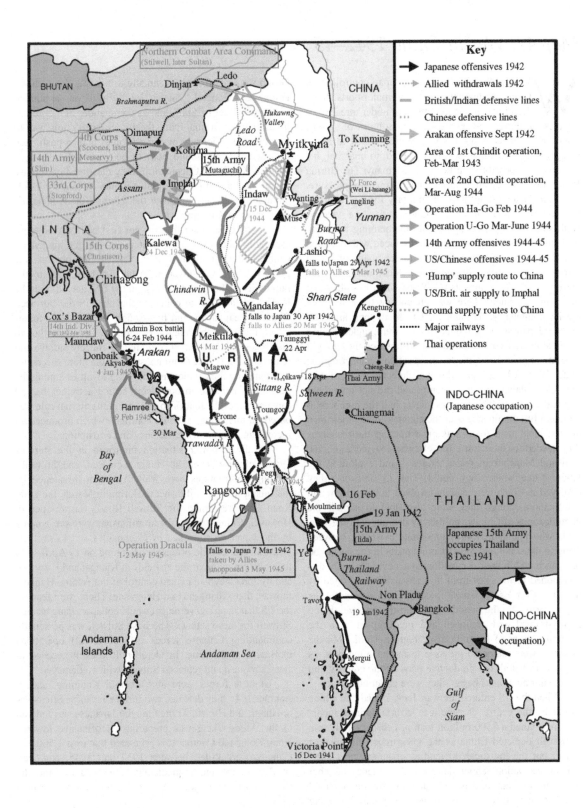

Key

→ Japanese offensives 1942
⋯ Allied withdrawals 1942
━ British/Indian defensive lines
⋯ Chinese defensive lines
→ Arakan offensive Sept 1942
▨ Area of 1st Chindit operation, Feb-Mar 1943
▨ Area of 2nd Chindit operation, Mar-Aug 1944
→ Operation Ha-Go Feb 1944
→ Operation U-Go Mar-June 1944
→ 14th Army offensives 1944-45
→ US/Chinese offensives 1944-45
→ 'Hump' supply route to China
⋯ US/Brit. air supply to Imphal
⋯ Ground supply routes to China
⋯ Major railways
→ Thai operations

BHUTAN

Northern Combat Area Command
(Stilwell, later Sultan)

Ledo
Dinjan
Brahmaputra R.

CHINA

Hukawng Valley

4th Corps
(Scoones, later Messervy)

Dimapur

14th Army
(Slim)

Kohima

Ledo Road

Myitkyina

To Kunming

15th Army
(Mutaguchi)

33rd Corps
(Stopford)

Assam

Imphal

Indaw

15 Dec 1944

Wanting

Muse

Lungling

Y. Force
(Wei Li-huang)

Yunnan

I N D I A

15th Corps
(Christison)

Kalewa
24 Dec 1944

Chindwin R.

Mandalay
falls to Japan 30 Apr 1942
falls to Allies 20 Mar 1945

Lashio
falls to Japan 29 Apr 1942
falls to Allies 7 Mar 1945

Burma Road

Shan State

Kengtung

Chittagong

Cox's Bazar
14th Ind. Div.
Sept 1942-Mar 1945

Maundaw

Donbaik
Akyab
4 Jan 1945

Arakan

B U R M A

Admin Box battle
6-24 Feb 1944

Meiktila
4 Mar 1945

Magwe

Taunggyi
22 Apr

Loikaw 18 Apr

Chieng-Rai

Thai Army

Ramree I.
19 Feb 1945

30 Mar

Sittang R.

Salween R.

Prome

Toungoo

Chiangmai

INDO-CHINA
(Japanese occupation)

Bay of Bengal

Irrawaddy R.

Pegu
6 May 1945

Rangoon

Moulmein

16 Feb

19 Jan 1942

THAILAND

15th Army
(Iida)

Operation Dracula
1-2 May 1945

falls to Japan 7 Mar 1942
taken by Allies
unopposed 3 May 1945

Ye

Burma-Thailand Railway

Japanese 15th Army
occupies Thailand
8 Dec 1941

Andaman
Islands

Andaman Sea

Tavoy

19 Jan 1942

Non Pladu

Bangkok

INDO-CHINA
(Japanese occupation)

Mergui

Gulf of Siam

Victoria Point
16 Dec 1941

Map 42: War in China 1942–45

When the Pacific War began, Japan controlled all China's industrial centres and major ports. Jiang Jieshi was in a poor situation, under threat from Japanese airpower and with dwindling sources of supply. Soviet aid stopped after 1940 as Stalin wished to avoid antagonising the Japanese, and wanted to marshal his resources for possible conflict with Germany. The Burma Road was sporadically closed under Japanese pressure. However, Japan did not have the military force to conquer the rest of China, or even achieve a decisive victory. Both sides were pre-occupied with maintaining authority in their spheres. Jiang was continually faced with the need to exert his authority over his own forces, many of which owed at least partial allegiance to a local warlord. Then there were the Communists (CCP) based in Fushih. After the Sian agreement there was an uneasy truce between the Kuomintang (KMT) and CCP, to focus their attention on the Japanese. Communist forces were under Jiang's nominal overall command, though in practice they fought separate wars. In 1940, the Japanese set up a puppet regime under Wang Ching-Wei (who had defected from Jiang), but held collaborators in contempt and did not give them any real authority. The Japanese never had the numbers to maintain full dominance over the countryside by their own efforts: their main focus was on extracting the resources they needed for their war effort elsewhere – rice, minerals, coal and Manchurian manufactures – and exploiting the labour force where they could. The 25 divisions they deployed in China were mainly involved in occupation and pacification, though they were also able to exploit the complications of Chinese politics by dealing with the warlords who maintained an autonomous existence between Jiang in the south and Mao's Communists in the north and resistance within their occupation zone never seriously discommoded them, apart from in a few areas penetrated by the CCP. Conversely, Jiang's forces, though nominally the largest army in the world, were mostly passive, being poorly-trained and equipped and preoccupied with the internal politics of his militaristic regime. Until 1944 the Japanese were under no pressure to mount offensives, as they controlled all the productive parts of the country and until major air attacks began, they were under no threat.

When the US entered the war, Jiang hoped that China would be the centre of American efforts against Japan. Congress voted a $500 million loan in February 1942 and Roosevelt depicted China as the US's major ally against Japan, but the logistical difficulties of supplying China, British reservations about Jiang and the urgency of other fronts meant that this never came to fruition. General Claire Chennault's aviators in the American Volunteer Group were reinforced (eventually to become the 14th Air Force), and General 'Vinegar Joe' Stilwell was appointed as Jiang's Chief of Staff, and as commander of US forces in the China–Burma–India theatre. Stilwell's job was to improve the efficiency of Jiang's forces and to push back the Japanese. He found both to be very difficult tasks. Jiang, Stilwell and Chennault bitterly disagreed on the use to put the limited (15,000 tons a month in January 1944) amount of aid coming in over the 'Hump' (the Himalayas) from India to Kunming.

In any case, other theatres got first call on resources, especially once American strategy no longer hinged on China, with their advances in the Pacific. The obvious low priority China was given in Allied strategy, despite the popularity of Jiang and his wife in the US, helped both the KMT and the CCP to conclude that the US did not need China to beat Japan, and they sought to keep their forces intact, ready for the renewal of their own conflict, though also recognising that they could not be entirely passive and retain credibility. The Communists were the more successful in organising their region and building loyalties among the peasantry, and also in organising armed activities behind Japanese lines. In Jiang's sphere, his authoritarian rule was based on managing factional conflicts, which produced an increasing amount of inefficiency and corruption.

As the airpower situation improved at the start of 1944, deliveries over the Hump increased, and Stilwell's training programmes bore fruit. Although threatened by the Japanese U-Go offensive in Burma in March, the Ledo Road (later re-named the Stilwell Road) was re-opened. However, Chinese plans for an offensive were pre-empted by the Japanese, provoked by Chennault's attacks on their bases. In the Ichi-Go offensive beginning on 17 April 1944 they overran many of the airfields in Kiangsi and Kwangsi, and by June they had gained control of the Peking–Hankow railway, then Changsha and Hengyang. There were fears in the US that Jiang's government would collapse. Jiang blamed Stilwell for these setbacks, because Stilwell was personally commanding Chinese forces in (successful) operations in Burma at the time. In October, Roosevelt acceded to Jiang's request and replaced Stilwell with Wedemeyer.

Chinese forces were able to hold Kunming, and in summer 1945 they defeated two further Japanese offensives in Hunan and Hupeh. At the time the Japanese surrendered to the Allies, Jiang was preparing an offensive towards Hong Kong and Canton. It is estimated that over 1,500,000 Chinese were killed between 1937 and 1945, and with conflict re-opening immediately between Jiang and the Communists, there were to be four more years of war in China.

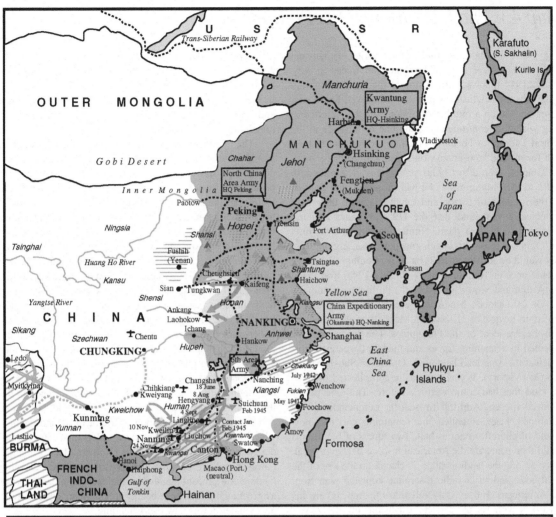

Key

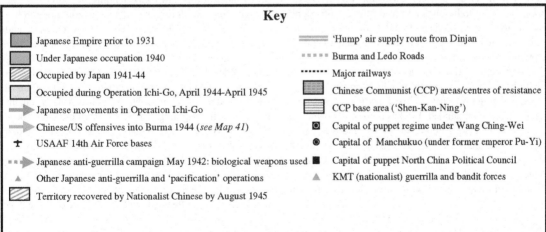

Japanese Empire prior to 1931	'Hump' air supply route from Dinjan
Under Japanese occupation 1940	Burma and Ledo Roads
Occupied by Japan 1941-44	Major railways
Occupied during Operation Ichi-Go, April 1944-April 1945	Chinese Communist (CCP) areas/centres of resistance
Japanese movements in Operation Ichi-Go	CCP base area ('Shen-Kan-Ning')
Chinese/US offensives into Burma 1944 (see Map 41)	Capital of puppet regime under Wang Ching-Wei
USAAF 14th Air Force bases	Capital of Manchukuo (under former emperor Pu-Yi)
Japanese anti-guerrilla campaign May 1942: biological weapons used	Capital of puppet North China Political Council
Other Japanese anti-guerrilla and 'pacification' operations	KMT (nationalist) guerrilla and bandit forces
Territory recovered by Nationalist Chinese by August 1945	

Map 43: The Liberation of the Philippines

After the Battle of the Philippine Sea, Tinian and Guam were secured by American forces in July, 1944 followed, after some of the fiercest fighting of the war, by Peleliu in September (Map 35). These successes opened up a number of options for the Americans. King wished to continue along the line of advance in the Central Pacific, to Formosa (Taiwan), which would be a base for air and land attacks on Japan and a linkage with the Chinese war effort. MacArthur was determined to return to the Philippines as he had promised, and pressed for the invasion of Luzon and Leyte, claiming they were strategically vital, and that the US was under a moral obligation to liberate them. Nimitz wished for Iwo Jima and Okinawa to be the targets, not Formosa, arguing that they would be equally good as bases for bombing Japan. In a conference on Honolulu on 27–28 July 1944, Roosevelt, MacArthur and Nimitz agreed on the Philippines route.

On 20 October, MacArthur and Halsey's forces converged on Leyte. On 21 October, MacArthur waded ashore with the President of the Philippines. The Japanese Navy collected its remaining forces and made a desperate effort to defeat the American landings – Operation Sho-1, part of Sho-Go (Victory). It was a typically complicated plan, of the kind that had come unstuck before. This one nearly achieved success. Admiral Toyoda, the commander of the Combined Fleet, intended the remaining carriers, now devoid of aircraft, to act as bait. Two forces of battleships would then penetrate the American inshore fleet and wreak havoc among the landing ships. A change in the key of the naval code and strict radio discipline kept the plan from the Americans. Halsey duly fell into the trap, taking his 3rd Fleet, with 16 fast carriers, off in pursuit of Ozawa's four carriers. The light carriers and destroyers off Samar protecting the landing suddenly found themselves under the fire of Japanese battleships. However, so strong a fight did they put up, that the Japanese commander, Kurita, victory in his grasp, concluded that stronger US forces were present, and withdrew, fearful of the safety of his ships.

The pincer anyway never closed, for the second force of battleships, commanded by Nishimura, was met in Surigao Strait by a squadron of the older American battleships, some of them re-floated after the Pearl Harbor attack. In the last ever battleship-to-battleship confrontation, the two aged Japanese ships, *Yamashiro* and *Fuso*, unlike their colleagues off Samar, sailed on undaunted, and were both sunk.

Overall, Leyte Gulf was the largest naval engagement in history. Aided by Halsey's misjudgement, the Japanese came close to success, but failed to seize their opportunity when it came. When Halsey caught up with Ozawa's fleet off Cape Engaño all four Japanese carriers were sunk. Although Halsey was forced by news of Kurita's attack to break off before sinking all Ozawa's fleet, Leyte Gulf was in the final analysis a great defeat for the Japanese Navy, and rendered its surface fleet a negligible factor for the remainder of the Pacific War.

The Japanese Army was far from defeated, however, though its strategy had been reduced to inflicting maximum damage on the enemy, in preference to retreating from positions it could not hope to hold – clinging on to the belief that the Americans would not have the stomach for high casualties and might be persuaded to offer terms rather than take the losses that an invasion of the Japanese mainland could be expected to bring. It took over two months to secure Leyte, as the Japanese Army poured in 50,000 reinforcements. Eighty thousand Japanese were killed; less than 1,000 surrendered. Their tactics were shown graphically in the appearance of a new weapon over the invasion beaches: the *kamikaze*. Japanese pilots were hopelessly under-trained, there being a shortage of gasoline and aircraft, and their planes were outclassed. They began deliberately crashing into ships of the invasion fleets, and soon special *kamikaze* units were set up, taking their name from the 'divine wind' that had saved Japan from invasion in the thirteenth century. These were essentially piloted bombs, and were a fearsome weapon, difficult to defend against, which struck horror into American sailors, and caused great destruction. The tendency of the pilots to attack warships, however, rather than the less prestigious troop-carrying landing craft, meant that their actual tactical impact was not as great as it might have been, for American superiority in naval matériel was now overwhelming.

On land, the Philippines campaign continued until the end of the war. In January 1945, the Americans landed at Lingayen Gulf on Luzon, and embarked on the largest land campaign of the Pacific War. Yamashita, the Japanese commander, like MacArthur in 1942, dispersed his units into the mountains – though unlike MacArthur, he also chose to defend Manila. The city was finally taken in February, after fighting that left it in ruins, with 100,000 Filipino civilians killed. Bataan, Corregidor and Mindanao were all recaptured. Elsewhere, contrary to his 'leap frogging' tactic, MacArthur also deployed sizeable forces to re-take the other Philippine Islands, though they were strategically unimportant. On Luzon, Japanese resistance persisted to the bitter end, with Yamashita fighting a skilful delaying campaign. The message was clear: despite devastating defeats and the decimation of their naval and air forces, the Japanese would fight harder and harder, the nearer the enemy came to Japan itself.

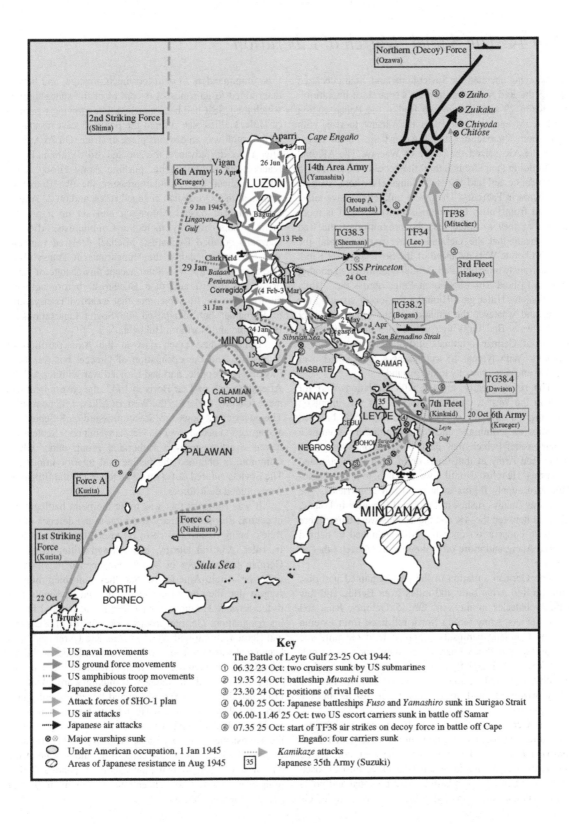

Key

The Battle of Leyte Gulf 23-25 Oct 1944:

US naval movements	
US ground force movements	
US amphibious troop movements	
Japanese decoy force	
Attack forces of SHO-1 plan	
US air attacks	
Japanese air attacks	
⊗ ⊗ Major warships sunk	
◯ Under American occupation, 1 Jan 1945	
◯ Areas of Japanese resistance in Aug 1945	
Kamikaze attacks	
35 Japanese 35th Army (Suzuki)	

① 06.32 23 Oct: two cruisers sunk by US submarines
② 19.35 24 Oct: battleship *Musashi* sunk
③ 23.30 24 Oct: positions of rival fleets
④ 04.00 25 Oct: Japanese battleships *Fuso* and *Yamashiro* sunk in Surigao Strait
⑤ 06.00-11.46 25 Oct: two US escort carriers sunk in battle off Samar
⑥ 07.35 25 Oct: start of TF38 air strikes on decoy force in battle off Cape Engaño: four carriers sunk

Map 44: The Soviet 'March of Liberation'

Having liberated the Soviet homeland, Stalin declared the Red Army was now on a 'march of liberation'. On 29 July Kosciuszko Radio, the Polish station in Moscow, appealed for Poles in Warsaw to rise, with Soviet help approaching. On 1 August the Polish Home Army, the AK, seized the centre of Warsaw. The AK had been building their strength until they could reassert Polish independence and had initiated risings elsewhere, such as in Volhynia in February. They were unlikely to have taken any lead from Polish Communists in Moscow. It is more likely that they assumed that the proximity of the Red Army meant that the Germans were in retreat, and the time to liberate Warsaw ahead of the Soviets was at hand. They seriously miscalculated. Model had mustered enough strength to hold Rokossovsky at Praga across the Vistula from Warsaw. Hitler gave Himmler the job of crushing the rising, and whatever the situation at the front, Himmler could always find units for such a job: they included a brigade of German criminals and another of anti-Soviet Russians. With typical SS ruthlessness they killed over 200,000 and razed the city to the ground.

The rising greatly strained Allied relations and for some in the West it confirmed that Stalin was intent on imposing his own rule on eastern Europe. Stalin branded the Poles as 'criminals' and refused either to attempt a military relief (which may have been beyond the means of the Red Army at that time) or to keep them supplied with arms. He refused, until it was too late, to allow Anglo-American supply flights to land on Soviet airfields. The rising was finally crushed in October. Elsewhere in Poland, relations between the AK and the Soviets were tense: there was little cooperation once the NKVD moved in behind the Red Army, and more often they regarded each other as enemies.

The German situation in the east remained perilous, with the Red Army only 400 miles from Berlin, and few natural obstacles in the way. On 15 October, Riga fell to the Soviets. Army Group North fell back from Estonia into the Courland peninsula, where it held out until the end of the war. East Prussia was now open to assault by Rokossovsky's 2nd Byelorussian Front, and fearful of brutality, rape and looting, 2 million Germans fled for safety westwards and to the coast for rescue by the *Kriegsmarine*.

The German position was in fact under most immediate threat in the south. Stalin preferred a broad front approach, much as did Eisenhower in the west: both feared the German capability for counter-attack against exposed flanks. In Stalin's case, it is likely that personal and political calculations also intruded; he did not wish any of his Front commanders to gain too much prestige, and he was determined to gain post-war control of the states through which the USSR had been attacked. The growing weakness of Hitler's allies also offered the point of least resistance, so the south was an obvious place to strike. On 25 August, after a five-day advance, the 2nd and 3rd Ukrainian Fronts reached the Danube delta, pushing Army Group South Ukraine ahead of it. Under pressure the two Romanian armies in that Group had changed sides, and on 23 August King Michael ousted Antonescu and set up a government of national unity, including Communists. After the Germans bombed Bucharest, Michael declared war, and sent his armies against the Hungarians in Transylvania. The Soviets at first would not accept this change of sides, occupying Ploesti and then Bucharest, before agreeing an armistice on 12 September that awarded Transylvania to Romania, but recognised the Soviet annexations of Bessarabia and Northern Bukovina.

Bulgaria had taken part in the Axis partition of Yugoslavia and the occupation of Greece, but was traditionally Russophile, and had avoided war with the USSR. After the death of Tsar Boris in 1943, the government had made tentative feelers to the Western Allies, with no results. The government bowed to Soviet pressure on 8 September and agreed to declare war on Germany, but on 9 September, it was overthrown by a Fatherland Front, under which Communists obtained the justice and interior ministries. The Soviets entered Sofia on 18 October and the Bulgarian Army joined their forces.

It was Hungary that was to be the main battleground in central Europe. Hungary was vital to the defence of the Reich, being its last source of oil after Romania was lost. Its ruler, Admiral Horthy, had allowed Hitler to station German troops there in March. He opened negotiations with the Anglo-Americans, but they informed him in August that they could not help him, and he should talk to the Soviets. He did so, but Hitler found out and forced his resignation. German troops took control of Budapest and fierce fighting with Malinovsky's 2nd Ukrainian Front began that was to last for months. German forces withdrew from Greece in October, 1944, and protected the flanks of Army Group South in Hungary. Tolbukhin's 3rd Ukrainian Front had driven into Yugoslavia and linked up with Tito's partisans: they faced a stiff fight for Belgrade, which fell on 20 October. Tolbukhin then moved into Hungary, leaving Yugoslavia to the partisans. From November, fighting centred on Budapest, which came fully under siege at the end of December. At that point Stalin suspended further offensives in order to concentrate on the main line of advance towards Berlin.

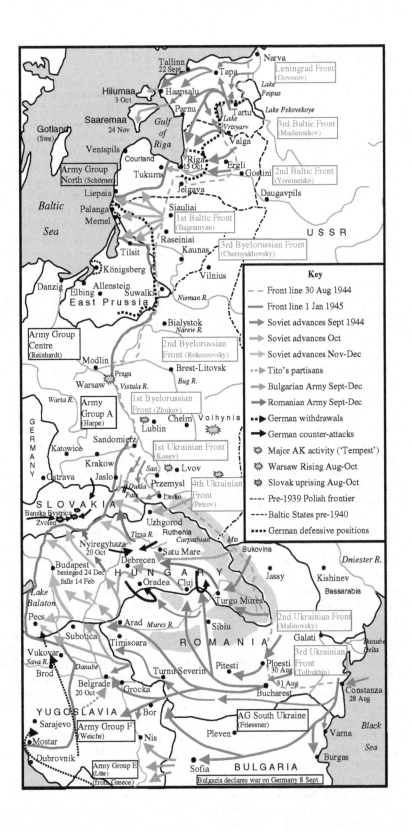

Map 45: The Big Three: from Teheran to Yalta

Discussions between the Big Three on political issues were pushed aside after June 1942 in the interests of focusing on immediate military issues. Most Allied–Soviet contact had been over Lend-Lease and the Arctic convoys and were characterised by bitterness and mutual suspicion. The Soviets suspected the Allies were holding back and hoping the Soviets would exhaust themselves in defeating Germany, and were planning a separate peace. The Allies also had their separate peace suspicions, and found the Soviets unappreciative of their efforts and unwilling to supply information or facilities that would advance their mutual cause. There were signs of an improvement in relations when the foreign ministers met in Moscow in October 1943. Little concrete was decided, but the atmosphere was cordial and Molotov was surprisingly cooperative. They did set up the European Advisory Commission in London to settle certain post-war issues: this was to be the forum where occupation zones for Germany and Austria were decided.

The Teheran Conference ('Eureka'), from 28 November to 1 December, 1943, mainly focused on military strategy, and the increasing need to coordinate it between the Soviets and the Anglo-Americans. Roosevelt, who stayed at the Soviet Embassy because the Soviets claimed there was a security threat, was at pains to build a close relationship with Stalin, if necessary at Churchill's expense. He was now prepared to agree to Stalin's pre-1941 frontiers, though not ready to say so in public, and there was agreement that Poland should have its borders moved westwards to compensate for the loss of territory to the Soviets in the east. Stalin said that he would enter the war against Japan after Germany was defeated. Relations were generally good, though the problem of Poland was not really solved, as they could not agree on who should be the Polish government: the Soviets had withdrawn recognition from the London Polish government-in-exile after they had supported German proposals for a Red Cross inquiry into the graves of Polish officers uncovered at Katyn, near Smolensk, in April.

After Eureka, relations remained on a more cordial basis into 1944, with Stalin's suspicions temporarily allayed by Overlord in June. He even allowed American bombers to operate from Soviet airfields (Operation Frantic). Relations soured over Poland again in August, when the Soviets refused to help the Warsaw rising. The future of Germany was becoming a subject of increasing debate, and at Quebec in September 1944 ('Octagon') a plan by Roosevelt's Treasury Secretary, Henry Morgenthau, to pastoralise it by destroying its industrial base was temporarily favoured. The more enduring issue was whether to keep Germany one state or to temporarily or permanently partition it.

The Soviet advances into Poland and the Balkans, and the approach of Allied and Soviet front-lines towards each other, meant that political issues that had previously been kept in the background could no longer be ignored. As before, it was Churchill who took the active role. He travelled to Moscow in October 1944, to make another effort to repair relations between the London Poles and Stalin. Faced with Stalin's mistrust of any Poles (including the ones he himself controlled) and the London Poles' refusal to accept any territorial changes, Churchill's efforts were fruitless. Polish Premier Mikolajczyk, under pressure, did agree to the proposed frontier movements, but back in London was forced to resign when his colleagues would not accept them.

Apparently without consultation with Roosevelt, Churchill also raised the issue of the Balkans. Military practicalities, such as the risk of bombing each others' forces (this was already happening in Yugoslavia) necessitated some delineation of spheres of activity – but Churchill's main concern was political: primarily the fate of Greece and Yugoslavia. He proposed to Stalin that influence should be apportioned on the following lines: in Romania 90 per cent to the Soviets, Greece 90 per cent to the Allies. Bulgaria would be 80 per cent Soviet, Hungary and Yugoslavia 50–50. There is much uncertainty as to what Churchill meant by the percentages, and no formal agreement was signed, though Molotov and Eden haggled over the percentages the following day, altering those for Hungary in favour of the Soviets. The important thing to Churchill was that he had made clear to Stalin that Britain was interested in Greece. Heeding the signal, Stalin made no attempt to interfere when the British sent troops to Greece, which by December were engaged in skirmishes with the Greek Communist resistance. The meaning of the discussion for elsewhere was less clear-cut, and considerable ill-will between the wartime allies was to grow up regarding high-handed Soviet actions in the countries they occupied: though they might well have argued that they were keeping to the Moscow arrangement and that the Allies had themselves managed political affairs in Italy in 1943–44, keeping the Soviets away from any influence when they negotiated with Badoglio, and when they set up a multi-party provisional government after the liberation of Rome. Allied policy was hardly consistent. Roosevelt's agreement with Stalin at Teheran that he was entitled to 'friendly governments' on his borders, and his 'four policemen' concept for managing world affairs sat uncomfortably with American unwillingness to concede that there was any part of Europe to which they should not have full economic access. They were suspicious that Churchill, as much as, if not more than, Stalin, wished to carve a 'sphere of influence', and they would seek an alternative approach at the next Big Three meeting, at Yalta.

Kirkenes
Petsamo
Murmansk
ICELAND
Germans evacuate Lapland 23 Nov 1944
Arkhangelsk
FINLAND
Russo-Finnish Treaty 19 Sept 1944
4 Mar 1945
3-Power European Advisory Commission meets from 14 Jan 1944: discusses armistice terms and occupation zones
NORWAY
SWEDEN
Leningrad
Churchill-Stalin conference 9-19 Oct 1944
North Sea
absorbed into USSR
Velikye Luki
Moscow
Courland
Riga
Daugavpils
Union of Polish Patriots (Wasiliewska)
GREAT BRITAIN
DENMARK
Vitebsk
Smolensk
Polish Government-in-Exile (Mikolajczyk)
Königsberg
Danzig
Minsk
USSR
Bobruisk
Kursk
Hamburg
Berlin
Potsdam
NETH
Rotterdam
London
Bergen-Belsen
POLAND
Chelmno
Treblinka
Warsaw
Lodz
Lublin
Majdanek
Sobibor
Belzec
Kiev
Khar'kov
Poltava
Zhitomir
6 June 1944
Antwerp
BELG
GERMANY
Cologne
Breslau
Auschwitz
Krakow
Lvov
Zaporozhye
Caen
Paris
Brest
Leipzig
Prague
SLOVAKIA
Uzhgorod
Strasbourg
Vienna
Bratislava
Jassy
Odessa
FRANCE
Dachau
Munich
Budapest
Debrecen
80/20
SWITZ.
Lake Balaton
HUNGARY
ROMANIA
Crimea
Yalta
Lyons
Milan
Salo
Ljubljana
Venice
Subotica
25 Aug 1944
90/10
Bucharest
29 Aug 1944
Sevastopol
Zagreb
Bologna
Ravenna
Belgrade
Black Sea
Churchill-Roosevelt-Stalin conference 4-11 Feb 1945
Ancona
YUGOSLAVIA
50/50
BULGARIA
8 Sept 1944
Marseilles
15 Aug 1944
Pisa
Adriatic Sea
Sofia
80/20
SPAIN
Rome
Cassino
Anzio
Bari
ALBANIA
Istanbul
TURKEY
1 Mar 1945
Mussolini's Italian Social Republic from 15 Sept 1943
22 Jan 1944
Naples
10/90
British take Cos, Leros, Samos 9-16 Sept 1943, fail to take Rhodes. Germans retake islands by end Oct
13 Oct 1943
GREECE
Mediterranean Sea
Samos
Athens
Leros
Cos
Sicily
Algiers
Rhodes
Roosevelt-Churchill pre-Yalta conference 31 Jan-2 Feb 1945
Malta
British troops land in Greece 5 Oct 1944
Crete
CYPRUS
Key
Allied territory Dec 1943
Liberated by Allies Dec 1943-Feb 1945
Controlled by Axis Feb 1945
Front line 31 Dec 1943
Front line 31 Mar 1944
Front line 4 July 1944
Front line 10 Oct 1944
Front line 4 Feb 1945
Allied landings
Major German counter-attacks
German withdrawals Oct 1944
Concentration camps (see Map 34)
Death marches
Territory restored to Romania
8 Sept Dates of declaration of war on Germany
Pre-1939 frontiers of Poland, Baltic States
90/10 Percentages (Soviet first) as agreed by Eden and Molotov, Moscow Oct 1944
Churchill's preferred strategy
American strategy
Montgomery's strategy
Eisenhower's strategy
Communist partisans take control
Governments set up by USSR
Governments set up by Britain and US

Map 46: The Noose Tightens Around Japan

One of the main purposes of Japanese expansion was to procure raw materials. These materials needed to be transported to Japan by sea, and materials and men to defend the new acquisitions dispatched in the opposite direction. Japan had a sizeable merchant fleet, but had neglected the need to protect this traffic. The Navy was built for fleet actions, including the submarine force; there were few escort vessels, and methods of convoying and anti-submarine warfare were not developed until it was too late. From 1943 Vice-Admiral Lockwood's Submarine Command in Pearl Harbor was able to deploy an increasing number of fine ocean-going submarines, which took a heavy toll of Japanese shipping. Supply to the island bases, then to Japan itself, was dislocated, with damaging impact on Japan's domestic economy. The rubber, oil and other resources that were the reason for the war in the first place ceased to flow into Japan. Aided by radar and signals intelligence, the American submarine blockade on Japan by the end of 1944 was one of the most effective naval blockades ever mounted. Over 1,200 Japanese merchant ships were sunk, and 20 major warships, for a loss of 52 US submarines out of 288.

Whatever the depletion of Japan's material capacity to make war, the resistance of the armed forces remained strong. With the fighting still raging on the Philippines, Nimitz's forces landed on Iwo Jima in March 1945. The defenders of this small volcanic island followed the established strategy, whereby the Japanese did not attempt to defend the beaches, which can lead to a dispersion of forces. Instead they built formidable defensive positions inland, taking advantage of the natural terrain. The Americans then had to overrun each of these. In terms of grand strategy, the American planners had found the solution to this by bypassing many Japanese island strongholds and striking more directly towards Japan itself – and Iwo Jima was the latest point on that line of advance. On the islands that were targets of attack, however, there was no alternative to costly assaults on these strongholds. Despite the destruction involved, American material resources were more than sufficient for such attritional warfare, and the Japanese hope that American willpower would weaken in the face of such destruction failed to take into account the determination for complete victory that the Pearl Harbor attack had raised. Such battles were, however, a terrible burden on the front-line troops, of whom there was a sufficiency but not an abundance, meaning that the same units were deployed again and again on island assaults. Sixty thousand Marines and 800 warships were deployed to take Iwo Jima. Over a third of the Marines were killed or wounded. The Japanese fought in their strongholds on Hill 382 and 'Bloody Gorge' to the last man. Iwo Jima took 36 days to capture, rather than the anticipated 14. The campaign produced the iconic photograph of Marines raising the flag over Mount Suribachi, and provided a useful air base, but its major significance was probably in strengthening the belief among American servicemen in the Pacific and policy-makers in Washington, that an invasion of Japan itself would be a very costly undertaking.

Okinawa had been Japanese territory since 1895 and contained a significant Japanese civilian population. It was the central island of the Ryukyus and only 340 miles (550 km) from Japan itself. On 1 April 1945, four divisions of US 10th Army attacked in the most costly American assault operation of the Pacific War – and also the last. Over half a million troops and over 1,200 warships – including the newly arrived British Pacific Fleet (TF57) participated. More than 170,000 US troops were actually landed on the island. They faced 77,000 Japanese, with 22,000 local militia, commanded by General Ushijima. He intended to attack the landings only with *kamikaze*, and concentrated his forces inland around Naha and on the Motobu peninsula. The aim was to inflict as many casualties as possible on the Americans, until all his own men were dead. Consequently, the Marines quickly captured the airfields that were a major objective. They advanced speedily until they came up against Ushijima's formidable defensive positions in rocky terrain and caves that were immune to air or sea bombardment.

Supporting Ushijima, Toyoda launched Operation Ten-Go: waves of *kamikazes*, which from 6 April to 22 June flew nearly 2,000 sorties and caused great damage to the Allied armada. The surface fleet sortied on its own *kamikaze* mission – but less effectively; the giant battleship *Yamato* and most of the seaworthy remnants of the Mobile Fleet, with fuel only for a one-way voyage, were sunk by aircraft in the East China Sea before they could reach Okinawa.

Meanwhile, the Marines reached the northern tip of Okinawa on 13 April and cleared Motobu by 20 April. They then joined 24th Corps confronting the strongholds in the south. Two infantry divisions were badly mauled, but Ushijima's defence strongpoint at Shuri was broken through and Naha capitulated on 27 May. The Japanese fell back onto the Oruku peninsula, which they defended stoutly. They were only finally defeated on 22 June. Ushijima committed suicide that day; only 7,400 of his troops survived to become prisoners. On the Allied side, 36 warships and landing ships had been sunk and nearly 5,000 sailors killed. Some 7,613 soldiers were killed. With the fall of Okinawa, Japan's inner defence perimeter had been breached.

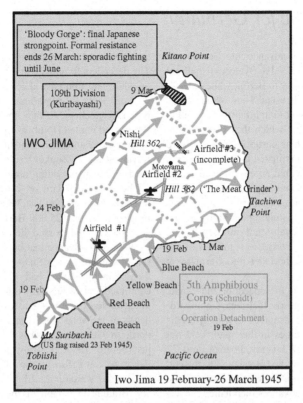

'Bloody Gorge': final Japanese strongpoint. Formal resistance ends 26 March: sporadic fighting until June

Kitano Point

109th Division (Kuribayashi)

9 Mar

IWO JIMA

Nishi
Hill 362

Airfield #3 (incomplete)

Motoyama
Airfield #2

Hill 382 ('The Meat Grinder')

Tachiwa Point

24 Feb

Airfield #1

19 Feb   1 Mar

Blue Beach

Yellow Beach

19 Feb

Red Beach

5th Amphibious Corps (Schmidt)

Operation Detachment
19 Feb

Green Beach

Mt. Suribachi
(US flag raised 23 Feb 1945)

Tobiishi Point

Pacific Ocean

Iwo Jima 19 February–26 March 1945

Okinawa 26 March–30 June 1945

Hedo Point

Kamikaze attacks on covering fleet from 6 April

Hedo
13 Apr

East China Sea

IE SHIMA   Bise
Motobu Pen.
12 Apr

Aha
19 Apr

16–21 Apr

20 Apr
8 Apr

11 Apr

8 Apr

Operation Iceberg
1 Apr 1945

10th Army (Buckner)

4 Apr

Ishikawa Isthmus

Pacific

3rd Amphibious Corps (Geiger)

TAKABANARE

Yontan
Hagushi
Kadena

Ocean

24th Corps (Hodge)

Katchin Pen.   10/11 Apr

Hagushi Bay

TSUGEN SHIMA

KEISE SHIMA

4 June   Naha

4 Apr
19 Apr

Japanese counter-attacks

26 Mar

Oruku Pen.   Shuri   Yonabaru

Japanese withdraw from Shuri Line
21 May

18 June

Kiyamu   Mabuni

Feint 1 Apr

32nd Army (Ushijima):
resistance ends 30 June

Map 47: The Battle for Germany

Stalin assigned two axes of advance into Germany at the start of 1945: Zhukov's 1st Byelorussian Front would proceed from Warsaw to Berlin, while Konev's 1st Ukrainian headed towards Breslau. They outnumbered Army Groups A and Centre twofold in infantry, fourfold in tanks, and sevenfold in artillery, which they had come to use in blistering preludes to their unsubtle direct forward advances. The Red Air Force dominated the air. Konev got off to a start on 12 January behind an enormous barrage. Zhukov's advance began on 14 January. Warsaw was encircled and fell on 17 January. On 21 January, Hitler created a new army, the Army of the Vistula, under Himmler: an appointment determined by loyalty not military talent. Himmler's forces were mainly *volkssturm* – militias of old men and boys. Konev crossed the Oder into Germany at Steinau on 22 January.

By now, the only limit to the speed of the Soviet advance was their own supply needs: their heavy bombardment tactics ate rapidly into the resources arriving from the east in US-made trucks. The cities in their path held out like fortresses: Memel until 27 January, Poznan until 22 February, Königsberg until April, and Breslau until the end of the war. However, by February, Konev and Zhukov were established on the Oder. Their advances then halted for two months, during which they consolidated their position in Poland, at the same time supervising the forcible resettlement of Poles in place of Germans, and arresting AK leaders.

Berlin was a formidable target. It was not fortified, but its nineteenth- and twentieth-century structures had stood up well to Allied bombing, and were eminently defensible. The Soviets marshalled huge forces for the assault. As they were doing so, the fierce fighting in Hungary around Lake Balaton finally concluded as Malinovsky and Tolbukhin broke out onto the plain and by 8 April were fighting in the heart of Vienna: the SS units there fought tenaciously and great destruction had been done by the time the city fell on 13 April. Three days later the attack on Berlin began, Konev and Zhukov racing each other to be the first to take the city. Zhukov's assault was led by Chuikov's 8th Guards Army – formerly the 66th Army, the defenders of Stalingrad. Some 464,000 Soviet soldiers prepared for the final battle. Contrary to what he had written to Eisenhower, Stalin regarded Berlin as of major significance.

Within Berlin, Hitler rejected the advice of his entourage and determined to remain there until the finish. He was, though, slipping out of touch with reality in his underground bunker, giving orders to non-existent units. The defenders fought street by street against the advancing Soviets, who poured a deluge of shells into the city. By 29 April they were less than a quarter of a mile from the Reich Chancellery. As they approached, Hitler married Eva Braun, and named Dönitz as his successor. On 30 April, he took poison, and then shot himself. On 2 May, Alyosha Kovalyov, one of Zhukov's soldiers, raised the red flag over the Reichstag, providing another great iconic photograph of the war. At 3 p.m. on 2 May, a cease-fire came into force. The Soviets had lost 300,000 men killed or wounded in taking Berlin; 125,000 Berliners had died in the battle.

Once he had crossed the Rhine and encircled the Ruhr, Eisenhower's advance had been remarkably fast across the German plain, giving Stalin cause to suspect a deal with the Germans. There had been no deal and resistance continued, but certainly by this point, Germans were eager to surrender to the western Allies, rather than fall into the hands of the vengeful Soviets. Montgomery struck across northern Germany towards Denmark, getting to Lübeck just before the Red Army. Further south, by 10 April Patton was at Erfurt on the Elbe, and by 12 April 1st and 9th Armies were on the Elbe too. Leipzig fell on 19 April and Bradley then held his position to await the Soviets. With plentiful news cameras present, Soviet and American soldiers met at Torgau on 24 April, embraced and toasted the Grand Alliance. Germany had been crushed between two giant pincers and for the soldiers the moment symbolised peace, even if relations between their superiors were becoming sour. Further south, Patton's forces found no National Redoubt, and by the time fighting ended had made a junction with Clark's 5th Army in Austria.

On 5 May, from his headquarters near Flensburg, Dönitz sent Field Marshal Jodl to Eisenhower's headquarters in Rheims to arrange a surrender to the western Allies. Eisenhower insisted on complete unconditional surrender, and with nothing to bargain, Jodl agreed the surrender at 2.41 a.m. on 7 May. Churchill and Truman declared 8 May as Victory in Europe (VE) Day – but Stalin still suspected a deal and insisted on a repeat signing in Berlin. This was done just before midnight on 8 May, meaning that for the USSR VE Day was 9 May. Fighting continued in Prague, as the Czech National Army resistance group attempted to seize the city to hand to the Americans. Patton had been ordered to halt short of the Czech capital, however, and it was the Red Army that entered Prague on 9 May, and took its surrender on 11 May.

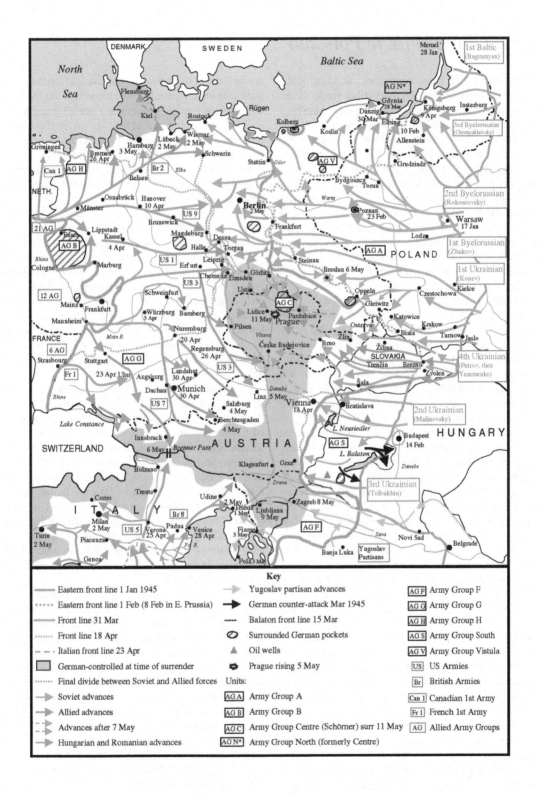

Key

—— Eastern front line 1 Jan 1945	➤ Yugoslav partisan advances
···· Eastern front line 1 Feb (8 Feb in E. Prussia)	➤ German counter-attack Mar 1945
—— Front line 31 Mar	···· Balaton front line 15 Mar
···· Front line 18 Apr	⬭ Surrounded German pockets
– – Italian front line 23 Apr	▲ Oil wells
▨ German-controlled at time of surrender	✿ Prague rising 5 May
···· Final divide between Soviet and Allied forces	Units:
➤ Soviet advances	AG A Army Group A
➤ Allied advances	AG B Army Group B
➤ Advances after 7 May	AG C Army Group Centre (Schörner) surr 11 May
➤ Hungarian and Romanian advances	AG N* Army Group North (formerly Centre)

AG F Army Group F
AG G Army Group G
AG H Army Group H
AG S Army Group South
AG V Army Group Vistula
US US Armies
Br British Armies
Can 1 Canadian 1st Army
Fr 1 French 1st Army
AG Allied Army Groups

Map 48: From Yalta to Potsdam

The second Big Three conference, at Yalta in the Crimea from 4 to 11 February 1945 (code-named Argonaut), has been the subject of great controversy. To many during the Cold War, Yalta became a symbol of Roosevelt's naïveté and was the point at which his weakness or misguided optimism towards Stalin produced the post-war division of Europe and encouraged Stalin to believe that he could embark on a programme of expansionism with impunity. Alternatively, the conference can be seen as the high-point of the Grand Alliance: the participants seem to have come away believing that was so, and it certainly looked like a triumph of the spirit of compromise in the face of the task that still needed to be completed – the Axis powers were in their last throes, but Allied unity was still needed to finish the job.

In particular, Roosevelt was concerned to gain Stalin's assurance that the promise to enter the war against Japan held good. The Americans were anxious that the Red Army should be brought into battle against the still sizeable Japanese forces in China and Manchukuo. In return, Roosevelt agreed that the Soviets would receive the southern part of Sakhalin and the Kurile islands, as well as confirmation of their control of Outer Mongolia and certain concessions in Manchuria.

With regard to Europe, it was agreed to set up an Allied Control Commission for Germany and Austria; Austria's independence was confirmed, and war criminals would be tried. France would receive, at Churchill's request, an occupation zone in Germany. The most difficult discussions were on Poland: the Big Three were already agreed on the eastern frontier; in the west, the Oder–Neisse line was agreed, though without specifying the western or eastern branch of the Neisse. Stalin asserted that there would be no problem with a German minority in Poland, since all the Germans had left – in fact his armies would make that so in the next two months. The issue of the Polish government was more contentious: the Soviets wished for the provisional government they had set up in Lublin, who were mostly Communists, to be recognised. A compromise was reached whereby this was to be expanded with the addition of Poles from London and from the AK – but it remained a matter of dispute what the proportions would be. It seemed, however, to be a satisfactory compromise, and generally there was pleasure that political matters could be discussed without catastrophic divergences. Agreement was reached on voting rights in the United Nations. On the Soviet demand for reparations, the western Allies conceded the principle, and a general figure was mentioned, which the Soviets later regarded as a firm agreement. On the subject of the liberated territories, a US State Department proposal was adopted as the Declaration on Liberated Europe, guaranteeing that all countries liberated from the enemy would have speedy elections to form democratic governments (this was probably directed at Britain and its activities in Greece as much as at the Soviets). Stalin signed it, though probably regarding it as a public relations exercise that did not supersede the percentages arrangement.

Be that as it may, the participants came away generally happy. The mood did not last. The Soviets immediately bullied King Michael into changing the Romanian government. Anglo-American representatives in Bulgaria had to watch passively as Communists moved into positions of power. The Soviets began arguing that the Poland agreement meant that their Polish committee in Lublin would be the basis for the new government, with a few additions. Furthermore, they objected to most western nominees and arrested representatives of the AK when they arrived in Moscow, claiming they had engaged in anti-Soviet activities.

Churchill, worried by these signs that the Soviets no longer felt the need to take Allied views into account, argued to Roosevelt that their forces should press ahead to take politically important cities like Berlin, Prague and Vienna, and should hold their line as far east as possible, not retreating to their designated zones without better behaviour from the Soviets. Churchill was furious about Eisenhower's dealings with Stalin over Berlin, which he regarded as a political, not a military, matter. The US Joint Chiefs of Staff were glad to be able to state flatly that military expediency came foremost in their calculations, and both Roosevelt and his successor Truman were unwilling to antagonise the Soviets in advance of their participation in the war with Japan.

Roosevelt died on 12 April, and Truman received advice to be tough with the Soviets. The Soviets themselves voiced suspicions that the Allies had made peace deals with the Germans and complained bitterly at contacts in Berne between SS General Wolff and Allen Dulles of the American Office of Strategic Services to arrange a surrender in Italy. It was in this context that the war in Europe came to an end. It was agreed to meet in Germany to discuss the future, but Truman successfully stalled the meeting until the atomic bomb could be tested. He was able to announce the success of the Trinity test (without saying what the bomb was) to Stalin at the conference at Potsdam, though Stalin's only response was to say he hoped it would be used on Japan.

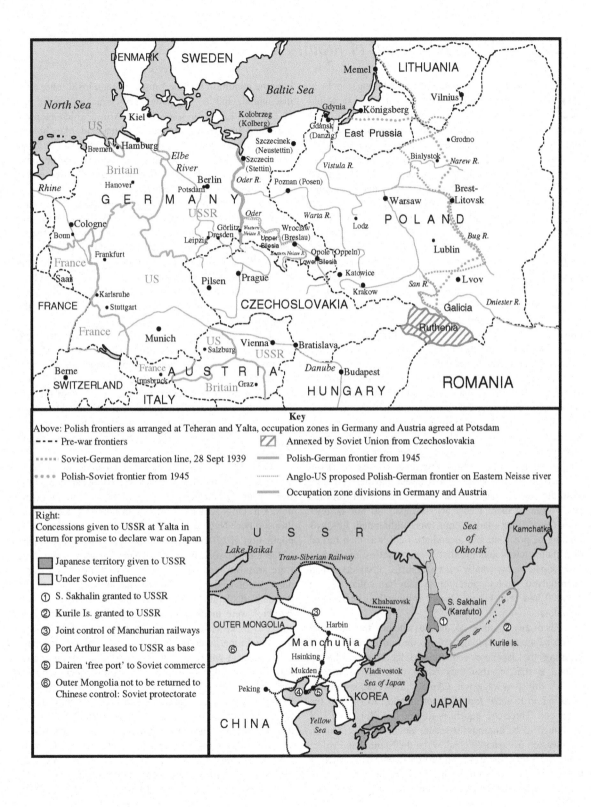

Key

Above: Polish frontiers as arranged at Teheran and Yalta, occupation zones in Germany and Austria agreed at Potsdam

- - - - Pre-war frontiers

//// Annexed by Soviet Union from Czechoslovakia

••••• Soviet-German demarcation line, 28 Sept 1939

——— Polish-German frontier from 1945

•••• Polish-Soviet frontier from 1945

········ Anglo-US proposed Polish-German frontier on Eastern Neisse river

——— Occupation zone divisions in Germany and Austria

Right:
Concessions given to USSR at Yalta in return for promise to declare war on Japan

■ Japanese territory given to USSR

□ Under Soviet influence

① S. Sakhalin granted to USSR

② Kurile Is. granted to USSR

③ Joint control of Manchurian railways

④ Port Arthur leased to USSR as base

⑤ Dairen 'free port' to Soviet commerce

⑥ Outer Mongolia not to be returned to Chinese control: Soviet protectorate

Map 49: The Final Defeat of Japan

Since 1940, the US had been developing the B-29 bomber specifically for the distances that would be involved in a Pacific campaign. On 15 June 1944 attacks with it began from India, on targets in Manchukuo and Korea. The campaign only started in earnest when the capture of the Marianas put Japan itself within range. High-level attacks from there began on 24 November, targeting the aircraft industry. After two months, results were poor, for the winds that prevail at high altitudes over Japan, cloud cover and Japanese fighters (no American escorts could accompany the bombers) made precision bombing virtually impossible. On 3 January tactics were switched to incendiary attacks on the highly inflammable Japanese cities, with a night raid on Nagoya. General LeMay took over the campaign, and on 25 February 150 B-29s burnt out a square mile in the centre of Tokyo in a day-time raid. LeMay then switched to low-level night raids, enabling heavier loads to be carried: gunners could be dispensed with, because the Japanese had not developed effective radar/night-fighter defence systems.

The results were devastating. On the night of 9/10 March 300 B-29s started a firestorm in residential areas of Tokyo that destroyed nearly a quarter of the city, including 20 military targets, and killing 85,000 people. Osaka, Kobe and Nagoya followed, before the bombers returned to Tokyo. After a break to support the landings on Okinawa, the assault re-started in May, this time with escorts from the airfield on Iwo Jima, which swept Japanese fighters from the sky. This allowed the B-29s and aircraft from the task forces to roam freely across Japan. In 500-bomber raids 66 of Japan's larger cities were obliterated. LeMay's mixture of precision and incendiary raids was then turned on smaller towns and installations, so that by the end of July, Japan was virtually at a standstill. Production had been halved, the transportation system had collapsed and 300,000 had been killed. Over 8 million had been made homeless.

Historians continue to debate whether the bombing or the submarine campaigns were the more important in bringing the Japanese economy to its knees. What is certain is that together they had a dramatic impact on Japan's ability to wage war. Okinawa, however, seemed in Washington to show Japan's determination to fight to the bitter end. Three consequences flowed from this. The JCS continued to be anxious to secure Soviet involvement in the invasion of Japan. Second, when the Manhattan Project came to fruition, there was no serious debate as to whether the atomic bomb should be used. Third, Japanese peace-feelers through the Soviets, with hints that they would seek only the condition that the Emperor retain his throne, were discounted. Opinion in Japanese policy-making circles was in fact divided, with some in the Army, which retained large and undefeated armies in China and Manchukuo, believing that American fear of high casualties in an invasion could bring a negotiated peace, while some civilians in the government believed that the war had to be ended before Japan was totally destroyed.

The US continued to insist on unconditional surrender – some have suggested that from the time of the successful test of the atomic bomb on 16 July there was a desire to use the bomb in action in order to intimidate the Soviets – and at Potsdam issued a declaration refusing any terms to the Japanese. This allowed the Japanese Army to claim that Japanese society and culture would be destroyed by the Americans in any event, so that fighting on was the only honourable course.

Events therefore moved to their terrible conclusion. On 6 August a lone B-29 flew from Tinian and at 8.15 a.m. dropped a 5-ton uranium bomb, 'Little Boy', over Hiroshima. An area of 5 square miles (13 sq km) was devastated. Sixty-two per cent of the buildings of the city were destroyed. Out of a population of 322,000, by August 1946 118,000 had died as a result of the bomb, and the effects of radiation were subsequently to push this figure towards 150,000.

On 8 August, in accordance with the undertaking given at Yalta, a massive Soviet attack was launched across the frontier into Manchuria, and swept the Kwantung Army before it. On 9 August, a plutonium bomb, 'Fat Man' was dropped over Nagasaki. About 74,000 were killed out of a population of 270,000. There was a delay while the impact of these blows sunk in among Japanese leaders – and there were army officers still prepared to fight on. The government announced on 10 August that it would accept the Potsdam declaration, provided the prerogatives of the Emperor were unaffected. The Americans were now prepared to make clear, in a way they had not done before, that the Emperor could remain on his throne. Japanese delay, at least partly because there was no strong central leadership in Tokyo, meant that the fire-bombers returned to Tokyo on the night of 13–14 August. This prompted the Emperor to make an unprecedented intervention, ordering his government to surrender and announcing on the radio that the war was 'no longer proceeding to Japan's advantage'. This was on 14 August, though it was not until 2 September that the surrender was signed on board USS *Missouri* (and the last Japanese soldier did not surrender until 1974). The Second World War was finally at an end.

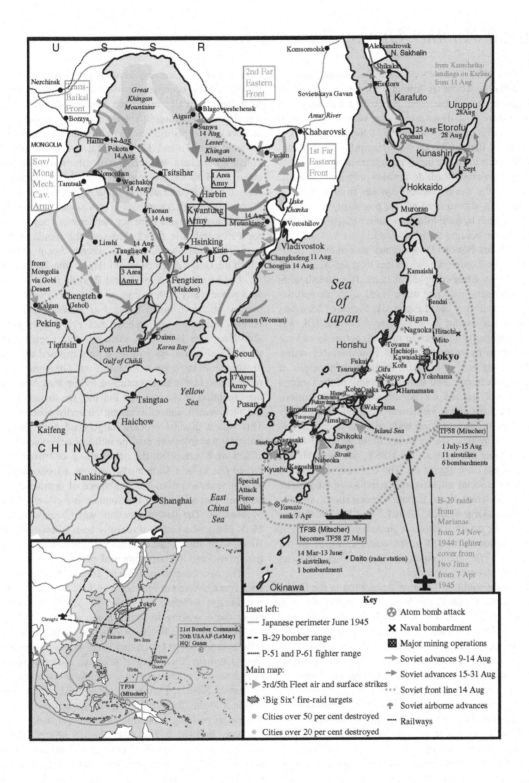

U S S R

Nerchinsk
Trans-Baikal Front
Borzya

Komsomolsk
Aleksandrovsk
N. Sakhalin
Shikuka
Esitoru
Karafuto

from Kamchatka: landings on Kuriles from 11 Aug

Uruppu 28 Aug

MONGOLIA

2nd Far Eastern Front

Great Khingan Mountains

Blagoveshchensk
Aigun
Sunwu 14 Aug

Sovietskaya Gavan

Amur River

Khabarovsk

Fuchin

1st Far Eastern Front

Etorofu 28 Aug
Otomari 25 Aug
Kunashiri
1 Sept

Hokkaido

Muroran

Sov/ Mong Mech. Cav. Army

Hailar 12 Aug
Pokotu 14 Aug
Nomonhan
Tamtsak
Wuchakou 14 Aug
Taonan 14 Aug

Tsitsihar

Lesser Khingan Mountains

1 Area Army

Harbin

Kwantung Army

Lake Khanka

14 Aug
Mutankiang
Voroshilov

Vladivostok

Changkufeng 11 Aug
Chongjin 14 Aug

Kamaishi

Sendai

Linshi
Tungliao 14 Aug

M A N C H U K U O

Hsinking
Kirin

3 Area Army

Fengtien (Mukden)

Sea of Japan

Niigata
Nagaoka
Hitachi
Mito

from Mongolia via Gobi Desert

Kalgan
Chengteh (Jehol)

Peking

Tientsin

Port Arthur
Dairen
Korea Bay
Gulf of Chihli

Gensan (Wonsan)

Seoul

17 Area Army

Honshu

Toyama
Hachioji
Kawasaki
Fukui
Kofu
Tsuruga
Gifu
Nagoya
Yokohama

Tokyo

TF58 (Mitscher)

1 July-15 Aug
11 airstrikes
6 bombardments

Tsingtao

Yellow Sea

Pusan

Himeji
Okayama
Fukuyama
Kobe Osaka
Wakayama
Hamamatsu

Kaifeng

Haichow

Hiroshima
Tokuyama

Imabari

Shikoku

Inland Sea

C H I N A

Nanking

Sasebo Nagasaki
Kyushu Kagoshima
Nabeoka
Bungo Strait

Special Attack Force (Ito)

East China Sea

Yamato sunk 7 Apr

TF38 (Mitscher) becomes TF58 27 May

14 Mar-13 June
5 airstrikes,
1 bombardment

Daito (radar station)

B-29 raids from Marianas from 24 Nov 1944: fighter cover from Iwo Jima from 7 Apr 1945

Shanghai

Okinawa

Key

Inset left:
— Japanese perimeter June 1945
- - - B-29 bomber range
······· P-51 and P-61 fighter range

Main map:
▶▶▶ 3rd/5th Fleet air and surface strikes
✺ 'Big Six' fire-raid targets
● Cities over 50 per cent destroyed
● Cities over 20 per cent destroyed

⊛ Atom bomb attack
✕ Naval bombardment
▦ Major mining operations
➤ Soviet advances 9-14 Aug
➤ Soviet advances 15-31 Aug
······· Soviet front line 14 Aug
⚲ Soviet airborne advances
···· Railways

Chengtu

Tokyo

21st Bomber Command, 20th USAAF (LeMay) HQ: Guam

Okinawa
Iwo Jima
Saipan
Tinian
Guam
Ulithi

TF38 (Mitscher)

Map 50: Another Uneasy Peace

In July 1944 a conference met at Dumbarton Oaks in Washington, where the format for a new international organisation was discussed. Agreement was only partial, and there was dispute over the veto for the great powers and over membership for the 16 Soviet republics of the USSR. At Bretton Woods, New Hampshire, new financial institutions to ensure better management of the world's economy were established: designed chiefly to transfer the direction of the world financial system from London to New York, but also to head off the possibility of another great depression by establishing the International Monetary Fund and what became the World Bank.

The United Nations Organization was founded at the San Francisco Conference, which ran from 25 April to 26 June, and was attended by 50 nations. It established an organisation designed to be more based upon the realities of power than the old League of Nations. Members renounced war except in self-defence, but the UN was given the authority to organise military action to enforce its resolutions by requesting forces from member states. The UN enshrined at its heart Roosevelt's principle of the 'four policemen': onto the 'democracy' of the General Assembly was grafted the dominance of the victorious allies, who were given permanent seats on the Security Council, the decision-making body, and the power of veto over actions by the UN, including those affecting themselves. Without this proviso, the USSR, and probably the US, would not have signed up. The UN also took over a number of the social and economic activities of the League (such as the International Labour Organization), and the World Health Organization, UNICEF and UNESCO were arguably to be the most effective elements of the UN as its central function foundered in the post-war world on the breakdown of the great power unanimity upon which its political effectiveness depended.

The tense relations that were developing in the Grand Alliance were evident at the final conference of the war. Code-named Terminal, it took place between 17 July and 2 August 1945 in Potsdam, a suburb of Berlin. On 28 July, Churchill was replaced by Clement Attlee who had won the British general election. On 26 July the Potsdam Declaration was issued to Japan, calling on Japan to surrender unconditionally and remove those who had led Japan's aggression or face 'complete and utter destruction' – though the atomic bomb was not specifically mentioned. Japan would be limited to the four home islands, would be disarmed, and war criminals would be punished. The Big Three had long and profitless discussions on German reparations. It was agreed that individual occupying powers would decide the amounts themselves and take them from their own zones; Germany would not be permanently partitioned, but the occupying powers would be sovereign in their zones, and all would have a veto on the ACC. Berlin was also to be partitioned. The territorial arrangements made at Yalta were confirmed and 6 million Germans were to be resettled from Poland, Hungary and Czechoslovakia. The Polish government was recognised, after a mission by US envoy Hopkins to Moscow in June (the Americans had refused to allow the Lublin Poles to represent Poland at San Francisco), though Soviet-backed provisional governments in Bulgaria and Romania were not; neither was a Soviet request for a trusteeship in Libya. Although the facade of Allied unity remained, the lines were already being drawn on which the Grand Alliance would fissure into the Cold War.

Unlike after the First World War, there was never to be a peace treaty with Germany. Nazi war criminals were tried at an international tribunal at Nuremberg in 1946. Foreign Ministers conferences met every three months until December 1947 in an attempt to reach agreement on the residual issues, but instead simply exposed the failure to agree on the long-term future of Germany and on reparations. In the areas occupied by the Red Army, with the exception of Austria and Finland, the Soviets carried out their stated aim of securing 'friendly governments'. This was a gradual process, largely *ad hoc*. The basic principle was to ensure that the military, police and foreign affairs were controlled: the only willing, or trusted agents turned out to be Communists, and one by one, coalition governments and even the semblance of democracy were replaced by regimes run by Communists closely directed by Moscow. The last to succumb was Czechoslovakia in 1948. Many who had until recently been fellow-resisters to Hitler, were imprisoned or murdered and forced 'socialisation' of national infrastructure took place.

The new frontiers of Europe, as agreed at the wartime conferences, were put in place, and for four years after the war Europe witnessed a stream of 'displaced persons'; either those seeking to return home after being used as forced labour in the Reich, or expelled ethnic Germans, or peoples in the Soviet Union that Stalin saw as traitors: Balts, Volga Germans, Circassians, Chechens, and many who had been prisoners of the Germans, who were either murdered or sent to Siberia. Europe lay devastated, and it was in response to this that the British and Americans began the process of reviving economic autonomy in their zones of Germany in 1946 and in 1947 the US offered Marshall Aid. These moves provoked more Soviet distrust, and the responses on both sides effectively cemented the wartime positions of the two halves of Europe, divided by an 'iron curtain' in a long but uneasy peace for the next 45 years.

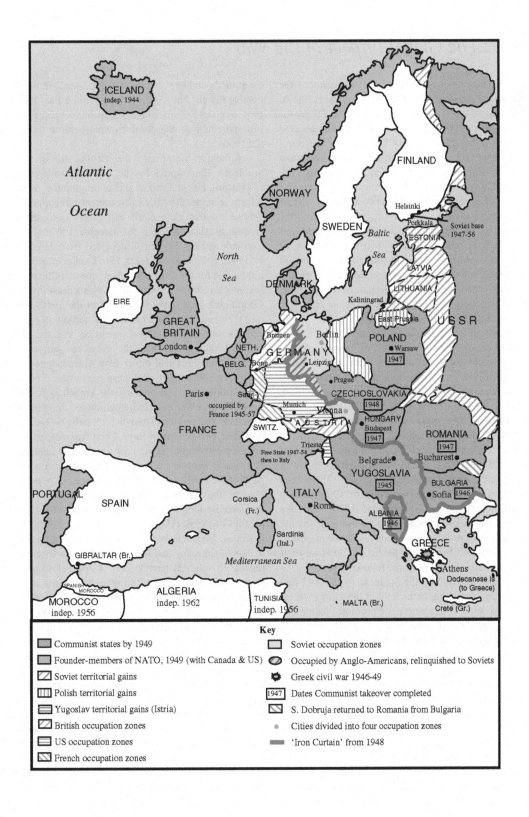

ICELAND
indep. 1944

Atlantic

Ocean

NORWAY

FINLAND

SWEDEN

Helsinki

Porkkala

Soviet base
1947-56

ESTONIA

Baltic

Sea

LATVIA

North
Sea

DENMARK

LITHUANIA

Kaliningrad

EIRE

GREAT
BRITAIN

London

Bremen

NETH.

Berlin

GERMANY

BELG.

Bonn

Leipzig

East Prussia

POLAND

Warsaw

1947

U S S R

Paris

Saar

occupied by
France 1945-57

Munich

Prague

CZECHOSLOVAKIA

1948

FRANCE

SWITZ.

A U S T R I A

Vienna

HUNGARY

Budapest

1947

ROMANIA

1947

Trieste

Free State 1947-54
then to Italy

Belgrade

Bucharest

YUGOSLAVIA

1945

BULGARIA

1946

PORTUGAL

SPAIN

Corsica
(Fr.)

ITALY

Rome

Sofia

ALBANIA

1946

GREECE

Sardinia
(Ital.)

GIBRALTAR (Br.)

Mediterranean Sea

Athens

Dodecanese Is
(to Greece)

SPANISH
MOROCCO

ALGERIA
indep. 1962

TUNISIA
indep. 1956

MALTA (Br.)

Crete (Gr.)

MOROCCO
indep. 1956

Key

Communist states by 1949

Soviet occupation zones

Founder-members of NATO, 1949 (with Canada & US)

Occupied by Anglo-Americans, relinquished to Soviets

Soviet territorial gains

Greek civil war 1946-49

Polish territorial gains

1947 Dates Communist takeover completed

Yugoslav territorial gains (Istria)

S. Dobruja returned to Romania from Bulgaria

British occupation zones

Cities divided into four occupation zones

US occupation zones

'Iron Curtain' from 1948

French occupation zones

Map 51: The Global Impact of the War

On the face of it, the end of the war restored the political status quo in Asia, with the exception of the dissolution of the Japanese Empire. There was not seen to be a need to convene a peace conference to agree a post-war settlement. The US took on the occupation of Japan with a small Commonwealth contingent that had no influence. American acceptance that the Emperor would remain on his throne meant that there was an element of constitutional continuity in Japan. While MacArthur, who was put in command, introduced reforms to transform Japan into a capitalist democracy, and war crimes trials were held that resulted in the execution of Tojo, there was not a radical transformation of Japanese society. Indeed, it became possible for Japanese to regard the militarist expansionist period as merely an interlude. Post-war Japan easily regained its position as the economic great power of the Far East.

Elsewhere in Asia, however, the war had, in fact, unleashed forces of radical change. Korea was occupied by the Soviets in the north and the Americans in the south. Both set up regimes according to their own preferences, and the Communist North invaded the South in June 1950, precipitating the Korean War, and a theatre for Cold War confrontation that outlasted the Cold War itself. In China, Jiang's forces were almost immediately involved in renewed conflict with Mao's Communists. In spite of American aid, and large armies trained during the war, the KMT were defeated and fled to Taiwan. There they declared themselves the true Republic of China, being recognised as such by the US until the 1970s, and like Japan, with American protection and investment became one of Asia's most prosperous economies. In China itself, Mao proclaimed the People's Republic of China in 1949 and became an ally of the USSR the following year.

The defeats inflicted by the Japanese in 1941–42 had been immensely damaging to the hold of the Europeans on their Asian colonies. The Japanese had promoted nationalist movements, and allowed some local autonomy. After their defeat, western-educated elites sought independence, drafting programmes for liberation based on a mixture of democratic and socialist principles. The British regained control of Burma, Malaya, Singapore and Borneo, and helped the French back into Indo-China, preferring their occupation to that of the Chinese, which the Americans, for a time, favoured. The Vietnamese declared their independence at the end of the war, expecting American support, but instead, after prolonged negotiations with the French, embarked on a war for independence which in various forms was to last for 30 years. The Americans granted independence to the Philippines, though they retained bases there, and kept certain strategic islands in the Pacific, notably Guam. The Dutch returned to the East Indies, but they, like the French, found it impossible to reassert control and finally withdrew from what became Indonesia in the 1950s.

Although victorious, the British faced the same problems. Bankrupted by the war and with occupation responsibilities in Europe and a programme of socialist reform at home, the Attlee government came quickly to the conclusion that they could not hold on to the British Empire in Asia. In return for agreement to remain in the Commonwealth, the British departed from India in haste in 1947. Burma and Ceylon (Sri Lanka) proved equally impossible for the British to retain, now that the population had lost any respect for them. They successfully fought a Communist insurgency in Malaya in the 1950s, but their rule there and elsewhere in Asia was rapidly to come to an end. The same phenomenon was to be repeated in Africa, and by 1960, 15 years after the end of the war, most of the European empires had either won independence or were well-advanced on that road, despite resistance on the part of the imperialists, particularly the French in Algeria. The Second World War had fatally humiliated these powers and materially reduced their strength so that they could no longer hold their possessions by force. Their hasty departure, without properly establishing a post-imperial settlement, meant that decolonisation produced independence, but in many parts of the world neither stability, peace nor prosperity.

On the positive side, the Second World War did undoubtedly accelerate the process by which the majority of peoples of the world gained greater control over their own destinies. Begun in order to halt the self-aggrandisement of Japan, Germany and Italy, the war was a success in that regard, although at terrible cost. Western Europe, after a short period of economic disorder, entered into a period of unprecedented peace, and attempts to resolve the issue of Germany in a new way brought movement to voluntary rather than forced European integration. For the United States, the war ushered in a period of greater prosperity than it had ever known. The price for all this was heavy: the immense human and material cost of the war, the unimaginable horrors that it unleashed in the Nazi genocides and in new terrible ways of waging war without mercy, and the fact that many of the peoples involved most closely in the struggle emerged from the war without freedom, but under the tyranny of Stalin. Even after Soviet rule was finally removed from the USSR and its satellites, older conflicts re-surfaced, many of them inflamed during the war and kept suppressed only by the Cold War, particularly in Yugoslavia and the Caucasus.

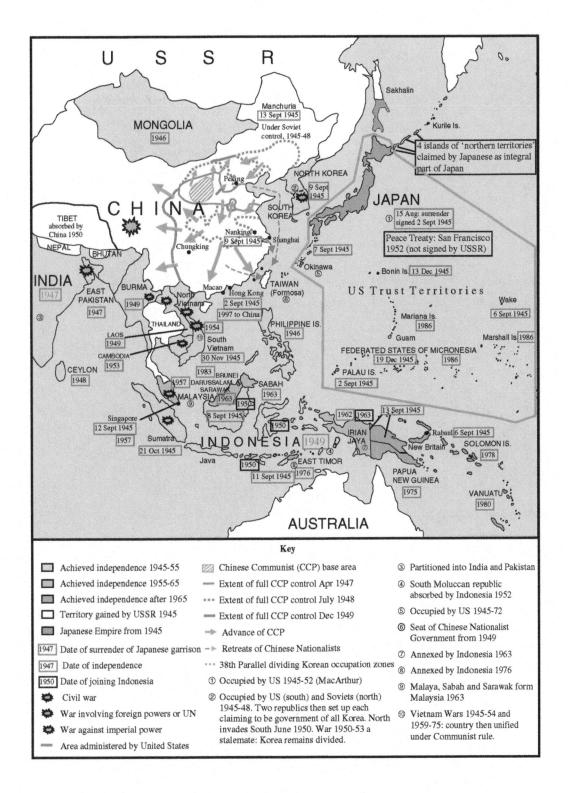

U S S R

MONGOLIA
1946

Manchuria
13 Sept 1945
Under Soviet
control, 1945-48

Sakhalin

Kurile Is.

4 islands of 'northern territories'
claimed by Japanese as integral
part of Japan

Peking

C H I N A

NORTH KOREA
② 9 Sept
1945

SOUTH
KOREA

JAPAN
① 15 Aug: surrender
signed 2 Sept 1945

TIBET
absorbed by
China 1950

Nanking
9 Sept 1945

Shanghai

Peace Treaty: San Francisco
1952 (not signed by USSR)

NEPAL

Chungking

7 Sept 1945

Okinawa
⑤

Bonin Is. 13 Dec 1945

BHUTAN

INDIA
1947

EAST
PAKISTAN
1947

BURMA
1949

North
Vietnam

Macao

TAIWAN
(Formosa)
⑥

Hong Kong
2 Sept 1945
1997 to China

US Trust Territories

Wake
6 Sept 1945

③

THAILAND

1954

PHILIPPINE IS.
1946

Mariana Is.
1986

LAOS
1949

South
Vietnam
30 Nov 1945

Guam

Marshall Is. 1986

CAMBODIA
1953

CEYLON
1948

1983

1957

BRUNEI
DARUSSALAM
SARAWAK
MALAYSIA 1963

SABAH
1963

FEDERATED STATES OF MICRONESIA
19 Dec 1945   1986

PALAU IS.
2 Sept 1945

Singapore
12 Sept 1945
1957

8 Sept 1945

1950

1950

1962 1963

13 Sept 1945

Sumatra
21 Oct 1945

INDONESIA
1949

IRIAN
JAYA
⑦

Rabaul 6 Sept 1945

New Britain
SOLOMON IS.
1978

Java

1950

EAST TIMOR

11 Sept 1945 ⑧ 1976

PAPUA
NEW GUINEA
1975

VANUATU
1980

AUSTRALIA

Key

▢ Achieved independence 1945-55	▨ Chinese Communist (CCP) base area
▢ Achieved independence 1955-65	— Extent of full CCP control Apr 1947
▢ Achieved independence after 1965	··· Extent of full CCP control July 1948
▢ Territory gained by USSR 1945	— Extent of full CCP control Dec 1949
▢ Japanese Empire from 1945	➤ Advance of CCP
1947 Date of surrender of Japanese garrison	➤ Retreats of Chinese Nationalists
1947 Date of independence	··· 38th Parallel dividing Korean occupation zones
1950 Date of joining Indonesia	① Occupied by US 1945-52 (MacArthur)
✹ Civil war	② Occupied by US (south) and Soviets (north)
✹ War involving foreign powers or UN	1945-48. Two republics then set up each
✹ War against imperial power	claiming to be government of all Korea. North
— Area administered by United States	invades South June 1950. War 1950-53 a
	stalemate: Korea remains divided.

③ Partitioned into India and Pakistan

④ South Moluccan republic
absorbed by Indonesia 1952

⑤ Occupied by US 1945-72

⑥ Seat of Chinese Nationalist
Government from 1949

⑦ Annexed by Indonesia 1963

⑧ Annexed by Indonesia 1976

⑨ Malaya, Sabah and Sarawak form
Malaysia 1963

⑩ Vietnam Wars 1945-54 and
1959-75: country then unified
under Communist rule.

Selected Bibliography

General

Addison, Paul, and Angus Calder, eds, *Time to Kill: The Soldier's Experience of War in the West 1939–1945* (London, 1997)

Cowley, Robert, ed., *No End Save Victory: Perspectives on World War II* (New York, 2001)

Dear, I. C. B., and M. R. D. Foot, eds, *The Oxford Companion to the Second World War* (Oxford, 1995)

Fussell, Paul, *Wartime* (Oxford, 1989)

Keegan, John, *The Second World War* (London, 1989)

Keegan, John, *The Battle for History. Re-Fighting World War II* (New York, 1995)

Murray, Williamson, and Allan R. Millett, *A War to be Won. Fighting the Second World War* (Cambridge, MA, 2000)

Overy, Richard, *Why the Allies Won* (New York, 1995)

Weinberg, Gerhard L., *A World at Arms: A Global History of World War II* (Cambridge, 1994)

Wint, Guy, Peter Calvocoressi and John Pritchard, *The Penguin History of the Second World War* (rev. edn. of *Total War*) (London, 2001)

Origins of the War

Bell, P. M. H., *The Origins of the Second World War in Europe* (London, 1986)

Feis, Herbert, *The Road to Pearl Harbor: The Coming of War Between the United States and Japan* (Princeton, 1950)

Iriye, Akira, *The Origins of the Second World War in Asia and the Pacific* (London, 1987)

Reynolds, David, *From Munich to Pearl Harbor: Roosevelt's America and the Origins of the Second World War* (Chicago, 2001)

Rothwell, Victor, *The Origins of the Second World War* (Manchester, 2001)

Taylor, A. J. P., *The Origins of the Second World War* (London, 1963)

Utley, Jonathan G., *Going to War with Japan, 1937–1941* (Knoxville, TN, 1985)

Watt, D. Cameron, *How War Came* (London, 1989)

War in the West

Ambrose, Stephen E., *D-Day, June 6, 1944: The Climactic Battle of World War II* (New York, 1994)

Ambrose, Stephen E., *Citizen Soldiers: The US Army from the Normandy Beaches to the Bulge to the Surrender of Germany, June 7, 1944–May 7, 1945* (New York, 1998)

Barnett, Corelli, *The Desert Generals* (London, 1983)

d'Este, Carlo, *Decision in Normandy* (New York, 1984)

Gilbert, Martin, *Finest Hour. Winston S. Churchill, 1939–41* (London, 1983)

Gilbert, Martin, *Road to Victory. Winston S. Churchill, 1941–45* (London, 1986)

Graham, Dominick, and Shelford Bidwell, *Tug of War: The Battle for Italy, 1943–45* (London, 1986)

Hastings, Max, *Overlord and the Battle of Normandy, 1944* (London, 1984)

Horne, Alistair, *To Lose a Battle: France 1940* (London, 1969)

Keegan, John, *Six Armies in Normandy* (London, 1982)

MacDonald, Charles B., *A Time for Trumpets: The Untold Story of the Battle of the Bulge* (New York, rev. edn., 1997)

Macksey, Kenneth, *Crucible of Power: The Fight for Tunisia 1942–43* (London, 1969)

Pitt, Barrie, *The Crucible of War* (3 vols) (London 1982–86)

Ryan, Cornelius, *The Last Battle* (London, 1966)

Weingarten, Stephen, ed., *The Greatest Thing We Have Ever Attempted: Historical Perspectives on the Normandy Campaign* (Wheaton, IL, 1998)

Wilmot, Chester, *The Struggle for Europe* (London, 1952)

The Soviet–German War

Beevor, Anthony, *Stalingrad* (London, 1998)

Beevor, Anthony, *The Battle for Berlin* (London, 2002)

Clark, Alan, *Barbarossa. The Russian–German Conflict, 1941–1945* (London, 1965)

Erickson, John, *The Road to Stalingrad* (London, 1975)

Erickson, John, *The Road to Berlin* (London, 1983)

Glantz, David M., and Jonathan House, *When Titans Clashed. How the Red Army Stopped Hitler* (Kansas, 1995)

Overy, Richard, *Russia's War. Blood on the Snow* (New York, 1997)

Roberts, Geoffrey, *Victory at Stalingrad* (London, 2002)

Salisbury, Harrison, *900 Days. The Siege of Leningrad* (London, 1969)

Seaton, Albert, *The Russo-German War, 1941–45* (London, 1971)

Grand Strategy

Higgins, Trumbull, *Soft Underbelly: The Anglo-American Controversy Over the Italian Campaign, 1939–1945* (New York, 1968)

Howard, Michael, *The Mediterranean Strategy in the Second World War* (London, 1968)

Kimball, Warren F., *The Most Unsordid Act: Lend-Lease, 1939–1941* (Baltimore, 1969)

Stoler, Mark, *The Politics of the Second Front: American Military Planning and Diplomacy in Coalition Warfare, 1941–43* (Westport, CT, 1977)

Stoler, Mark, *Allies and Adversaries: The Joint Chiefs of Staff, the Grand Alliance and US Strategy in World War II* (Chapel Hill, NC, 2000)

Thorne, Christopher, *Allies of a Kind: The United States, Britain and the War Against Japan, 1941–1945* (Oxford, 1978)

Politics of War

Beitzell, Robert, *The Uneasy Alliance: America, Britain and Russia, 1941–1943* (New York, 1972)

Berthon, Simon, *Allies at War: The Bitter Rivalry Among Churchill, Roosevelt and De Gaulle* (New York, 2001)

Buhite, Russell D., *Decision at Yalta: An Appraisal of Summit Diplomacy* (Wilmington, DE, 1986)

Clemens, Diane S., *Yalta* (New York, 1970)

Edmonds, Robin, *The Big Three. Churchill, Roosevelt and Stalin in Peace and War* (New York, 1991)

Hildebrand, Robert, C., *Dumbarton Oaks: The Origins of the United Nations and the Search for Postwar Security* (Chapel Hill, NC, 1990)

Kimball, Warren, F., *Forged In War: Roosevelt, Churchill and the Second World War* (New York, 1997)

McNeill, William H., *America, Britain and Russia: Their Cooperation and Conflict, 1941–1946* (Oxford, 1953)

Mee, Charles L., *Meeting at Potsdam* (London, 1975)

Reynolds, David, *The Creation of the Anglo-American Alliance, 1937–41* (Chapel Hill, 1981)

Sainsbury, Keith, *The Turning Point: Roosevelt, Stalin, Churchill and Chiang Kai-Shek, 1943 – the Moscow, Cairo and Tehran Conferences* (Oxford, 1985)

Sainsbury, Keith, *Churchill and Roosevelt at War. The War They Fought and the Peace They Hoped to Make* (New York, 1994)

Smith, Gaddis, *American Diplomacy During the Second World War 1941–1945* (New York, 2nd edn., 1985)

van Tuyll, Hubert P., *Feeding the Bear: American Aid to the Soviet Union, 1941–1945* (Westport, CT, 1989)

Wilson, Theodore A., *The First Summit: Roosevelt and Churchill at Placentia Bay 1941* (Boston, 1969)

The Naval and Air War

Dull, Paul S., *A Battle History of the Imperial Japanese Navy, 1941–1945* (Cambridge, 1978)

Hastings, Max, *Bomber Command* (London, 1987)

Hough, Richard, *The Longest Battle: The War at Sea* (London, 1986)

Middlebrook, Martin, *Convoy* (London, 1976)

Morison, Samuel E., *The Two-Ocean War* (Boston, 1963)

Overy, Richard, *The Air War 1939–45* (London, 1987)

Roskill, Stephen, *The War at Sea* (3 vols) (London, 1954–61)

Schaffer, Ronald, *Wings of Judgement: American Bombing in World War II* (New York, 1985)

Schofield, B. B., *The Russian Convoys* (London, 1964)

van der Vat, Dan, *The Pacific Campaign in World War II, the US–Japanese Naval War, 1941–1945* (London, 1992)

von der Porten, Edward, *The German Navy in World War Two* (London, 1970)

Werrell, Kenneth P., *Blankets of Fire: US Bombers over Japan During World War II* (Washington, DC, 1996)

The Civilian War

Addison, Paul, *The Road to 1945* (London, 1975)

Anderson, Karen, T., *Wartime Women: Sex Roles, Family Relations, and the Status of Women During World War II* (Westport, CT, 1981)

Barber, John, and Mark Harrison, *The Soviet Home Front, 1941–1945. A Social and Economic History of the USSR in World War II* (London, 1991)

Calder, Angus, *People's War Britain 1939–1945* (London, 1969)

Folly, Martin H., *The United States in World War II. The Awakening Giant* (Edinburgh, 2002)

Gilbert, Martin, *Auschwitz and the Allies* (New York, 1981)

Grunberger, Richard, *A Social History of the Third Reich* (London, 1971)

Havens, T. R. H., *Valley of Darkness. The Japanese People and World War Two* (New York, 1978)

O'Neill, William L., *A Democracy at War: America's Fight at Home and Abroad in World War II* (New York, 1993)

Rings, Werner, *Life with the Enemy: Collaboration and Resistance in Hitler's Europe 1939–45* (London, 1982)

Shillony, B., *Politics and Culture in Wartime Japan* (Oxford, 1991)

Stern, J. P., *Hitler. The Führer and the People* (Berkeley, 1975)

Takaki, Ronald, *Double Victory: A Multicultural History of America in World War II* (Boston, 2000)

Thorne, Christopher, *The Far Eastern War, States and Societies* (London, 1986)

The War in the East

Borg, Dorothy, and Shumpei Okamoto, eds, *Pearl Harbor as History: Japanese–American Relations, 1931–1941* (New York, 1973)

Chang, Iris, *The Rape of Nanking: The Forgotten Holocaust of World War II* (London, 1998)

Costello, John, *The Pacific War* (New York, 1983)

Dower, John W., *War Without Mercy: Race and Power in the Pacific War* (New York, 1986)

Feifer, George, *Tennozan: The Battle of Okinawa and the Atomic Bomb* (New York, 1992)

Frank, Richard, *Guadalcanal. The Definitive Account of the Landmark Battle* (New York, 1990)

Fuchida, Mitsuo, *Midway. The Japanese Story* (London, 2002)

Hersey, John, *Hiroshima* (New York, 1946)

Hoyt, Edwin P., *Japan's War: The Great Pacific Conflict* (New York, 1986)

Iriye, Akira, *Power and Culture: The Japanese–American War, 1941–1945* (Cambridge, MA, 1981)

Jones, F. C., *Japan's New Order in East Asia: Its Rise and Fall, 1937–1945* (Oxford, 1954)

Love, Robert W., ed., *Pearl Harbor Revisited* (New York, 1994)

Prange, Gordon W., *At Dawn We Slept: The Untold Story of Pearl Harbor* (New York, 1981)

Prange, Gordon W., *Miracle at Midway* (New York, 1982)

Rhodes, Richard, *The Making of the Atomic Bomb* (New York, 1986)

Schaller, Michael, *Douglas MacArthur: The Far Eastern General* (New York, 1989)

Spector, Ronald H., *Eagle Against The Sun: The American War With Japan* (New York, 1985)

Takaki, Ronald, *Hiroshima: Why America Dropped the Bomb* (Boston, 1995)

Tuchman, Barbara, *Stilwell and the American Experience in China, 1911–1945* (New York, 1971)

Walker, John S., *Prompt and Utter Destruction: Truman and the Use of Atomic Bombs Against Japan* (Chapel Hill, NC, 1997)

Willmott, H. P., *Empires in the Balance* (London, 1982)

Atlases

Badsey, Stephen, ed., *The Hutchinson Atlas of World War II Battle Plans: Before and After* (London, 2000)

Gilbert, Martin, *The Routledge Atlas of the Holocaust* (London, 3rd edn., 2002)

Griess, Thomas, E., ed., *West Point Atlas for the Second World War* (2 vols) (New York, 1987)

Keegan, John, ed., *The Times Atlas of the Second World War* (London, 1989)

Overy, Richard, *The Penguin Historical Atlas of the Third Reich* (London, 1996)

Smurthwaite, David, *War Atlas of Asia and the Pacific 1941–1945* (Shrewsbury, 2000)

Young, Peter, ed., *Atlas of the Second World War* (London, 1973)

First-Hand Accounts

Field Marshal Lord Alanbrooke, *War Diaries 1939–1945* (eds Alex Danchev and Daniel Todman, London, 2001)

Axell, Albert, *Stalin's War Through the Eyes of his Commanders* (London, 1997)

Bendiner, Elmer, *The Fall of Fortresses. A Personal Account of the Most Daring, and Deadly, American Air Battles of World War II* (London, 1980)

Chuikov, V. I., *The Beginning of the Road* (London, 1963)

Churchill, Winston S., *History of the Second World War* (6 vols) (London, 1947–53)

Colville, John, *Fringes of Power. Downing Street Diaries 1939–1955* (2 vols) (London, 1985)

Djilas, Milovan, *Wartime* (London, 1977)

Gardner, Brian, *Terrible Rain. The War Poets 1939–45* (London, 1987)

Gilbert, G., *Nuremberg Diary* (London, 1963)

Harriman, Averell W., and Elie Abel, *Special Envoy to Churchill and Stalin, 1941–1946* (New York, 1975)

Khaldei, Yevgeny, *Witness to History. The Photographs of Yevgeny Khaldei* (New York, 1997)

Lomax, Eric, *The Railway Man* (London, 1995)

Macintyre, Donald, *U-Boat Killer* (London, 1976)

Magee, John, *The Pilot Poet* (London, 1996)

Sajer, Guy, *The Forgotten Soldier* (New York, 2000)

Sledge, E. B., *With the Old Breed: At Peleliu and Okinawa* (Novato, CA, 1981)

Speer, Albert, *Inside the Third Reich* (London, 1970)

Trevor-Roper, Hugh, ed., *The Goebbels Diaries* (Secker & Warburg: London, 1978)

Vassilitchikov, Marie, *The Berlin Diaries 1940–1945* (London, 1985)

Warlimont, W., *Inside Hitler's Headquarters* (London, 1964)

Covert Activities

Beesly, Patrick, *Very Special Intelligence: The Story of the Admiralty's Operational Intelligence Centre, 1939–1945* (London, 1977)

Bennett, Ralph, *Ultra in the West* (London, 1979)

Drea, Edward J., *MacArthur's Ultra: Codebreaking and the War Against Japan, 1942–1945* (Lawrence, KS, 1992)

Foot, M. R. D., *SOE* (London, 1984)

Hinsley, F. H., *The History of British Intelligence in World War II* (5 vols) (London, 1979–90)

Jones, R. V., *Secret War* (London, 1978)

Lewin, Ronald, *Ultra Goes to War. The Secret Story* (London, 1978)

Lewin, Ronald, *The American Magic: Codes, Ciphers and the Defeat of Japan* (New York, 1982)

Michael, H., *The Shadow War* (London, 1972)

Smith, Bradley F., *The Ultra-Magic Deals and the Most Special Relationship, 1940–1946* (Novato, CA, 1993)

Smith, Bradley F., *Sharing Secrets with Stalin. How the Allies Traded Intelligence 1941–1945* (Kansas, 1996)

Tarrant, V. E., *The Red Orchestra* (London, 1995)

The End of the War and Post-war Problems

Bailey, Paul, *Postwar Japan: 1945 to the Present* (Oxford, 1996)

Calvocoressi, Peter, *Fallout: World War II and the Shaping of Postwar Europe* (London, 1997)

Gaddis, John L., *The United States and the Origins of the Cold War, 1941–47* (New York, 1972)

Harbutt, Fraser, *Iron Curtain: Churchill, America and the Origins of the Cold War* (Oxford, 1986)

Kennedy-Pipe, Caroline, *Stalin's Cold War. Soviet Strategies in Europe, 1943 to 1956* (Manchester, 1995)

Lowe, Peter, *Origins of the Korean War* (London, 2nd edn., 1997)

Painter, David, *The Cold War. An International History* (London, 1999)

Rose, Lisle A., *Dubious Victory: The United States and the End of World War II* (Ohio, 1973)

Sharp, Tony, *The Wartime Alliance and the Zonal Division of Germany* (Oxford, 1975)

Sherwin, Martin J., *A World Destroyed. Hiroshima and the Origins of the Arms Race* (New York, rev. edn., 1987)

Smith, Bradley F., *The War's Long Shadow. The Second World War and Its Aftermath* (New York, 1986)

Smith, Joseph, *The Cold War, 1945–1991* (Oxford, 1997)

Vaizey, John, *The Squandered Peace. The World, 1945–1975* (London, 1983)

Index

CPSIA information can be obtained
at www.ICGtesting.com
Printed in the USA
LVOW05s0538151217

559597LV00031B/30/P